Writing Effective Sentences

Writing Effective Sentences

. . . .

George E. Bell
Cecil Community College

Allyn & Bacon
Boston London Toronto Sydney Tokyo Singapore

Executive Editor: Joe Opiela
Series Editorial Assistant: Brenda Conaway
Production Administrator: Susan McIntyre
Editorial-Production Service: DMC & Company
Text Designer: Donna Merrell Chernin
Copy Editor: Sandra Sizer Moore
Cover Administrator: Linda Dickinson
Manufacturing Buyer: Louise Richardson

Copyright ©1993 by Allyn & Bacon
A Division of Simon & Schuster
160 Gould Street
Needham Heights, MA 02194

Bell, George (George E.)
    Writing effective sentences / George Bell.
        p. cm.
    Includes index.
    ISBN 0-205-14037-8
    1. English language—Sentences. 2. English language—Rhetoric.
I. Title.
PE1441.B44 1993
428.2—dc20   92-22630
                                                                  CIP

Printed in the United States of America
10 9 8 7 6 5 4 3 2 1   96 95 94 93 92

Dedication

To my first and best teachers,
my parents,
Edward and Ruth Bell.

Brief Contents

Preface to the Instructor   xv
Preface to the Student   xvii

PART I

Understanding English Grammar

Chapter 1	Basic English Grammar and the Sentence	1
Chapter 2	Nouns and Pronouns	10
Chapter 3	Verbs	30
Chapter 4	Adjectives and Adverbs	64
Chapter 5	Conjunctions	82
Chapter 6	Prepositions and Prepositional Phrases	95
Chapter 7	Verbals and Verbal Phrases	105
Chapter 8	Subordinating Conjunctions, Relative Pronouns, and Subordinate Clauses	124
Chapter 9	Types and Classes of Sentences	142

PART II

Writing Unified and Coherent Sentences

Chapter 10	Fragments and Run-On Sentences	155
Chapter 11	Agreement of Subject and Predicate	170
Chapter 12	Pronoun Case	185
Chapter 13	Agreement of Pronoun and Antecedent	196
Chapter 14	Vague, General, and Unclear Pronoun Reference	204
Chapter 15	Misplaced and Dangling Modifiers	210
Chapter 16	Parallel Structure	221
Chapter 17	Shifts in Person, Number, and Tense	234

PART III

Punctuating Sentences Effectively

Chapter 18 End Marks, Dashes, Parentheses, and
                Quotation Marks   242

Chapter 19 Comma   260

Chapter 20 Semicolon and Colon   276

PART IV

Writing Mechanically Correct Sentences

Chapter 21 Capital Letters, Apostrophes, and Underlining   286

PART V

Becoming a Better Speller

Chapter 22 Becoming a Better Speller   309

INDEX   325

C O N T E N T S

. . . .

Preface to the Instructor   xv
Preface to the Student   xvii

PART I

Understanding English Grammar

Chapter 1	**Basic English Grammar and the Sentence**	**1**
	The Grammatical Functions of Words	1
	Naming	2
	Expressing Action, Possession, or State of Being	2
	Modifying	3
	Joining	3
	Expressing Passion or Emotion	4
	The Main Parts of a Sentence	4
	The Subject	4
	The Predicate	6
Chapter 2	**Nouns and Pronouns**	**10**
	Nouns	10
	Pronouns	13
	The Properties of Nouns and Pronouns	14
	Person	14
	Number	14
	Gender	15
	Types of Pronouns	18
	Personal Pronouns	18
	Demonstrative Pronouns	20
	Interrogative Pronouns	21
	Indefinite Pronouns	22
	Reflexive and Emphatic Pronouns	23
	Reciprocal Pronouns	24
	The Pronouns at a Glance	24
Chapter 3	**Verbs**	**30**
	Active and Passive Voice	32
	Tense	35

The Tenses Defined   36
   Present, Past, and Future Tenses   36
   Present Perfect, Past Perfect, and
      Future Perfect Tenses   37
The Principal Parts of Verbs   40
   Regular Verbs   40
   Irregular Verbs   40
Tense Formation   44
Special Tense Forms   48
   The Progressive Tense   48
   Emphatic Verb Forms   55
Helping (or Auxiliary) Verbs   55
Person and Number   56
Mood   57
   The Indicative Mood   57
   The Imperative Mood   57
   The Subjunctive Mood   57
Transitive, Intransitive, and Linking Verbs   60

Chapter 4   Adjectives and Adverbs   64
Adjectives   64
   Descriptive Adjectives   65
   Definitive Adjectives   67
Adverbs   73
   Adverbs of Time, Manner, Place, and Degree   73
Comparison of Adjectives and Adverbs   76
   Comparison of Adjectives   77
   Comparison of Adverbs   79

Chapter 5   Conjunctions   82
Coordinating Conjunctions   83
Correlative Conjunctions   88
Conjunctive Adverbs   89

Chapter 6   Prepositions and Prepositional Phrases   95
Prepositions   95
Prepositional Phrases   96
Functions of Prepositional Phrases   98
Special Usage Problems   102

Chapter 7   Verbals and Verbal Phrases   105
Gerunds and Gerund Phrases   106
Participles and Participial Phrases   111
Infinitives and Infinitive Phrases   117

Chapter 8   **Subordinating Conjunctions, Relative Pronouns,**
and Subordinate Clauses   **124**
Subordinating Conjunctions and
Relative Pronouns   126
    Introducing Adjectival Clauses   126
    Introducing Adverb Clauses   127
    Introducing Noun Clauses   127
Recognizing Subordinate and Independent Clauses 127
The Functions of Subordinate Clauses   131
    The Adjectival Clause   131
    The Adverbial Clause   134
    The Noun Clause   137

Chapter 9   **Types and Classes of Sentences**   **142**
Types of Clauses   142
Types of Sentences   143
    The Simple Sentence   143
    The Compound Sentence   144
    The Complex Sentence   144
    The Compound-Complex Sentence   145
Classes of Sentences   150
    The Declarative Sentence   150
    The Interrogative Sentence   150
    The Imperative Sentence   151
    The Exclamatory Sentence   151

PART II

Writing Unified and Coherent Sentences

Chapter 10   **Fragments and Run-On Sentences**   **155**
Fragments   155
Run-On Sentences   160
    Avoiding the Comma Splice   160
    Avoiding the Fused Sentence   165

Chapter 11   **Agreement of Subject and Predicate**   **170**
Agreement When Phrases Come Between
    Subject and Predicate   171
Agreement With Subjects Joined by *And*   172
Agreement With Subjects Joined by *Or, Nor,*
    Either...Or, Neither...Nor, or
    Not Only...But Also   172
Agreement With Indefinite Pronouns   174

Agreement With Collective Nouns   176
Agreement When a Subject Complement Is Present 178
Agreement With *There Is/Are, There Was/Were*,
    and the Expletive *It*   178
Agreement With a Subject That Is the Name
    of a Book, Play, Newspaper, etc.   80
Agreement With Nouns That Are Plural in
    Form But Singular in Meaning   180
Agreement With *The Number* and *A Number*   181
Agreement With the Relative Pronouns
    Who, Which, and *That*   182

Chapter 12 Pronoun Case   **185**
The Personal Pronouns   186
    Subjective Case   186
    Objective Case   187
    Possessive Case   188
Relative and Interrogative Pronouns   192
    Subjective and Objective Case   192
    Possessive Case   193
Indefinite and Reciprocal Pronouns   194

Chapter 13 Agreement of Pronoun and Antecedent   **196**
Agreement When Two or More Antecedents
    Are Joined by *And*   197
Agreement When Antecedents Are Joined by
    Or, Either...Or, and *Neither...Nor*   198
Agreement When the Antecedent Is a Singular
    Indefinite Pronoun   198
Agreement When the Antecedent Is a
    Collective Noun   199
Agreement When the Antecedent Is Plural
    in Form But Singular in Meaning   200

Chapter 14 Vague, General, and Unclear Pronoun Reference   **204**
Vague and General Pronoun Reference   204
Unclear Pronoun Reference   206

Chapter 15 Misplaced and Dangling Modifiers   **210**
Misplaced Modifiers   210
Dangling Modifiers   214

Chapter 16 Parallel Structure   **221**
Achieving Parallel Structure   221
Avoiding Faulty Parallel Structure   229

Chapter 17 Shifts in Person, Number, and Tense   234
Shifts in Person and Number   234
Shifts in Tense   236

PART **III**

Punctuating Sentences Effectively

Chapter 18 End Marks, Dashes, Parentheses, and
Quotation Marks   242
End Marks   242
The Period   242
The Question Mark   247
The Exclamation Mark   248
The Dash   250
Parentheses   251
Quotation Marks   253
The Use of Quotation Marks   253
With Direct Quotations   253
With Quotations Within Quotations   254
With Titles of Songs, Poems, etc.   254
With Words Used in a Special Sense   254
Placement of Other Marks of Punctuation   255
Periods and Commas   255
Colons and Semicolons   255
Question Mark and Exclamation Mark   255

Chapter 19 Comma   260
Setting Off Independent Clauses   260
Separating Items in a Series   262
Setting Off Introductory Words, Phrases,
and Clauses   263
Setting Off Nonessential Words, Phrases,
and Clauses   267
Other Standard Uses of the Comma (Dates,
Addresses, Numbers, etc.)   271
To Assist Clarity in Other Ways   272

Chapter 20 Semicolon and Colon   276
Semicolon   276
Colon   281

PART IV

Writing Mechanically Correct Sentences

Chapter 21	**Capital Letters, Apostrophes, and Underlining**	**286**
	Capital Letters	286
	For First Words	286
	For Proper Nouns	288
	Apostrophes	294
	To Show Possession	294
	To Show Omission of Letters or Numbers	299
	To Form Some Plurals	301
	Underlining	302
	Underline Certain Publications, Titles, and Names	302
	Other Uses of Underlining	305
	Underline Certain Foreign Terms and Expressions	305
	Underline Letters, Words, Numbers, and Symbols Treated as Such	306
	Underline to Emphasize a Word or Words	306

PART V

Becoming a Better Speller

Chapter 22	**Becoming a Better Speller**	**309**
	Step 1: Record and Learn the Correct Spellings of Your Misspelled Words	309
	Step 2: Match Spelling and Meaning When You Use Words Having Similar Sounds	309
	Step 3: Learn the Basic Spelling Rules	315
	IE and *EI* Words	315
	Words Ending in *E*	318
	Words Ending in *Y*	319
	Doubling a Final Consonant	321
	A Final Note on Prefixes and Suffixes	322
	Words Often Misspelled	323
	INDEX	**325**

P R E F A C E

. . . .

TO THE INSTRUCTOR

Writing Effective Sentences is designed for developmental English composition courses and concentrates on developing sentence-level writing and editing skills.

The goals of the book are:

1. To give students the knowledge and skills needed for effectively applying the basic principles of grammar, sentence structure, punctuation, mechanics, and spelling to their own writing.

2. To help students understand what hinders effective written expression at the sentence level.

3. To give students confidence in their ability to write well-developed sentences.

To help students achieve these goals, *Writing Effective Sentences* is based on the following assumptions:

1. The students' knowledge of the principles of grammar, sentence structure, punctuation, mechanics, and spelling is valuable only insofar as that knowledge is thorough and is put into practice.

2. Students benefit from having principles underlying effective sentence composition illustrated amply and explained simply.

3. The study of writing effective sentences should proceed sequentially from simple to complex material.

4. The students' learning is enhanced by a book which has a large variety of exercises intended to heighten student interest and to avoid monotony. These exercises should include recognizing and employing correct usage, composing effective sentences, and editing paragraphs.

5. College-level developmental English students learn the value of concrete detail from a book that has varied, readable, high-interest content in its illustrations and exercises. This content should be drawn from news, sports, and traditional academic subjects such as political science, environmental science, music, biology, and history.

6. A college-level book on writing effective sentences should recognize that developmental students include older adults as well as teenagers.

7. As members of a multicultural nation and a world community, students deserve a book whose illustrations and exercises are sensitive to both the unity and the diversity of America, and to the interdependence of nations.

8. Practicing writing sentences that are unified and coherent, that are punctuated effectively, and that are mechanically correct is the surest way for students to improve their writing abilities.

The text is structured as follows:

PART I: The first part of *Writing Effective Sentences* is concerned with the grammatical functions of words and with combining words to make phrases and clauses. Through simple definitions and well-explained examples, Part I outlines the basic principles of grammar and how to apply those principles to writing. Since Part I moves sequentially, students acquire their knowledge and skills in a step-by-step process. Chapters 1-5 move from the single-word parts of speech and simple subject-predicate sentences to compound sentences. An instructor need not be bound by this sequence, however. The Instructor's Manual contains syllabi suggesting alternate approaches to using the book. Chapters 6-7 explain prepositional and verbal phrases, and how they can be used to effectively communicate meaning within a sentence. In Chapters 8-9, subordinate and independent clauses, along with complex and compound-complex sentences, are introduced. Most important, through a rich variety of exercises, students are given many opportunities to practice writing effective sentences of their own. Special emphasis is placed on writing sentences that show logical subordination and coordination.

PART II: The knowledge and skills that students acquired in Part I are directly applicable to Part II: **Writing Unified and Coherent Sentences**. Students build on and apply their knowledge of the parts of speech, of subjects and predicates, and of phrases and clauses to write sentences that are grammatically correct, smooth-flowing, and complete. The chapters end with paragraph-editing exercises. In Chapter 10, students are given extensive opportunities to change fragments into sentences and to employ various options to avoid run-on sentences. Part II also contains chapters on subject-verb agreement (Chapter 11) and pronoun usage (Chapters 12, 13, and 14). These chapters are more comprehensive than those found in most other developmental English books. Chapters 15 and 16 emphasize writing sentences employing appropriately placed modifiers and logically balanced parts. Since understanding and achieving parallel structure is especially difficult for most students, Chapter 16 begins with many exercises intended to reinforce both the value and use of parallelism. Chapter 17 continues the emphasis on writing coherent sentences. Students are given thorough instruction and practice in writing sentences that have consistent usage of person, number and tense.

PARTS III and IV: Chapters 18-21 in Parts III and IV deal with punctuation and mechanics. Much of the material in these chapters will be familiar to students, for the effective use of end marks, commas, semicolons, and capital letters is introduced as appropriate throughout the book. However, the coverage in these chapters—coverage that includes the dash, parentheses, quotation marks, apostrophes, and underlining—is more extensive than that found in most other developmental books. Through numerous sentence- and paragraph-editing exercises, these chapters offer students comprehensive instruction and practice in the placement of marks and the use of capital letters to make the meaning of a sentence clear.

PART V: Chapter 22, **Strategies for Improving Spelling**, offers students a step-by-step process for becoming better spellers. In addition to thorough coverage of the basic rules of spelling, the chapter offers extensive coverage of words often misspelled, as well as practice in using those words correctly. The aim is to have students realize that our system of spelling is, for the most part, predictable and that they can become confident spellers by putting into practice a few simple steps.

The Instructor's Manual includes sample syllabi, a correction symbol chart, student's progress sheet, answers to exercises, and three post-tests per chapter.

TO THE STUDENT

When I was a student in college, my American history instructor began the semester with these words: "Most of you bring to this class a basic knowledge of the subject, but I also hope you bring with you the ability to write an effective sentence." For his class, we had to write a book report, essay exams, and a research paper. These assignments required writing hundreds of sentences, and my instructor never failed to examine each of them with care. Naturally, he also examined my papers for their overall unity and organization and for their supporting reasons and facts. He told us that disunified, incoherent, or poorly supported paragraphs and essays would not earn good grades in his class. But he also told us that frequent errors in grammar, sentence structure, punctuation, mechanics, and spelling would result in low grades. What was true for this instructor was true for others. They respected good writing, and they rewarded it. Your instructors will do the same.

At the heart of successful writing in college and in the workplace is the effectively written sentence. Writing such sentences is a skill you can acquire by understanding how a sentence works and by applying that knowledge to your own writing. Only by putting into practice the principles of grammar, sentence unity and coherence, punctuation, mechanics, and spelling can you improve your writing. This book offers you simple definitions and detailed illustrations of the principles that you will need to know in order to write effective sentences. More important, this book contains numerous exercises to help you put that knowledge into practice. They include finding and correcting errors, writing sentences of your own, and editing paragraphs.

When you complete this book, you should have a much better understanding of what makes a sentence effective, and you should have significantly improved your sentence-writing skills. You may not find that writing is easy. However, you will be a more confident writer and a more richly rewarded one.

ACKNOWLEDGMENTS

I am indebted to many people for their advice and encouragement during the preparation of this book.

At Cecil Community College I am grateful to President Robert L. Gell and the Board of Trustees for their enthusiastic support in the sahbbatical year during which I wrote the first draft. I am also very grateful for the insightful responses by Cecil's English instructors—Sidney Campbell, Dennis Fabella, Dorothy Lehman, Joan-Marie Powers Moss, and Joseph Rose—and their students to early drafts of this book. Special thanks go to Carolyn Farkas for patiently reviewing the manuscript and making many helpful suggestions.

Among the many others who reviewed the manuscript at various stages, I am particularly grateful to Roslyn J. Harper, Trident Technical College; Cynthia Horgan, Ulster County Community College; Steven Katz, State Technical Institute at Memphis; Susan Lagunoff, St. Louis Community College at Florissant Valley; Patsy MacDonald, Northeastern University; Timothy Miank, Lansing Community College; Gretchen B. Niva, Western Kentucky University; Joanne Pinkston; Virginia H. Thigpen, Volunteer State Community College; and Betty Jean Wallace, Sinclair Community College.

At Allyn & Bacon, I thank my editor Joe Opiela and production administrator Susan McIntyre for their invaluable guidance and encouragement. I also thank Donna Merrell Chernin and copy editor Sandra Sizer Moore of DMC & Company for their design skills and perceptive editing.

Lastly, to my secretary Betty Adams, for her attention to detail and for her unfailing encouragement, I am deeply appreciative.

. . . .

Basic English Grammar and the Sentence

Every subject that you study has its own special terms to describe its various elements. The computer scientist speaks of DOS commands, directories, and subdirectories; the psychologist speaks of the id, the ego, and the superego; the mathematician speaks of rational numbers and real numbers. English grammar, too, has some special terms that you should know.

Knowing these terms will help you to understand how words function—alone and in groups—to make meaning. This knowledge will enable you to evaluate the strengths and weaknesses of your own writing and the writing of others. So the terms are not ends in themselves; rather, they are means to an end: to understand your own writing and that of others. In short, they are tools to be used to determine what is correct and effective in written expression.

The first part of this chapter will introduce you to eight basic terms: **noun, pronoun, verb, adjective, adverb, preposition, conjunction,** and **interjection.** Then it will introduce the basic parts of a sentence: the **subject** and the **predicate.** Although you are probably already familiar with a number of these terms, this chapter and the rest of this book will help you to increase and to deepen your knowledge of these and a few others. This will help you to understand and to apply the rules of grammar and mechanics.

In short, these terms are important because they concern how words, the basic building blocks of meaning, function (or act), and combine to form the basic, independent, and larger unit of meaning known as the sentence.

THE GRAMMATICAL FUNCTIONS OF WORDS

Each word acts in one of several ways to express thought:
1. Naming
2. Expressing action, possession, or state of being
3. Modifying
4. Joining
5. Expressing passion or emotion

Traditionally, the ways that words function are categorized into eight parts of speech. Specifically, a word's part of speech is a function of the role it plays in a sentence.

1

According to *The American Heritage Dictionary*, for example, the word *like* can play the role of several parts of speech, depending on how the word is used in a sentence. **Noun**: His *likes* are Sue's dislikes. **Verb**: She *likes* English. **Adjective**: I want a ton of crushed stones and a *like* amount of sand. **Preposition**: Sam is *like* me. Be aware, then, that the following lists may contain words that, depending on circumstances, may function as more than one part of speech. A standard college dictionary is a useful guide to a word's part(s) of speech.

Naming

1. NOUN
A noun is a word (or word group) that names a person, place, thing, or idea.

> **Examples**
> Johnny Thomas, Sheryl Rodriguez, South Carolina, house, horse, cassette, citizen, freedom, compassion, justice, way, area, center, mode, group [*Johnny Thomas* races *horses*. *Sheryl Rodriguez* bought a *house*. The *group* of *citizens* demanded *justice*.]

2. PRONOUN
A pronoun is a word that takes the place of a noun.

> **Examples**
> I, she, it, they, him, her, them, one, something, many, myself, one another, which, what, who, whomever [*They* took *something*. *I* know *who you* are.]

Expressing Action, Possession, or State of Being

3. VERB
A verb is a word (or word group) that expresses action, possession, or state of being.

> **Examples**
> Action: ran, will go, has walked
> Possession: have, had, will own
> State of Being: is, was, seems, appears
> [Brian *has walked* a mile. I *have* five dollars. Tina *appears* happy.]

Modifying

4. ADJECTIVE
An adjective is a word (or word group) that modifies a noun or pronoun.

> **Examples**
>
> small   (small house)
> dry   (dry champagne)
> nine   (nine justices)
> red   (red pen)
> fast   (fast car)
> [I own *a small* house. *The* court has *nine* justices.]

5. ADVERB
An adverb modifies a verb, an adjective, or another adverb.

> **Examples:**
>
> peacefully   (lived peacefully)
> quickly   (walked quickly)
> too   (too slow)
> extremely   (extremely happy)
> very   (very quickly)
> [They lived *peacefully*. Eric spoke *very quickly*.]

Joining

6. CONJUNCTION
A conjunction is a word (or word group) that joins other words (or word groups).

> **Examples**
>
> and, or, for, nor, but, either...or, not only...but also, while, as if, than, as soon as, since, although, thus, therefore, indeed, moreover [Dirk *and* Kate enjoyed the party. She is taller *than* I am.]

7. PREPOSITION
A preposition is a word (or word group) that relates a noun or pronoun, called the object of the preposition, to another word (or word group).

> **Examples**
>
> from   (girl from Thailand)
> on   (books on the desk)
> of   (homes and apartments of Russell Johnson)

around (chain around its neck)
but   (no one but Sunny)
[The girl *from* Thailand is the new exchange student. The books *on* the desk are mine.]

Expressing Passion or Emotion

8. INTERJECTION
An interjection is a word (or words) that expresses passion or emotion; in brief, it is a mild or strong exclamation.

Note: In the first of these examples, since *oh* is a mild interjection, a comma is used. Since *Fire!* and *Ouch!* are strong interjections, an exclamation mark is required.

Examples
Oh   [*Oh*, I thought you knew.]
Fire! [*Fire!* The house is on fire!]
Ouch! [*Ouch!* That injection hurt!]

THE MAIN PARTS OF A SENTENCE

A sentence is an independent grammatical unit that is composed of a subject and a predicate and that expresses a complete thought. The sentence begins with a capital letter and ends with a period, a question mark, or an exclamation mark.

Examples
Scott enjoyed his vacation.
Does Vanessa speak Russian?
They've won!

The Subject

The person, place, thing, or idea that the sentence is about is called the *simple subject*. The simple subject can be a noun or a pronoun.

Examples
Person: *She* spoke quickly.
Place: *Trump Plaza* is a city within a city.
Thing: The *statue* of President Kennedy cost $175,000.
Idea: *Innocence* was lost on the battlefield.
[In these examples the person, place, thing, and idea (the simple subjects) are *She, Trump Plaza, statue,* and *Innocence,* respectively.]

The *complete subject* is the simple subject plus its modifiers.

Examples

> *The angry mob* shouted defiance.
> *The man in the white lab coat* is my uncle.
> *The only drawing created by all four Beatles* has a value of
> four million dollars.

[In these examples the complete subjects are as follows: *The angry mob*, *The man in the white lab coat*, and *The only drawing created by all four Beatles*. The simple subjects are *mob*, *man*, and *drawing*.]

The subject, then, is *the who* or *the what* that the sentence is about. To locate the subject, ask yourself *who or what is acting, possessing, or simply being something.*

Examples

> John's *work day* begins at 6 A.M. [When you ask "Who or what begins at 6 A.M.?" you get *work day* as the answer. *Work day* is the simple subject. The complete subject is *John's work day*.]

> The fast-paced *race* took its toll on the runners. [When you ask "Who or what took its toll on the runners?" you get *race* as the answer. *Race* is the simple subject, and *The fast-paced race* is the complete subject.]

E X E R C I S E   1 - 1

Fill in the blanks with a suitable subject.

1. _____ is my favorite sport.

2. A(n) _____ costs a great deal of money.

3. The _____ ended tragically.

4. A(n) _____ is needed on campus.

5. A(n) _____ will occur next year.

6. An _____ has eight arms, each bearing
   two rows of suckers.

7. The _____ did not disappoint me.

8. _____ is my favorite film star.

9. A(n) _____ makes me happy.

10. The _____ always begins on time.

. . . .

E X E R C I S E	**1 - 2**

Circle the *complete subject* in the following sentences. **Remember:** Ask yourself who or what is acting, possessing, or simply being something.

Examples

(The Brooklyn Bridge) spans the East River between Brooklyn and Manhattan.

1. Bo Jackson won the Heisman Trophy in 1985.

2. Iran and Iraq fought a bitter war from 1980 to 1988.

3. The Republic of South Africa has huge supplies of gold, chrome, and diamonds.

4. The National Baseball Hall of Fame and Museum opened in Cooperstown, New York, in 1939.

5. The chief exports of Senegal are peanuts and fish.

6. Thousands of people die each year from famine in Ethiopia.

7. Reruns of *The Love Boat* air in nearly one hundred countries.

8. Over ninety million Americans from children to grandparents ride bicycles.

9. A single B-1 bomber costs $300 million.

10. The city of Rome, Italy, surrounds Vatican City, a Roman Catholic state.

. . . .

The Predicate

The predicate is a verb (or verb group) that makes an assertion about the subject or asks a question about the subject.

Examples

Sasha *enjoyed* her visit to Los Angeles.
Cannes *is* famous for its yearly film festival.
Did Mark *complete* the report?

[The predicates in these sentences are *enjoyed, is,* and *did complete,* respectively. Each of these verbs is known as the *simple predicate.* The simple predicate can consist of one verb (*enjoyed* or *is*) or a verb group (*did complete*).]

The *complete predicate* consists of a verb or verb group and all other words connected to the verb or verb group. In the three examples, *enjoyed her visit to Los Angeles, is famous for its yearly film festival,* and *did complete the report* are all complete predicates.

To locate the simple predicate of a sentence, ask yourself what word or word group asserts action, possession, or state of being.

Examples

David designed a better mousetrap. [The action word is *designed*, the simple predicate. The complete predicate is *designed a better mousetrap*.]

The "miniature" Christmas garden is fifty feet square. [The simple predicate, *is*, expresses state of being. *Is fifty feet square* is the complete predicate.]

Laura owns fifty shares of IBM stock. [*Owns*, a verb that asserts possession, is the simple predicate, and *owns fifty shares of IBM stock* is the complete predicate.]

Note: Subjects and predicates may be compound:

Amy, Melissa, and Neil walked and then ran to the nearest exit. [The simple subject is *Amy, Melissa,* and *Neil*; the simple predicate is *walked* and *ran*.]

E X E R C I S E   1 - 3

Fill in the blank with a suitable predicate.

1. I _____ to win the race tomorrow.

2. Viktor and Vladimir _____ their travels throughout the United States.

3. Cigarette smoking _____ not on _____ commercial airplanes.

4. The physics textbook _____ long and difficult.

5. The dentist _____ my gums with a pain-killing drug.

6. Eli _____ awake for twenty-four hours.

7. Last Halloween my younger brothers _____ trick-or-treating together.

8. Gene _____ one dollar's worth of nails at the store.

9. Jacob _____ his right to speak.

10. My parents _____ for Philadelphia this afternoon.

· ·

EXERCISE 1-4

Circle the complete subject and underline the complete predicate in each of the following sentences.

Example

(The Haitians) face numerous social, economic and political problems.

1. Few Cherokee Indians live in Tennessee.

2. In the 1830s, the federal government removed the entire Cherokee tribe to Oklahoma.

3. One hundred and eleven nuclear plants operate in the United States today.

4. Indoor air pollution plagues many modern buildings.

5. The mighty Nile is the longest river in the world.

6. America's pro wrestlers attract large television audiences.

7. The Spanish-American War started in 1898 after the destruction of the battleship *Maine* under strange circumstances.

8. The United States Postal Service has over 800,000 employees.

9. President John F. Kennedy created the Peace Corps through an executive order on March 1, 1961.

10. Major League baseball players earn, on average, nearly $975,000 per year.

. . . .

EXERCISE 1-5

Circle the simple subject and underline the simple predicate in each of the following sentences. **Reminder:** The *simple subject* is the subject without its modifiers. The *simple predicate* is the verb (or verb group) that asserts action, possession, or state of being.

Example

(Neil Armstrong) walked on the moon on July 20, 1969.

1. A tunnel links Britain and France.

2. Twenty million Hispanics live in the United States today.

3. Greenland is the largest island in the Atlantic Ocean.

4. *The Bonfire of the Vanities* by Tom Wolfe concerns, among other things, crime in the Bronx.

5. In *Do the Right Thing*, a film about racial disharmony, Spike Lee touched the conscience of America.

6. Only thirty to fifty panthers inhabit Florida's Everglades today.

7. The United States Navy found no definite cause for the explosion of a gun turret on the battleship *Iowa* in 1989.

8. In Operation Desert Storm twenty-six nations formed an alliance against Iraq.

9. The spine of a human being contains twenty-four movable bones.

10. Elimination of air, water, and soil pollution requires the active involvement of all of us.

· ·

E X E R C I S E   1 - 6

In the following paragraph, circle the simple subject and the simple predicate in each sentence. The sentences are numbered for easy identification.

(1) Bangkok and Los Angeles have several similarities. (2) For one, the name of each community means "City of Angels." (3) For another, serious traffic problems make car travel difficult. (4) The numerous cars and buses in both cities foul the air and cause smog. (5) Despite these problems, the cities attract thousands of new residents, as well as tourists, each year. (6) Both rank high as great industrial and business centers. (7) Moreover, residents and visitors enjoy numerous cultural attractions, such as art galleries, museums, and world-class theaters. (8) The cities possess an international flavor and are home to people from all over the world. (9) Lastly, Bangkok and Los Angeles offer a warm and snow-free climate!

Nouns and Pronouns

Having a good understanding of the eight parts of speech—**nouns, pronouns, verbs, adjectives, adverbs, prepositions, conjunctions**, and **interjections**—is important. Like bricks that build a house, the parts of speech are the materials that build a sentence. In this chapter you will learn more about the parts of speech known as **nouns** and **pronouns**, and you will also learn several important properties (or characteristics) shared by nouns and pronouns.

NOUNS

A noun is the name of a person, place, thing, or idea. As used here, the word *idea* includes a concept, an emotion, or an event.

Examples

Person:	man, woman, singer, Betsy Ross
Place:	city, store, Puerto Rico, Grand Canyon
Thing:	desk, money, Statue of Liberty
Concept:	immortality, role, authority, notion, rule
Emotion:	love, hate, despair, fear
Event:	Great Depression, earthquake, concert

One way to tell whether words are nouns (or can be used as nouns in a sentence) is to put *the, an,* or *a* in front of them and see if the combination makes sense. The best way to do this is to use the combination in a sentence. **Caution:** The test is not perfect. For example, you would not ordinarily use it to identify the name of a specific person as a noun: I know *the John Brown* you mean.

Examples

The singer	(Tina Turner is a singer.)
A city	(Houston, Texas, is a city.)
The money	(I lost the money.)

The rule   (What is the rule?)
A love   (Wendy has a love.)
The concert   (New Kids on the Block performed at the concert.)

EXERCISE 2-1

Some of the following words are nouns, and some are other parts of speech. To determine which words are nouns, put *the*, *an*, or *a* in front of each of the following words and see if the combination makes sense. If it does, write a sentence using those two words as the *last two* in it. If the combination does not make sense, leave the space blank.

1. _____ sugar _____

2. _____ ate _____

3. _____ chair _____

4. _____ very _____

5. _____ Vietnam War _____

6. _____ as _____

7. _____ their _____

8. _____ location _____

9. _____ police _____

10. _____ my _____

11. _____ bullfight _____

12. _____ meeting _____

13. _____ chapter _____

14. _____ for _____

15. _____ lasted _____

16. _____ well _____

17. _____ occurs _____

18. _____ newspaper _____

19. _____ yet _____

20. _____ seriously _____

The function of a word in a sentence determines its part of speech. As you have seen in the above exercise, not all words can act as nouns. However, some of the words that you used as nouns could function (act) as other parts of speech in a sentence.

Examples

I chair the meetings of the local PTA. [In this case, *chair* serves as the simple predicate, the main verb of the sentence.] Maria sings well. [*Well* serves as an adverb modifying the predicate *sings.*]

In the following chapters you will learn how to recognize the parts of speech; as a result, you will be better able to understand and to put into practice the rules of grammar and mechanics.

There are two main classes of nouns: **common nouns** and **proper nouns**. A **common noun** names one of a general class of persons, places, or things. A **proper noun** names a particular and individual person, place, or thing and is always capitalized. Study the following examples:

Note: A proper noun is often a word group. *World War II*, for example, is one noun, one event.

Common Nouns	Proper Nouns
people	Magic Johnson, Chris Evert
nations	Mexico, Kuwait, Latvia
buildings	Empire State Building, the White House
events	Boston Tea Party, World War II, Super Bowl XXV

EXERCISE 2-2

Write a proper noun that matches each of the following common nouns.

1. man _____

2. woman _____

3. ocean _____

4. river _____

5. musician _____

6. building _____

7. nation _____

8. holiday _____

9. language _____

10. event _____

. . . .

E X E R C I S E   2 - 3

Underline the nouns in the sentences below. Above each noun write *C* for common noun or *P* for proper noun.

1. The Baltimore Colts won Super Bowl V.

2. Australia is a continent and a country.

3. Benjamin Franklin wanted the turkey as the symbol of the United States.

4. Vatican City is a nation within the city of Rome.

5. Concern for the environment is at the heart of the celebration of Earth Day.

6. Sports such as football and basketball have become big businesses at many universities.

7. Farmers in Vietnam earn about fifteen dollars per month.

8. Liberia was founded by ex-slaves from America.

9. Thomas Jefferson died on the Fourth of July, 1826, fifty years after the Continental Congress adopted the Declaration of Independence.

10. Orlando, Florida, is the home of Disney World.

· ·

PRONOUNS

A **pronoun** is a word that takes the place of a noun. As you have learned, a **noun** is the name of some person, place, thing,or idea. A **pronoun**, on the other hand, indicates a person, place, thing, or idea, but does not actually state its name.

Consider this question: Did the Statue of Liberty inspire the immigrants? Using pronouns, you could answer: Yes, *it* inspired *them.*

Or, consider this question: Did Tom give the flowers to Alice? Again, using pronouns, you could answer: *He* gave *them* to *her.*

The noun that the pronoun *stands for* (*pro-*) is termed the pronoun's **antecedent**. For example: The *girls* said that *they* would be back by noon. The noun *girls* is the antecedent of the pronoun *they*. (As you will learn later, some classes of pronouns have no stated antecedents.)

Pronouns are important because they can make your writing more concise and coherent. In this chapter you will learn several types of pronouns; in chapter 8 you will learn another type: relative pronouns. This may sound like a large task, but actually you already know most of the pronouns. Before learning the pronouns, you should know that nouns and pronouns share certain properties: *person, number, gender,* and *case.*

THE PROPERTIES OF NOUNS AND PRONOUNS

Nouns and pronouns share the characteristics known as *person, number, gender,* and *case.* For now, only the first three will be studied in detail; you will learn more about *case* in chapter 12.

Person

There are three persons: *first, second,* and *third.* When *I* or *we* speak, the first person is being used. When I speak to a person or thing, I use the second person: *you.* When I speak about a person, thing, or idea, I use the third person: *he, she, it,* and *they.*

Thus:
The person *speaking* is the FIRST PERSON (I, we).
The person or thing *spoken to* is the SECOND PERSON (you).
The person or thing *spoken about* is the THIRD PERSON (he, she, it, they).

In general, a noun is in the third person. However, if I name myself, my name is in the first person: *I, Manuel Gonzales,* am from Brazil. And if the noun is spoken to, that noun is in the second person: *You, Manuel Gonzales,* need a passport.

Number

How many? The answer to that question, in grammar, is number. One, two, three, or more. Thus, a noun or pronoun may be *singular* or *plural* in number.

A singular noun or pronoun refers to one person, place, thing, or idea.

Examples
boy, flower, sin, viewpoint, thought, I, he, she, it

A plural noun or pronoun refers to two or more persons, places, things, or ideas. Most singular nouns become plural by adding an "s" to the noun.

Examples
buildings, books, trees, girls, women, they

Note: A *collective noun* names a group: army, navy, committee, band, class, team, company, flock, jury. A collective noun is generally thought of as singular in number.

Example
The jury was selected this morning. [The *jury* is considered a single unit.]

However, a collective noun is plural in number if the members of the group act as individuals.

Example

> The jury took their seats. [In this case, since the members are acting as individuals, *jury* must be considered plural. To avoid such an awkward though technically correct sentence, add a suitable noun: The *members* of the jury took their seats.]

Gender

Gender refers to the sex indicated by the noun or pronoun: *masculine, feminine, neuter,* or *unspecified.*

The masculine gender refers to a noun or pronoun indicating the male sex.

Examples

> boy, man, actor, buck, he, him

The feminine gender refers to a noun or pronoun indicating the female sex.

Examples

> girl, woman, actress, doe, she

The neuter gender refers to a noun or pronoun having no sex.

Examples

> baseball, hotel, cake, liberty, style, song, it

A noun or pronoun may have an unspecified gender:

Examples

> cat, dog, fish, somebody, person [Clearly, the cat, the dog, the fish, the somebody, and the person may be male or female; the sex is *unspecified.*]

Now you know the meaning of person, number, and gender in relation to nouns and pronouns. Try the following exercise.

E X E R C I S E   **2 - 4**

Indicate the person, number, and gender of the underlined nouns and pronouns.

1. The <u>sound</u> of the <u>rooster</u> woke the <u>farmer</u>.
      a   b   c

	Person	**Number**	**Gender**
a)			
b)			
c)			

2. I saw three <u>bulls</u> and ten <u>cows</u> in the <u>barn</u>.
    a   b   c   d

	Person	Number	Gender
a)			
b)			
c)			
d)			

3. <u>You</u>, <u>Fred Patterson</u>, are late.
    a   b

	Person	Number	Gender
a)			
b)			

4. <u>They</u> bought three <u>hens</u> at the <u>auction</u>.
    a   b   c

	Person	Number	Gender
a)			
b)			
c)			

5. When <u>Tom</u> entered the <u>house</u>, <u>he</u> was bitten by a <u>dog</u>.
    a   b c   d

	Person	Number	Gender
a)			
b)			
c)			
d)			

6. <u>Kate</u> found the <u>wallet</u>, and <u>she</u> gave <u>it</u> to <u>Sara</u>.
    a   b   c   d   e

	Person	Number	Gender
a)			
b)			
c)			
d)			
e)			

7. <u>Tim</u>, <u>you</u> can have the <u>job</u>.
    a   b   c

	Person	Number	Gender
a)			
b)			
c)			

8. Do <u>you</u> know that <u>Donald Duck</u> is a <u>drake</u>?
      a   b   c

	Person	Number	Gender
a)			
b)			
c)			

9. <u>Stags</u> and <u>hinds</u> are found in many <u>countries</u>.
    a   b   c

	Person	Number	Gender
a)			
b)			
c)			

10. Do <u>people</u> really distinguish between a <u>goose</u> and a <u>gander</u>?
       a   b   c

       Person   **Number**   **Gender**

a) _____

b) _____

c) _____

. . . .

TYPES OF PRONOUNS

Now that you have studied the characteristics or properties of nouns and pronouns, you are ready to learn the types of pronouns.

Personal Pronouns

A personal pronoun takes the place of a person, place, thing, or idea. The personal pronouns in the following list are used as subjects of sentences and are thus in the *subjective case*. The word *case* refers to the form (or spelling) that a pronoun takes to indicate its function in a sentence.

    1st person singular: *I* (the person speaking)
    2nd person singular: *you* (the person or thing spoken to)
    3rd person singular: *he, she, it* (the person or thing spoken of)

    1st person plural: *we* (the persons speaking)
    2nd person plural: *you* (the persons or things spoken to)
    3rd person plural: *they* (the persons or things spoken of)

Examples

    I will travel to Zambia in March.
    You will need a passport.
    He has a fear of flying.
    We enjoyed the trip.
    You—John, Louis, and Carolyn—will take separate flights.
    They landed safely.

The *objective case* is used when a pronoun functions as the object of a verb or of a preposition. For now, your concern is the pronoun used as the object of a verb. (Chapter 6 discusses the use of the objective case in prepositional phrases.)

To locate the object, take the subject and the simple predicate of the sentence and attach What? or Whom? to them. For example, in the sentence, *I saw them*, you locate the object by asking, *I saw whom?* The answer, the *object*, is *them*. The personal pronouns listed below are used as objects and are thus in the *objective case*.

1st person singular: me
2nd person singular: you
3rd person singular: him, her, it

1st person plural: us
2nd person plural: you
3rd person plural: them

Examples

Judy took *me*.
I know *you*.
Tom loves *her*.
Ms. Parker taught *us*.
We ate *them*.

Note that the personal pronouns *you* and *it* are the same for the subjective case and for the objective case. The spelling does not change.

E X E R C I S E   2 - 5

Rewrite each of the following sentences using a personal pronoun in place of the italicized words. Write *S* above each subjective case pronoun and *O* above each objective case pronoun.

1. *Pauline* enjoyed the concert.

_____

2. *The soldiers* celebrated after the victory.

_____

3. Justin won *the lottery*.

_____

4. Lisa bought *the magazines*.

_____

5. *The snow* fell for hours.

_____

6. *Wayne and Jonathan* will join you.

_____

7. *Barry* lost the wallet at the beach.

_____

8. I love *Karen*.

_____

9. Michelle helped *Gary and Shannon*.

_____

10. *Roxann* was at the party.

_____

. . . .

EXERCISE 2 - 6

In each of the following sentences, underline the correct pronoun in the parentheses. Write *S* above each subjective case pronoun and *O* above each objective case pronoun.

1. William and (I, me) followed Paul's suggestions.

2. Al invited both Karl and (he, him).

3. Either (she, her) or Pauline will tutor Hazel.

4. Mr. Cleaver took Pablo and (I, me) to the game.

5. Will (he, him) and Bert finish the work today?

6. Neither Samantha nor (he, him) arrived on time.

7. Do Brad and John know (they, them)?

8. Could Mrs. Lopez sue (we, us) for damages?

9. Both Carla and (I, me) reached the goal.

10. (He, Him) and Susan suffered from eye strain.

. . . .

Demonstrative Pronouns

Demonstrative pronouns point to a specific person, place, or thing, or to a group of persons, places, or things. There are only four demonstrative pronouns:

    Singular: this, that
    Plural: these, those

Examples

> *This* is Mary's house.
> *That* is Tony's house.
> *These* are the right answers.
> *Those* are the wrong answers.

In the above examples, the demonstrative pronouns are used as subjects. These pronouns can also be used as objects:

Examples

> I bought *this.*
> I like *that.*
> I do not want *these.*
> I will buy *those.*

Note that these pronouns have the same form whether they are used as subjects or as objects.

Interrogative Pronouns

Interrogative pronouns ask a question: *what, which, who, whom, and whose.* Like the demonstrative pronouns, the antecedent of the interrogative pronoun is not specifically expressed. The antecedent of the demonstrative pronoun is implied, and the antecedent of the interrogative pronoun is actually the answer to the question.

Examples

> *What* do you want?   *Whom* do you know?
> *Which* is the answer?   *Whose* is this?
> *Who* is coming?

Who is used as a subject, and *whom* is used as an object. A sentence which reads *Whom do you want?* can be written *You do want whom?* By doing so, you can see that *whom* is the object.

E X E R C I S E   2 - 7

In the following sentences, underline the proper form of the interrogative pronouns *who* and *whom.*

1. (Who, Whom) went with you?

2. (Who, Whom) do you believe?

3. (Who, Whom) saw the accident?

4. (Who, Whom) did Jennifer select?

5. (Who, Whom) wrote *Born on the Fourth of July*?

6. (Who, Whom) does she like?

7. (Who, Whom) will she marry?

8. (Who, Whom) followed Wayne?

9. (Who, Whom) would accept such an invitation?

10. (Who, Whom) did Gary hurt?

. . . .

E X E R C I S E   2 - 8

In the following sentences, underline each pronoun. In the blank, write the name of the pronoun: *personal*, *demonstrative*, or *interrogative*.

1. _____   You will enjoy the play.

2. _____   Does John have those?

3. _____   This is a beautiful park.

4. _____   Suzanne met him at the party.

5. _____   She picked a winner.

6. _____   What does Christopher need?

7. _____   Whom did Wanda select?

8. _____   Kris never saw them.

9. _____   Who won the race?

10. _____   I selected this.

11. _____   They enjoyed the trip to Florida.

12. _____   I went to the concert with Sharon.

13. _____   Victor knows her.

14. _____   That is the dog with rabies.

15. _____   Did Paul have it?

. . . .

Indefinite Pronouns

Indefinite pronouns refer to no particular person, place, thing, or idea; rather, they refer to a group, type, or category.

Following is a list of common indefinite pronouns:

Always Singular		Always Plural	Singular or Plural
another	everything	both	all
anybody	neither	few	any
anyone	nobody	many	more
anything	no one	others	most
each	nothing	several	none
either	one		some
everybody	somebody		such
everyone	someone		

As you can see from the above list, most indefinite pronouns are singular in number.

Each needs help.
Nobody wants to go.

As the list also shows, some indefinite pronouns may be singular or plural. Their number depends on your intention. Often that intention is clear from the noun(s) or pronoun(s) that the indefinite pronoun refers to in the sentence.

Examples

Some of the sugar is ready for shipment. [Since *sugar* is considered as one unit, *some* is singular in number.]
Some of the horses were killed in the fire. [Since *horses* is plural in number, *some* is also plural in number.]

Reflexive and Emphatic Pronouns

Reflexive and emphatic pronouns always end in *–self* or *–selves*:

Singular	Plural
myself	ourselves
yourself	yourselves
herself, himself, itself	———
———	themselves
oneself	———

A *reflexive pronoun* refers back to the subject of the sentence and shows the subject of the sentence acting upon itself. The word(s) that the pronoun refers back to is called the *antecedent*.

Examples

I have *myself* to blame for the problem.
They gave *themselves* a raise.
The hunter shot *himself* by mistake.

In the above examples, *I*, *They*, and *hunter* are the antecedents of *myself*, *themselves*, and *himself*, respectively.

The *emphatic pronouns* stress the importance of their antecedents.

Examples

> The president *himself* decided to direct the invasion.
> You *yourself* will be responsible for the work.

Note: While reflexive pronouns are used as objects, emphatic pronouns are used as *appositives*. An *appositive* is simply a word (or word group) that is placed next to another word (or word group) and explains it. The emphatic pronouns function as appositives. In the first example, *himself* is an appositive for *president*, and *yourself* is an appositive for *you* in the second example. Consider the following example: Alice Mayer, the leader of the chorus, was given the award. *The leader of the chorus* is the appositive for *Alice Mayer*.

Reciprocal Pronouns

Reciprocal pronouns express a mutual relationship between persons, places, things, or ideas; these pronouns are *one another* and *each other*. *Each other* regularly refers to two items; *one another* is regularly used with reference to more than two items.

Examples

> Paul and Joan love *each other*.
> The tourists enjoyed *one another* during their trip to Japan.

THE PRONOUNS AT A GLANCE

Pronouns That Take the Place of a Person, Place, Thing or Idea

Personal Pronouns

	Subject	Object
1st person singular:	I	me
2nd person singular:	you	you
3rd person singular:	he, she, it	him, her, it
1st person plural:	we	us
2nd person plural:	you	you
3rd person plural:	they	them

Pronouns That Point to a Person, Place, Thing or Idea

Demonstrative Pronouns

Singular	Plural
this, that	these, those

Pronouns That Ask a Question

Interrogative Pronouns

what   who   whose   which   whom

Pronouns That Refer to a Group, Type, or Category

Indefinite Pronouns

Always Singular		Always Plural	Singular or Plural
another	everything	both	all
anybody	neither	few	any
anyone	nobody	many	more
anything	no one	others	most
each	nothing	several	none
either	one	some	
everybody	somebody	such	
everyone	someone	something	

Pronouns That Show the Subject of the Sentence Acting on Itself or That Emphasize the Antecedent

Reflexive or Emphatic Pronouns

Singular	Plural
myself	ourselves
yourself	yourselves
himself, herself, itself	——
——	themselves
oneself	

Pronouns That Express a Mutual Relationship between Persons, Places, Things, or Ideas

Reciprocal Pronouns

each other	(refers to two items)
one another	(refers to more than two items)

EXERCISE 2-9

In the following sentences, underline the pronouns. In the blank, write the type of pronoun you have underlined: *indefinite, reflexive, emphatic,* or *reciprocal.*

_____ 1. The captain himself called for the crew to abandon ship.

_____ 2. Both were ready to begin the race.

_____ 3. Al was not aware of the others in the room.

_____ 4. Did Ginger enjoy herself?

_____ 5. Donna herself will lead the march.

_____ 6. Some of the money was left on the table.

_____ 7. Everyone was prepared to win.

_____ 8. Something was clearly wrong.

_____ 9. The men restrained themselves during the strike.

_____ 10. Most of the snowy weather was in March.

. . . .

EXERCISE 2-10

Use each of the following pronouns in a sentence.

Example
The indefinite pronoun *no one*
No one followed the captain's order to open fire.

1. The indefinite pronoun *anyone*

_____

2. The reflexive pronoun *myself*

_____

3. The indefinite pronoun *nothing*

_____

4. The emphatic pronoun *ourselves*

_____

5. The indefinite pronoun *several*

_____

6. The indefinite pronoun *either*

_____

7. The reflexive pronoun *herself*

_____

8. The indefinite pronoun *none*

_____

9. The reciprocal pronoun *each other*

_____

10. The indefinite pronoun *nobody*

_____

11. The personal pronoun *I*

_____

12. The interrogative pronoun *who*

_____

· ·

E X E R C I S E 2 - 11

Underline the pronouns in the following sentences. Above each pronoun identify the type: personal (PER), interrogative (INTER), demonstrative (DEM), indefinite (IND), reflexive (REF), emphatic (EMP), or reciprocal (REC).

1. I did not know the others at the meeting.

2. You yourself will have to meet them.

3. We need to help one another.

4. Who said that?

5. This is it.

6. All of the gold belonged to them.

7. Is anything wrong?

8. Patricia and Paul intend to help each other.

9. She wants these and not those.

10. They told themselves not to worry.

. . . .

E X E R C I S E 2 - 1 2

Use each of the following pronouns in a sentence.

Example
> The personal pronoun *she*
> She correctly answered the questions.

1. The personal pronoun *me*

   _____

2. The reflexive pronoun *themselves*

   _____

3. The interrogative pronoun *which*

   _____

4. The emphatic pronoun *itself*

   _____

5. The indefinite pronoun *any*

   _____

6. The demonstrative pronoun *this*

   _____

7. The personal pronoun *he*

   _____

8. The reciprocal pronoun *one another*

   _____

9. The indefinite pronoun *such*

_____

10. The interrogative pronoun *what*

_____

11. The personal pronoun *them*

_____

12. The emphatic pronoun *herself*

_____

13. The indefinite pronoun *another*

_____

14. The personal pronoun *it*

_____

15. The indefinite pronoun *all*

_____

. . . .

Verbs

While nouns and pronouns are important parts of speech, the verb is even more important because, when it acts as the predicate of a sentence, it is the very heart of the sentence. In this chapter you will learn what a verb is, what its properties are, what its role is as the predicate in a sentence, and how to use it effectively.

A verb acting as a predicate is a word or words that say something about the subject of a sentence. The verb expresses an action (Tom *ate* an apple.), tells who or what owns something (Tom *has* two cars.), or tells what someone or something is (Tom *seems* happy.).

In general, it changes its form to indicate time. Knowing this fact will help identify the verb in a sentence.

Examples

> Today Sue *lives* in Maryland.
> Last year she *lived* in Texas.
> Next year she *will live* in Alaska.

All of the italicized verbs are called **simple predicates**. The **complete predicate** is the predicate plus its object(s) or complement(s) and any modifiers (adjectives and adverbs). In the examples above, *lives in Maryland*, *lived in Texas*, and *will live in Alaska* are the **complete predicates**. Note: Objects and complements are discussed at the end of this chapter.]

In a sentence, first locate the simple predicate by looking for the word that expresses action, ownership, or state of being. When you locate that word and ask **who?** or **what?**, your answer will be the **simple subject** of the sentence.

Consider the following examples:

1. Earl ran into the street.
   The action word is *ran*, the simple predicate. When you ask *Who ran?*, your answer is the simple subject, *Earl*.

2. Alice bought a new Ford.
The action word, the simple predicate, is *bought*.
When you ask *Who bought?*, your answer is *Alice*, the simple subject.

3. The Third National Bank has plenty of money on hand.
Has expresses ownership or possession and is the simple predicate. *Who has [the money]?* The answer is the simple subject, *Third National Bank*.

4. The voters of New York are happy about the election.
The simple predicate is *are*, a state-of-being word. *Who are [happy]?* The answer is the simple subject, the *voters*.

E X E R C I S E   3 - 1

In the following sentences, draw one line under the simple subjects and two lines under the simple predicates.

1. Marie, Darryl, and Jonathan look sad.

2. I live in the third house on Elm Street.

3. Philip Caputo wrote *A Rumor of War*.

4. My sister from Ohio gave birth to twins.

5. The train from New York crashed into a bus.

6. The gold coins were old and rare.

7. This book weighs nearly ten pounds.

8. A knowledge of verbs made me a more confident writer.

9. Some forms of life in the ocean exist on sulfur and not on oxygen.

10. Small earthquakes are a daily event in California.

. . . .

E X E R C I S E   3 - 2

For additional practice in locating simple subjects and simple predicates, draw one line under the simple subject and two lines under the simple predicate in each of the following sentences.

1. Twenty gallons of gasoline cost $5.40 in 1950.

2. Crude oil sold for only six cents a gallon in the same year.

3. American soldiers missing in action in the Vietnam War number over 2,250.

4. In August 1991, the captain of the Greek cruise ship *Oceanos* abandoned his sinking ship ahead of over one hundred and fifty passengers.

5. In 1912, Captain Smith of the *Titanic* went down with his ship.

6. In Roman mythology, the god of gates and doorways is Janus.

7. The Marshall Plan aided European recovery after World War II.

8. Robert F. Kennedy and Martin Luther King, Jr., died from assassins' bullets in 1968.

9. The United States launched *Columbia*, the world's first space shuttle, in 1981.

10. At maturity, some octopuses weigh nearly six hundred pounds.

. . . .

Because verbs are the **essential parts** of sentences, knowing as much as you can about verbs is important. Like nouns and pronouns, verbs have certain characteristics or properties which must be known. These properties are **voice, tense, person, number**, and **mood**.

VOICE

There are only two voices: **active** and **passive**. In the active voice the subject is doing the acting; in the passive voice, the subject is being acted upon. In each, the verb varies in form to show either active or passive voice.

Active Voice

A verb in the active voice shows that the subject is performing an action, owning something, or just existing (or existing in a certain way).

Examples
Iran *freed* fifty-two American hostages in 1981.
Cathy *owns* a Chevy.
Steve *appears* anxious.

Passive Voice

In the passive voice, the subject receives the action or ownership; in other words, the passive voice shows what is happening to the subject. The passive voice is composed of a form of the verb *to be* (*am, is, are, was, were*) and a verb's **past participle**, such as *freed, owned, invaded, written*. As you will learn later in this chapter, most verbs form their past participle by adding *–ed*, *–d*, or *–t* to the form of the verb used to express present time. Thus, the past participles of *love, live*, and *act* are *loved, lived*, and *acted*, respectively.

Examples

>   Fifty-two American hostages *were freed* by Iran in 1981.
>   The Chevy *is owned* by Cathy.
>   Grenada *was invaded* by American troops in 1983.
>   *The "Albany" novels were written* by William Kennedy.

As you can see, while the active voice places emphasis on the "actor" as subject of the sentence, the passive voice makes the recipient the subject and either deletes the actor or names the actor in a prepositional phrase. (A prepositional phrase is a group of related words introduced by a preposition, such as *in, by, on,* and *from*, and having an object, such as *Iran, Cathy, troops,* and *William Kennedy* in the sentences above.)

The passive voice is especially useful when you do not know who the actor is or if you have reason to conceal the actor. For example, Mrs. Tompkins *was* badly *scarred* in the attack. In this example, who scarred Mrs. Tompkins is not known.

Unless you have reason to use the passive voice, use the active voice. In general, the active voice has more energy, clarity, and intensity than the passive voice.

EXERCISE 3 - 3

In the following sentences, underline the simple predicates. Write *A* above each active voice predicate, and *P* above each passive voice predicate. The first one is done for you.

1. On December 28, 1890, Chief Big Foot, the leader of the Sioux, *surrendered* peacefully to troops of the Seventh Cavalry.

2. The Sioux, mostly old people and children, were surrounded and nearly disarmed by the troops on the following day.

3. One Sioux, apparently deaf, resisted.

4. A shot was fired by somebody, and a soldier screamed in pain.

5. The soldiers fired their automatic Gatling guns.

6. At least 200 Sioux adults and children were massacred by the troops.

7. Perhaps the troops were haunted by memories of Custer's defeat.

8. Perhaps they were motivated by racial hatred.

9. In truth, no reason justified the troops' action.

10. The Battle of Wounded Knee in South Dakota was no "battle."

EXERCISE 3-4

In each of the following sentences, draw one line under the subject and two lines under the passive voice predicate. The first one is done for you.

1. The <u>freedom</u> of the "United Colonies" <u><u>was declared</u></u> by the Continental Congress on July 2, 1776.

2. The Declaration of Independence was adopted by the delegates on the fourth.

3. In fact, "freedom" from England was opposed by many people in the colonies.

4. The colonies were occupied by English people.

5. Moreover, the colonies were ruled by those people.

6. Every colony was represented by a colonial agent in Parliament.

7. King George III was loved by many colonials.

8. Finally, the law was generally followed by King George.

9. Obviously, many unwise laws were enacted by Parliament to restrict the rights of the colonies to govern themselves.

10. In large part, however, the separation was caused by colonists who had become "Americans."

· ·

EXERCISE 3-5

Rewrite each of the following sentences by changing the predicate to the passive voice. In the passive voice, remember to use *is* and *are* to indicate present time, and *was* and *were* to indicate past time.

Examples

> The letter carrier delivers the mail at noon.
> The mail *is delivered* by the letter carrier at noon.
> Our committee drafted the budget.
> The budget *was drafted* by our committee.

1. Gerry loves Beverly.

2. Someone removed all the papers on my desk.

_____

3. Geraldo examines the reports on a daily basis.

_____

4. Your performance stunned the audience.

_____

5. I placed the money on the table.

_____

6. Vernon solved the puzzle.

_____

7. The strong winds prevent a smooth flight.

_____

8. The satellite orbits the earth every twenty-four hours.

_____

9. Jason rented the apartment.

_____

10. Connie needs two days to complete the work.

_____

· ·

E X E R C I S E   3 - 6

On separate paper, rewrite each sentence in Exercise 3-4 by changing the simple predicate from the passive voice to the active voice.

· ·

TENSE

A second characteristic that verbs have is tense, a word meaning **time**. The most often-used tenses in English grammar are the following: **simple present, simple past, simple future, present perfect, past perfect,** and **future perfect.**

Examples

Simple Present Tense:	I talk	I speak
Simple Past Tense:	I talked	I spoke

Simple Future Tense:	I shall talk	I shall speak
Present Perfect Tense:	I have talked	I have spoken
Past Perfect Tense:	I had talked	I had spoken
Future Perfect Tense:	I shall have talked	I shall have spoken

The Tenses Defined

What exactly does each of the tenses mean?

The Present Tense   The **present tense** means that the time of the speaking or writing is the same as the time of the action expressed in the sentence.

Example

I *drive* a truck. [The time of the driving and the time of the speaking or writing of the sentence are the same.]

The present tense is also used to express what is habitually or generally true.

Example

I *drive* my children to school.

The Past Tense   The **past tense** means that something has occurred and is now finished.

Example

I *drove* a taxi several years ago. [I am speaking or writing the sentence now; however, by the use of past tense, I am indicating prior, rather than present, action. The driving occurred and is now over.]

The Future Tense   The **future tense** means that the action will take place at some future date.

Example

I *shall drive* you to work next week. [Though I am speaking or writing the sentence now, I show, by the use of the future tense, that the act of driving will occur at some future time.]

In general, the future tense is formed by using *shall* or *will* with the present infinitive of the verb (without the *to*). This will be explained in the section covering the formation of the tenses.

Sometimes the present tense is used to signal the future: I join the company in March. A form of the verb *to be* and *going to* may be used to express the future: I am going to join the company in March.

EXERCISE 3-7

Draw one line under each simple subject, and two lines under the simple predicate in each of the following sentences. In the blank, indicate the tense of the predicate: *present*, *past*, or *future*.

_____ 1. A gourmet enjoys fine food and drink.

_____ 2. The Library of Congress was founded in 1800.

_____ 3. According to some politicians, the District of Columbia will become America's fifty-first state within the next ten years.

_____ 4. AIDS remains a serious health problem.

_____ 5. Mars was the Roman god of war.

_____ 6. India will exceed China in population by the year 2050.

_____ 7. In 1928, Walt Disney created the first Mickey Mouse cartoon.

_____ 8. Alaska has the highest mountain in America.

_____ 9. The world will remember the Tienanmen Square massacre for many years.

_____ 10. The United States signed peace agreements with Vietnam in 1973.

. . . .

The Present Perfect Tense **The present perfect tense and all other perfect tenses refer to a completed or perfected action.** All perfect tenses are constructed by combining a form of the verb *to have* with the past participle of a verb. The present perfect tense shows that an action was completed sometime prior to the present time.

Example
I *have driven* you home.

The present perfect tense may also indicate that an action started in the past and continues to the present time.

Example
I *have driven* a bus for many years. [The point is that I *still do* drive a bus.]

The Past Perfect Tense The **past perfect tense** shows that the action was completed prior to a specific point in the past.

Example

>   When I reached Atlanta, I *had driven* for nearly eight hours.
>   [The act of driving occurred before or was completed before
>   arrival in Atlanta.]

The past perfect tense may also be used to indicate a past hope or desire that is not fulfilled.

Example

>   They *had wanted* to drive Terry to the airport.

The Future Perfect Tense The **future perfect tense** shows that the action was completed before some future time.

Example

>   I *shall have driven* 2000 miles by next Tuesday. [The driving
>   will occur in the future and be completed prior to Tuesday]

E X E R C I S E   3 - 8

Draw one line under each simple subject, and two lines under the simple predicates in the following sentences. In the blank, indicate the tense of each predicate: *present perfect*, *past perfect*, *future perfect*.

_____ 1. The United States has belonged to the United Nations for many years.

_____ 2. Earlier they had mentioned their fears for the success of the project.

_____ 3. By December the Johnsons will have made their trip to France.

_____ 4. They have lived in Boston for many years.

_____ 5. I have heard that joke many times.

_____ 6. Ted had been to the altar nine times before his latest marriage.

_____ 7. By the end of our journey we will have seen most of the United States.

_____ 8. Florence has caught a cold.

_____ 9. Before the accident Thomas had appeared happy.

_____10. Alex has longed for victory for some time.

. . . .

E X E R C I S E   3 - 9

For additional practice in recognizing predicates, draw two lines under the simple predicates in the following sentences. Draw one line under the simple subjects. In the blank write the tense of each predicate.

1. The U.S. Postal Service handles 165 billion pieces of mail each year.

   Tense:_____

2. The Social Security Act became law on August 14, 1935.

   Tense:_____

3. Most American landfills will be full by the year 2005.

   Tense:_____

4. Only about a thousand giant pandas remain in China's forests.

   Tense:_____

5. By the year 2005, the giant panda may have become extinct in the wild.

   Tense:_____

6. The Boeing 747-400 will carry over 650 passengers.

   Tense:_____

7. The world's largest salamanders live in the streams of Western Maryland.

   Tense:_____

8. The United States has trusted Canada as a good neighbor for many years.

   Tense:_____

9. The President will have spoken to the Russians about the new trade agreement prior to the formal meeting in July.

   Tense:_____

10. Bishop Desmond Tutu received the Nobel Peace Prize in 1984 for his heroic efforts on behalf of racial justice in South Africa.

   Tense:_____

. . . .

The Principal Parts of the Verb

The principal parts of a verb are the **present infinitive**, the **past tense**, the **past participle**, and the **present participle**. Verbs are classified as **regular** or **irregular**, and form their principal parts accordingly.

A **regular verb** forms its past tense and past participle by adding *–ed*, *–d*, or *–t* to the present infinitive (without the *to* in front of it). The present infinitive is the "to" form of the verb; *to go, to run*, and *to walk* are examples of the present infinitive. The present participle for both regular and irregular verbs is formed by adding *–ing* to the present infinitive. Each of the six tenses also has a progressive form, which uses the present participle. You will learn about this form later in this chapter.

Fortunately, most verbs are regular. Consider these examples:

Present Infinitive	Past Tense	Past Participle	Present Participle
(to) act	acted	acted	acting
bake	baked	baked	baking
care	cared	cared	caring
eject	ejected	ejected	ejecting
fool	fooled	fooled	fooling
grab	grabbed	grabbed	grabbing
spend	spent	spent	spending
spy	spied	spied	spying
zip	zipped	zipped	zipping

Caution: If you are unsure of the spelling of a verb form, be sure to check a good dictionary.

Not all verbs form their past tense and past participle by adding *–ed*, *–d*, or *–t*. Those that do not are called **irregular verbs**. You already know many of them through using them over the years. For example:

Present Infinitive	Past Tense	Past Participle	Present Participle
(to) arise	arose	arisen	arising
become	became	become	becoming
begin	began	begun	beginning
blow	blew	blown	blowing
break	broke	broken	breaking
bring	brought	brought	bringing
burst	burst	burst	bursting
buy	bought	bought	buying
catch	caught	caught	catching
choose	chose	chosen	choosing
come	came	come	coming
cut	cut	cut	cutting
do	did	done	doing
draw	drew	drawn	drawing
drink	drank	drunk	drinking

Present Infinitive	Past Tense	Past Participle	Present Participle
drive	drove	driven	driving
eat	ate	eaten	eating
fall	fell	fallen	falling
find	found	found	finding
fly	flew	flown	flying
forget	forgot	forgot(ten)	forgetting
freeze	froze	frozen	freezing
get	got	got(ten)	getting
give	gave	given	giving
go	went	gone	going
grind	ground	ground	grinding
grow	grew	grown	growing
hang (execute)	hanged	hanged	hanging
hang (suspend)	hung	hung	hanging
have	had	had	having
hear	heard	heard	hearing
hide	hid	hidden	hiding
hold	held	held	holding
keep	kept	kept	keeping
know	knew	known	knowing
lay	laid	laid	laying
lead	led	led	leading
leave	left	left	leaving
let	let	let	letting
lie (rest)	lay	lain	lying
lie (falsify)	lied	lied	lying
pay	paid	paid	paying
put	put	put	putting
read	read	read	reading
ride	rode	ridden	riding
ring	rang	rung	ringing
rise	rose	risen	rising
run	ran	run	running
say	said	said	saying
see	saw	seen	seeing
seek	sought	sought	seeking
set	set	set	setting
shed	shed	shed	shedding
shine	shone	shone (shined)	shining
shrink	shrank	shrunk(en)	shrinking
sing	sang	sung	singing
sink	sank	sunk	sinking
sit	sat	sat	sitting
speak	spoke	spoken	speaking
spring	sprang	sprung	springing

Present Infinitive	Past Tense	Past Participle	Present Participle
stand	stood	stood	standing
steal	stole	stolen	stealing
stick	stuck	stuck	sticking
swear	swore	sworn	swearing
swim	swam	swum	swimming
swing	swung	swung	swinging
take	took	taken	taking
teach	taught	taught	teaching
tear	tore	torn	tearing
think	thought	thought	thinking
throw	threw	thrown	throwing
wake	woke	woke (waked)	waking
wear	wore	worn	wearing
weep	wept	wept	weeping
win	won	won	winning
wind	wound	wound	winding
wring	wrung	wrung	wringing
write	wrote	written	writing

E X E R C I S E   3 - 1 0

In each of the following sentences, fill in the correct past tense of the irregular verb. Use the chart above as a guide.

1. From 1840 to 1924, immigrants _____ (come) to the United States in great numbers and for many reasons.

2. In Ireland, a potato famine _____ (bring) starvation, and the Irish economy _____ (grind) to a halt.

3. As a result, nearly two million Irish _____ (leave) for America.

4. In Austria, Italy, Sicily, and Germany, serious political fights _____ (break) out.

5. Often, the blame for the turmoil _____ (fall) on the heads of innocent Jews.

6. In any event, Jew and non-Jew alike _____ (seek) relief in America.

7. Between 1900 and 1920, nearly fourteen and a half million immigrants _____ (choose) to seek a new life in the United States.

8. When these people arrived, they _____ (see) the Statue of Liberty.

9. It _____ (give) them hope.

. . . .

E X E R C I S E   3 - 1 1

For additional exercise, in each of the following sentences fill in the correct past tense form of the irregular verb. Use the chart above as a guide.

1. In 1892 Ellis Island _____ (become) the examining center for the new immigrants.

2. First, the immigrants _____ (hear) directions in German, Italian, Polish, and Yiddish, among others.

3. Next, doctors _____ (begin) physical examinations.

4. The immigrants _____ (know) that a serious health problem resulted in deportation.

5. Doctors _____ (write) such letters as *H* (heart trouble) and *E* (trachoma, an eye disease) on the backs of people who failed their physicals.

6. Eighty percent of the immigrants _____ (get) through this examination successfully.

7. Finally, an immigration inspector (or interpreter) _____ (read) a series of questions about work, legal problems, and so on.

8. If an immigrant _____ (lie) and was found out, he or she could be deported.

9. After successfully answering the questions, an immigrant _____ (get) a "landing card."

10. With it, he or she _____ (pay) a visit to the exchange office and received American money in place of foreign currency.

11. At this point, the immigrant _____ (win) entrance to the United States.

. . . .

EXERCISE 3-12

In the space below, write the present and past tense forms of the fifteen verbs that cause you the most difficulty.

Present Tense	Past Tense	Present Tense	Past Tense
1._____	_____	9._____	_____
2. _____	_____	10._____	_____
3. _____	_____	11._____	_____
4. _____	_____	12._____	_____
5. _____	_____	13._____	_____
6. _____	_____	14._____	_____
7. _____	_____	15._____	_____
8. _____	_____		

Using at least ten of the verbs you have just listed, write a paragraph. The paragraph can be serious or funny.

. . . .

Tense Formation

How are the various tenses formed? First, you need to know the principal parts of the verb. Second, you have to put the right part in the right place. Knowing the principal parts of the verb *to walk* (*walk, walked, walked, walking*), for example, you can easily form the tenses for the first person singular:

Simple present: *I + present infinitive* (I walk)
Simple past: *I + past tense* (I walked)
Simple future: *I + shall + present infinitive* (I shall walk)
Present perfect: *I + have + past participle* (I have walked)
Past perfect: *I + had + past participle* (I had walked)
Future perfect: *I + shall have + past participle* (I shall have walked)

Another way to show the tense formation is the following:

Present: I *walk*   (present infinitive)
Past: I *walked*   (past tense)
Future: I shall *walk*   (present infinitive)
Present perfect: I have *walked* (past participle)
Past perfect: I had *walked*   (past participle)
Future perfect: I shall have *walked* (past participle)

When you write out all the tenses, you **conjugate the verb**. The regular verb *to trust* is conjugated in the active voice in the following manner:

Present singular
I, you trust
he, she, it trusts

Present plural
we, you, they trust

Note that the verb in the present tense, third person singular, ends in s.

Past singular
I, you, he, she, it trusted

Past plural
we, you, they trusted

Future singular
I shall trust
you, he, she, it will trust

Future plural
we shall trust
you, they will trust

Present perfect singular
I, you have trusted
he, she, it has trusted

Present perfect plural
we, you, they have trusted

Past perfect singular
I, you, he, she, it had trusted

Past perfect plural
we, you, they had trusted

Future perfect singular
I shall have trusted
you, he, she, it will have trusted

Future perfect plural
we shall have trusted
you, they will have trusted

The same verb can, of course, be conjugated in the passive voice. In this case, you use the appropriate forms of the verb *to be* and the past participle of *to trust* (i.e., *trusted*).

An **irregular verb** is conjugated in the same way as a regular verb. However, you need to know the principal parts of the irregular verb. Following is the conjugation in the active voice of the irregular verb *to know*. The principal parts are (*to*) *know, knew, known, knowing*. (Of course, the verb *to know* can also be conjugated in the passive voice.)

Present singular
I, you know
he, she, it knows

Present plural
we, you, they know

Past singular
I, you, he, she, it knew

Past plural
we, you, they knew

Future singular
I shall know
you, he, she, it will know

Future plural
we shall know
you, they will know

Present perfect singular
I, you have known
he, she, it has known

Present perfect plural
we, you, they have known

Past perfect singular
I, you, he, she, it had known

Past perfect plural
we, you, they had known

Future perfect singular
I shall have known
you, he, she, it will have known

Future perfect plural
we shall have known
you, they will have known

The most irregular verb of all is the verb *to be*. It has eight forms: (*to*) *be*, *am*, *is*, *are*, *was*, *were*, *been*, *being*. Its present and past tenses are the most difficult:

Present singular
I am
you are
he, she, it is

Present plural
we, you, they are

Past singular
I was
you were
he, she, it was

Past plural
we, you, they were

Future singular
I shall be
you, he, she, it will be

Future plural
we shall be
you, they will be

Present perfect singular
I, you have been
he, she, it has been

Present perfect plural
we, you, they have been

Past perfect singular
I, you, he, she, it had been

Past perfect plural
we, you, they had been

Future perfect singular
I shall have been
you, he, she, it will have been

Future perfect plural
we shall have been
you, they will have been

E X E R C I S E   3 - 1 3

Fill in each blank with the appropriate *present*, *past*, or *future* tense of the indicated *irregular verb*. In some sentences, more than one answer is appropriate.

1. Yesterday I _____ (swim) for nearly two hours.

2. As a rule, Don _____ (be) ten minutes late for a meeting.

3. I _____ (keep) the secret until Marie died.

4. When I asked him, he just _____ (shake) his head.

5. Yesterday Kevin _____ (be) in a nasty mood.

6. At last week's trial Alex _____ (lie) to the jury.

7. Mary and Katie _____ (be) in Europe last summer.

8. When the doctor came, the child _____ (hide) behind a chair.

9. Last night, when William _____ (hear) the tragic news,

   he _____ (weep) for hours.

10. Water _____ (freeze) when it reaches 32° Fahrenheit.

11. While dieting last month, Elizabeth _____ (eat) only one

12. We _____ (be) at the picnic tomorrow.

13. The helium-filled balloon _____ (burst) just as it was landing.

14. Carl _____ (get) a raise next week.

15. Nancy _____ (be) unhappy when she learned of the accident.

16. Next February Paul _____ (fly) to Germany.

17. Ted _____ (fall) in love when he saw Kate.

18. Usually, I _____ (sing) in the shower.

19. Lou _____ (drink) eight beers at Janet's party yesterday.

20. Yesterday I _____ (sit) for two hours at the train station.

· ·

E X E R C I S E   3 - 1 4

Fill in each blank with the requested *present perfect*, *past perfect*, or *future perfect* form of the simple predicate.

1. I _____ (love, present perfect tense) you for many years.

2. By next year Pauline _____ (earn, future perfect tense) over $50,000 on her investments.

3. Bruce _____ (be, past perfect tense) ready for several hours before Lois arrived.

4. Kurt _____ (wear, present perfect tense) the same clothes for the last five days.

5. Judy _____ (write and mail, past perfect tense) her letter of resignation the day before she was fired!

6. I _____ (be, present perfect tense) with you for twenty years.

7. He _____ (spy, present perfect tense) for the CIA since 1989.

8. Alice _____ (hope, past perfect tense) to attend her class reunion.

9. The robbers _____ (take, past perfect tense) the money one hour before the bank opened.

10. We _____ (walk, future perfect tense) over 2,000 miles
    by the time we reach Alaska.

11. They _____ (expect, past perfect tense) to meet the president of
    IBM.

12. They _____ (do, future perfect tense) the work by next Saturday.

. . . .

SPECIAL TENSE FORMS

The simple and perfect tenses are known as the **common tenses**. They indicate simple present, future, or completed actions. To show action that is continuing requires the **progressive tense**; the **emphatic tense** of a verb gives emphasis to the point the verb is making.

The Progressive Tense

The progressive tense is formed by using the appropriate form of the verb *to be* and the present participle. Study the following conjugation of the verb *to play*.

Present progressive singular
I am playing
you are playing
he, she, it is playing

Present progressive plural
we, you, they are playing

Past progressive singular
I was playing
you were playing
he, she, it was playing

Past progressive plural
we, you, they were playing

Future progressive singular
I shall be playing
you, he, she, it will be playing

Future progressive plural
we shall be playing
you, they will be playing

Present perfect progressive singular
I, you have been playing
he, she, it has been playing

Present perfect progressive plural
we, you, they have been playing

Past perfect progressive singular
I, you, he, she, it had been playing

Past perfect progressive plural
we, you, they had been playing

Future perfect progressive singular
I shall have been playing
you, he, she, it will have been playing

Future perfect progressive plural
we shall have been playing
you, they will have been playing

How are these progressive tenses used?

The Present Progressive Tense   The present progressive tense means that an action is occurring even as you speak or write. This tense may also be used to indicate an action that is occurring, and which is presently and generally true.

Examples

> The ground *is moving*, and buildings *are falling*. [The actions are occurring even as you speak.]

> The murder rate *is increasing* in the nation's capital. [The rate may not increase today; however, the progressive tense is used to indicate a present and general truth about the nation's capital.]

The Past Progressive Tense   The past progressive tense shows an action continuing in the past. This tense may also be used to show that two past actions were happening at the same time.

Examples

> By late in 1781, General Washington *was becoming* more certain about victory over the British. [Here the past progressive tense indicates that Washington's thoughts were changing in a positive way.]

> The French fleet closed the Virginia waterway while General Washington *was encircling* the British forces at Yorktown. [In this example the past progressive tense is used to show that two actions were taking place at the same time.]

The Future Progressive Tense   The future progressive tense indicates a future action that will continue, either generally or at a set date.

Examples

> The Hubble Space Telescope *will be orbiting* the earth for many years. [The future progressive tense is here used to indicate a general and continuing action.]

> Jesse Jackson *will be addressing* the graduates on June 9. [The future progressive tense is used to indicate a continuing action at a set future date.]

EXERCISE 3-15

Rewrite each of the following sentences by changing the present tense to the present progressive tense.

Example

> **From:** I eat.
> **To:**   I am eating.

1. **From:** Troy watches MTV.

   To: _____

2. **From:** Charley and Laurie walk rapidly.

   To: _____

3. **From:** Brent reads mystery novels.

   To: _____

4. **From:** I expect visitors.

   To: _____

5. **From:** The men finish their job today.

   To: _____

. . . .

E X E R C I S E   3 - 1 6

Rewrite each of the following sentences by changing the past tense to the past progressive tense.

Example
> **From:** I slept.
> **To:**   I was sleeping.

1. **From:** Bert cooked.

   To: _____

2. **From:** I studied in the library.

   To: _____

3. **From:** Richard sought help at the clinic.

   To: _____

4. **From:** Brent and Ronald kept quiet.

   To: _____

5. **From:** They lied to the jury.

   To: _____

. . . .

EXERCISE 3-17

Rewrite each of the following sentences by changing the future tense to the future progressive tense.

Example
  From: I will help Bob.
  To: I will be helping Bob.

1. **From:** We will read *The Great Gatsby*.

   To:_____

2. **From:** Dave will do the assigned work.

   To:_____

3. **From:** Mr. Dreger will buy the needed supplies.

   To:_____

4. **From:** Thomas will cut the lawn tomorrow.

   To:_____

5. **From:** Vicki will choose the winner of the contest.

   To:_____

. . . .

The Present Perfect Progressive Tense The present perfect progressive tense shows an action starting in the past and continuing into the present.

Example
  The wetlands of the United States *have been decreasing* at an alarming rate in recent years.

The Past Perfect Progressive Tense The past perfect progressive tense indicates that a past action continued up to the start of another past action.

Example
  Before the American West was settled, the native buffaloes *had been growing* in number.

The Future Perfect Progressive Tense The future perfect progressive tense indicates that an action will progress up to a future time.

Example
  In 2001 *Voyagers I* and *II will have been exploring* deep space for nearly twenty-five years.

E X E R C I S E 3 - 1 8

Rewrite each of the following sentences by changing the present perfect to the present perfect progressive tense.

Example
> **From:** I have loved you.
> **To:** I have been loving you.

1. **From:** Paul has wanted an answer from you.

   To: _____

2. **From:** Lee has thought about making a change.

   To: _____

3. **From:** Betty and Mark have had an argument.

   To: _____

4. **From:** Martin has sat at his desk for five hours.

   To: _____

5. **From:** Carolyn has accepted all suggestions.

   To: _____

· ·

E X E R C I S E 3 - 1 9

Rewrite each of the following sentences by changing the past perfect to the past perfect progressive tense.

Example
> **From:** The work had taken too much of Sam's time.
> **To:** The work had been taking too much of Sam's time.

1. **From:** Frank had spoken for over two hours.

   To: _____

2. **From:** Don had thrown only strikes.

   To: _____

3. **From:** Jan had paid her bills.

   To: _____

4. **From:** Mike had lain on the pavement for an hour.

   To: _____

5. **From:** Mr. Goldfarb had hidden the money.

   To: _____

E X E R C I S E   3 - 2 0

Rewrite the following sentences by changing the future perfect to the future perfect progressive tense.

Example

From: I shall have heard.

To: I shall have been hearing.

1. **From**: Daniel will have known.

   To: _____

2. **From:** Alex will have seen.

   To:_____

3. **From:** Georgia will have run.

   To:_____

4. **From:** Andy and Harvey will have written.

   To:_____

5. **From:** Carlos will have received.

   To:_____

. . . .

E X E R C I S E   3 - 2 1

In the blank write the requested progressive tense of the indicated verb.

1. Future perfect progressive tense of *work*:

   In October I _____ for IBM for thirty years.

2. Present progressive tense of *rise* and *flee*:

   The river _____ , and the people _____ .

3. Future progressive tense of *study*:

   For the next several decades biologists _____ the effects of

   acid rain on the Chesapeake Bay.

4. Present perfect progressive tense of *decline*:

   The number of wild ducks on the Eastern Shore of Maryland _____

   since the 1960s.

5. Past progressive tense of *change*:

His appearance _____ on a daily basis.

6. Past perfect progressive tense of *pray*:

For months before sailing, the Puritans _____ for good weather.

7. Past perfect progressive tense of *enter*:

Fewer minority men and women _____ the teaching profession.

8. Future perfect progressive tense of *serve*:

Next month they _____ on this project for two years.

9. Present progressive tense of *plan*:

The astronauts _____ carefully for the next mission.

10. Future progressive tense of *watch*:

Californians _____ for any signs of a possible earthquake.

. . . .

E X E R C I S E   3 - 2 2

Fill in each blank with the requested progressive tense of the indicated verb.

1. The sun _____ (rise, present progressive), and the birds _____ (sing, present progressive).

2. Starting in two years, the team _____ (play, future progressive) in the new stadium.

3. Early in the race, Carol _____ (begin, past progressive) to think of winning.

4. The murder rate in many of America's big cities _____ (increase, present perfect progressive).

5. Next year Bob _____ (drive, future perfect progressive) the same car for twenty years.

6. While the marines _____ (prepare, past progressive) to attack, the navy bombarded the shoreline.

7. Herb _____ (talk, present progressive), but Al _____ not _____ (listen, present progressive).

8. Before the closing bell was rung, the stock market _____ (fall, past perfect progressive) for nearly six hours.

9. My neighbors _____ (travel, future progressive) throughout the Middle East next month.

10. Deaths from lung cancer _____ (climb, present perfect progressive) in the female population of the United States.

. . . .

Emphatic Verb Forms

These special verb forms emphasize the point made by a verb. Occurring in the present and past tenses only, the emphatic verb forms combine the verb *to do* with the present infinitive (minus the *to*) of the verb. Following is the conjugation of the verb *to enjoy*:

Present tense singular
I, you do enjoy
he, she, it does enjoy

Present tense plural
we, you, they do enjoy

Past tense singular
I, you, he, she, it did enjoy

Past tense plural
we, you, they did enjoy

HELPING (OR AUXILIARY) VERBS

A helping (or auxiliary) verb assists the main verb in making its point. The helping verb *to do* can be used to form questions or negative statements:
Does Diego own that car?
Did Georgia speak to you?
I do not know the answers to those questions.
The helping verbs *shall* and *will* are used to indicate the future:
I shall go   we shall go
you, he, she, it will go   you, they will go
Or, when shifted, these helping verbs can be used to indicate determination:
I will go   we will go
you, he, she, it shall go   you, they shall go
Other helping verbs are *may, can, must, could, might, ought, should,* and *would*. These helping verbs express what is needed, what is possible, what is demanded, or what is able to be done.

Examples
Joan must help her children.
Tom might go to the party.
Yes, Marie would have helped.
[*Must help, might go,* and *would have helped* are the simple predicates of these sentences.]

E X E R C I S E   3 - 2 3

Write a suitable helping verb in each of the blanks. Circle each simple predicate.

1. John _____ walked to the store.

2. Mary _____ walk to the store.

3. It _____ snow on Monday.

4. They _____ believe in equal justice for all.

5. I _____ lie down.

6. She _____ done the work.

7. Fred _____ try very hard to do well in English.

8. Melvin _____ not want a birthday party.

9. Laura _____ arrive on the next train.

10. He _____ rise at 6 A.M.

. . . .

PERSON AND NUMBER

As you have learned, nouns and pronouns have person and number. Thus, you can speak of first person, second person, and third person, and singular or plural in number. As you have also seen, a predicate must *agree* in person and number with its subject. Singular subjects require singular predicates, and plural subjects require plural predicates.

The forms of the verb *to be* show considerable changes regarding the person and number of the subject. Note the changes in form for the present tense, third person singular, of the following examples:

Present Tense

Singular	**Plural**
To be	
I am	we are
you are	you are
he, she, it is	they are
To have	
I have	we have
you have	you have
he, she, it has	they have
To do	
I do	we do
you do	you do
he, she, it does	they do

Present Tense
<u>Singular</u>   <u>Plural</u>
To carry
I carry   we carry
you carry   you carry
he, she, it carries   they carry

MOOD

Mood, another major characteristic of a verb, shows the speaker's or writer's intention toward the point made by the verb. There are three moods: the **indicative**, the **imperative**, and the **subjunctive**. Mood occasionally requires form changes in the verb.

The Indicative Mood

The indicative mood shows that the writer regards a statement as a fact, an opinion, or a question (about a fact). It is the mood used most often in this text and in most of the writing you will do now in college and later in your professional life.

Examples

> Our visit to Williamsburg was an exciting adventure.
> How, exactly, is a mint julep made?
> Though large in area, San Antonio, Texas, retains a small-town atmosphere.

The verb forms of the indicative mood are those used in the standard formation of the tenses.

The Imperative Mood

The imperative mood shows that the writer regards a statement as a command, a request, or an entreaty. The subject usually is implied rather than stated.

Examples

> Follow these directions exactly.
> Walk to the nearest exit.
> Run!
> Let's go on a picnic.
> Please let me know if Edna arrives.

The verb form of the imperative mood is always the same as the second person, present tense.

The Subjunctive Mood

The subjunctive mood shows that the writer regards a statement as contrary to fact, doubtful, wishful, hypothetical, possible, or probable. The subjunctive mood has the following verb forms:

Present subjunctive: infinitive form of the verb minus *to* (whatever the subject).

Past subjunctive: past tense of the verb; *to be* uses *were* whatever the person or number of the subject.

Past perfect subjunctive: past perfect of the verb.

The subjunctive has the following uses:

Conditional, Supposed, or Hypothetical Circumstances

Examples
> If I *were* Samuel, I would study hard for the test.
> I wish I *were* on Hilton Head Island now.

Note: If an *if* clause is followed by an independent clause that contains an effect that *is reasonably possible*, use the indicative mood:
> If Ted *stops* smoking, his chances of getting lung cancer will start to diminish.
> [It is possible that Ted will stop smoking.]

That Clauses Expressing Demands, Suggestions, Recommendations, and Requirements

Examples
> The committee demands that you *be* present at 8 A.M. for the hearing.
> The lawyer recommended that the defendant *be* given probation-before-verdict.
> Ms. Clark insisted that the student *take* more time to write the essay.

Special Expressions
Certain phrases or expressions traditionally use the subjunctive mood:

Examples
> *Be* that as it may.
> *Come* hell or high water.
> Far *be* it for me to intrude.

EXERCISE 3-24

For the following sentences, write the appropriate form of the subjunctive mood in the blanks.

1. If Mr. Sidel _____ (be) not ill, we would have had class.

2. I wish I _____ (be) a millionaire.

3. I wish I _____ (take) Judith's advice.

4. The judge demanded that the audience _____ (be) quiet.

5. The assistant manager acted as if he _____ (be) the president of the company.

6. _____ (come) what may, I will meet you at noon.

7. Shouts of "Long _____ (live) the King!" arose from the crowd.

8. If I _____ (be) Dr. Reid, I would speak more candidly to my patients.

9. My instructor requires that everyone _____ (listen) carefully.

10. Spot is, as it _____ (be), a dog that thinks he is human.

11. The hospital recommends that all members of the medical staff _____ (be) tested for the AIDS virus.

12. My ten-year-old brother behaves as if he _____ (be) a senior citizen.

13. If I _____ (be) in Haiti now, I would be looking for a way to leave.

14. I wish I _____ (have) more time to study before I took the test.

15. Maggie demanded that her son _____ (eat) all the food on his plate.

. . . .

EXERCISE 3-25

Use, as appropriate, the indicative, imperative, or subjunctive form of the verb in parentheses. Be able to explain your answers.

At the Alamo General Travis and his band of 187 Americans faced an army of thousands of Mexicans. Ordered to surrender, Travis _____ (shout) to the men near him, " _____ (fire) the cannon. _____ (wave) our flag proudly." From the men a shout _____ (arise), "Long _____ (live) Texas!" Then Travis quickly _____ (pen) his last letter, and it _____ (end) with these words: "If need (be), we _____ (fight) to the last man." Doubtless Travis then suggested

that each man _____(make) his peace with God. Though the defend-
ers of the Alamo _____ (slaughter), David Crockett among them,
the Mexicans _____ (be) eventually _____ (defeat)
by General Sam Houston and his army at San Jacinto River, not far from
Galveston Bay. Texas then _____ (become) the now-celebrated
Lone Star Republic before becoming a member of the United States in 1845,
nearly ten years after the fall of the Alamo.

. . . .

TRANSITIVE, INTRANSITIVE, AND LINKING VERBS

Finally, verbs can be classified as **transitive, intransitive**, or **linking**, depending on the relationship of the verb to the rest of the sentence.

The Transitive Verb

A **transitive verb** is one that requires a **direct object** for the completion of its
meaning in a sentence. The direct object receives the action of the subject of
the sentence. Like the subject, the direct object is a noun, a pronoun, or a
word group acting as a noun:

Simple Subject	Simple Predicate	Direct Object(s)
The men	played	baseball.
Cynthia	will tutor	Tony.
My horse	has won	it.

To locate the direct object, take the subject and the simple predicate and
attach **what?** or **whom?** to them. For example, *Cynthia will tutor whom?* The
answer is the direct object *Tony.* Another kind of object that can accompany a
direct object is termed an **indirect object.** The indirect object is a noun or a
pronoun and occurs after some types of transitive verbs, such as *give, grant,
order,* and *tell.* The indirect object answers the questions **to whom or what?
for whom or what?**

Simple Subject	Simple Predicate	Indirect Object	Direct Object
Arnold	tossed	Paul	the ball.
[You]	Grant	me	victory.
Lucy	gave	it	attention.
He	caused	Karl	injury.

EXERCISE 3-26

In each of the following sentences, write *SUB* above the simple subject, *PRED* above the simple predicate, *IO* above the indirect object (if any), and *DO* above the direct object (if any).

1. Hunters from England sent Australia a dozen pairs of European rabbits in 1859.

2. In less than eighty years, 600 million rabbits populated the country.

3. In the 1940s, disease reduced the rabbit population to a handful.

4. However, disease-resistant rabbits multiplied rapidly.

5. Today several hundred million rabbits inhabit Australia.

6. These animals give farmers and ranchers cause for alarm.

7. Yearly damages to crops and grasslands cost the landholders approximately $75 million.

8. The farmers and ranchers are fighting the rabbit explosion.

9. They are using shotguns, poison, and even bombs.

10. Meanwhile, the rabbit population is increasing.

. . . .

EXERCISE 3-27

Write five sentences using transitive verbs.

1. _____.

2. _____.

3. _____.

4. _____.

5. _____.

. . . .

The Intransitive Verb

An **intransitive verb** is one that does not require an object for the completion of its meaning. Such a verb itself asserts the whole point about the subject.

Simple Subject	Simple Predicate
Josephine	rejoiced.
Gilbert	sings.
The motor	runs.

[Many verbs can be either transitive or intransitive, such as *sing* and *run*: Gilbert *sings* ballads. She *runs* a store.]

E X E R C I S E   3 - 2 8

Write five sentences using intransitive verbs.

1. _____ .

2. _____ .

3. _____ .

4. _____ .

5. _____ .

. . . .

The Linking Verb

A **linking verb** is one that joins a subject to a noun or pronoun but does not show action. In effect, a linking verb is like an equals sign (=) in mathematics. The linking verb joins a subject to what is termed a **complement**, and that complement can be either a noun or pronoun (called a **subject complement**) or an adjective (called an **adjective complement**).

Note: A number of linking verbs, such as *appear*, *look*, *feel*, and *smell*, can also act as intransitive or transitive verbs. Adverbs follow intransitive and transitive verbs; however, adjectives follow linking verbs.

> **Examples**
> Ted looked intense; he wanted to win the race.
> Ted looked intensely at the stars; he wanted to see the Big Dipper.
> [In the first example, *intense* is an adjective following the linking verb *looked*; in the second example, *intensely* is an adverb following the intransitive verb *looked*. Use the *to be* or *to seem* test to determine if a verb is being used as a linking verb.]

To be (in its many forms) is the most frequently occurring linking verb. Such verbs as *to appear*, *to become*, *to feel*, *to grow*, *to look*, *to seem*, *to smell*, *to sound*, and *to taste* can be used as linking verbs.

To determine if a verb is a linking verb, use an appropriate form of the verb *to be* or *to seem* in place of the verb in the sentence. If the sentence makes sense, the verb is probably a linking verb.

Simple Subject	Linking Verb	Complement
Evelyn	is	captain. (noun)
Alvin	was	a golfer. (noun)
The study	will be	long. (adjective)
The trip	appears	difficult. (adjective)
The music	sounds	strange. (adjective)

E X E R C I S E   3 - 2 9

In the following sentences circle the linking verbs. Draw one line under each subject complement and two lines under each adjective complement. The first one is done for you.

1. During the wedding Jerome and Ruth (seemed) happy.

2. This onion tastes sweet.

3. The rug was old and dirty.

4. I felt nervous.

5. Paul will be a graduate in June.

6. William appeared anxious during his talk.

7. This animal is ugly.

8. Her expression grew somber during the funeral.

9. The diamond rings were beautiful.

10. His performance has been exceptional.

. . . .

E X E R C I S E   3 - 3 0

Write five sentences using linking verbs.

1. _____.

2. _____.

3. _____.

4. _____.

5. _____.

. . . .

. . . .

Adjectives and Adverbs

The basic building blocks of a sentence are nouns, pronouns, and verbs. You can write a sentence with a subject and a predicate in the active voice, or you can write a sentence in the passive voice. Sentences composed of just a subject and a predicate are the result:

Fish swim. (active voice)

Andrea is loved. (passive voice)

You can also write sentences with a subject, a predicate in the active voice, and a direct object or an indirect object and a direct object:

Lisa enjoyed the movie. (subject—predicate—direct object)

Billy gave me the money. (subject—predicate—indirect object— direct object)

You can write a sentence with a subject, a predicate using a linking verb, and a complement:

Jonathan was the winner. (subject complement)

Sondra looks happy. (adjective complement)

These examples are all **simple sentences,** and each contains at least a subject and a predicate and makes complete sense. However, the sentences contain only very basic meanings. To make a sentence have more meaning and thus be more exact, you can add modifiers—**adjectives** and **adverbs**—to the basic patterns. Effective writing is often concrete and specific, and modifiers can help you achieve that kind of writing.

ADJECTIVES

An adjective is a modifier of a noun or pronoun. Consider the following example:

adjective noun
warm day

[In this example, *day* is a **noun,** and *warm* is an **adjective** that modifies *day. Warm* tells what kind of *day* it is.]

As a general rule, you can identify what part of speech a word is by how that word functions in a sentence. In the example above, *warm* is an adjective because it functions as one; it modifies *day,* a noun.

Consider the following sentences:
I enjoyed the warm day.
The heaters warm the room.

In the first example, *warm* modifies day and is thus an adjective. In the second example, however, *warm* functions as a predicate, a verb. Basically, there are two types of adjectives; descriptive and definitive.

Descriptive Adjectives

A descriptive adjective makes a noun or pronoun more exact—more specific—by indicating one of its qualities. It gives your reader a clearer picture of a noun or pronoun.

Examples

I ordered a *large* salad.
The *white* Ford caused the accident.
A *dense* fog covered the airport.
I like *Chinese* food.

Note: A descriptive adjective formed from a proper noun is capitalized.

Examples

Asian elephant
Jeffersonian principles

The following are just a few of the words that can function as descriptive adjectives: small, medium, large; red, white, blue, black, orange; slow, fast, rapid; steel, concrete, wood, woody, wooden; dull, sharp, rough; frank, honest, sincere.

E X E R C I S E   4 - 1

Underline the descriptive adjectives in the following sentences.

1. An intense fire consumed the pine and oak forest.

2. A courageous policewoman rescued the small boy.

3. The unusual story was true.

4. He liked the colorful postcards.

5. A windy day greeted the kite flyers.

6. The long trail led to a high mountain.

7. The difficult questions were unfair.

8. The warm sunshine melted the ice.

9. The speech was short but powerful.

10. A Spanish cook prepared the tasty meal.

. . . .

E X E R C I S E   **4 - 2**

Make an interesting paragraph by inserting descriptive adjectives in the blanks.

As I entered the _____ and _____ house, I was greeted by

a _____ man, a _____ woman, and three _____

cats. The man wore a _____ hat, a _____

shirt, _____ pants, and _____ shoes. The woman

wore a _____ dress and _____ shoes. Curiously, the

cats wore _____ hats. I asked the _____ couple

where they had purchased their _____ clothes. They

replied, "We made them ourselves."

. . . .

E X E R C I S E   **4 - 3**

Using the following descriptive adjectives, write sentences.

sharp   1. _____

                     _____

blind   2. _____

                     _____

American   3. _____

                     _____

strange   4. _____

                     _____

little   5. _____

                     _____

. . . .

Definitive Adjectives

Definitive adjectives are such words as numbers, pronouns, and articles; they are used to quantify or otherwise identify a noun or pronoun.

The most commonly-used definitive adjectives are the **definite** and the **indefinite articles**. The **definite article** is the word *the*; the **indefinite articles** are the words *a* and *an*.

The refers to specific (identified) persons, places, things, or ideas.

Examples

In August 1991 the people of Russia demanded and won freedom and democracy. [The writer is referring to specific people.]

The rule of the Communist Party in Russia ended. [In this sentence the first *the* refers to a particular power or control, and the second *the* refers to a specific organization.]

The can also refer to a representative of a general group or class.

Example

The actor must know what to say and how to say it.

A and *an* are used in a general sense to refer to one person, place, thing, or idea of a type, in all other respects indefinite.

Example

Vickie and Kevin wanted to buy a house rather than rent an apartment. [*A* does not refer to a specific house; *an* does not refer to a specific apartment.]

A is used before words that start with a consonant sound, and *an* is used before words that start with a vowel sound (*a, e, i, o, u*) or with a silent *h*.

Examples

a high chair	an ally
a historic meeting	an elephant
a hurdle	an honest man
a use	an hour

Repeat the article when you are referring to two separate items.

Example

I ordered a ham and a cheese sandwich. (Two sandwiches were ordered.)

E X E R C I S E 4 - 4

In the following sentences insert the appropriate articles.

1. According to Benjamin Franklin, "_____ small leak will sink

   _____ great ship."

2. Melissa suffered from _____ infection of unknown origin.

3. _____ man kissing Danice is my brother Tom.

4. _____ student in Japan and West Germany must attend over 200

   days of school each year.

5. Is_____ picture truly worth _____thousand words?

6. Tammy visited_____ Kennedy Space Center in June.

7. She is_____ member of_____ United States Senate.

8. For my birthday I received_____ green and _____orange

   sweater.

9. George Washington was trained as _____ surveyor.

10. _____ man living in Harlem is less likely to reach age

    sixty-five than _____ man living in Bangladesh.

. . . .

Numerical adjectives simply indicate numbers: one, two, three, first, second, third, fourth, single, double, triple.

Examples
        I caught *five* bass.
        Alonzo had a *single* goal.

Demonstrative adjectives (*this*, *that*, *these*, and *those*) point out a specific noun, and they change form to indicate singular or plural number:

Singular	Plural
this car	these cars
that car	those cars

Examples
        Tiffany designed *this* lamp.
        That man is Mayor Dinkins.
        These gold coins are Canadian.
        Those alarms were false.

EXERCISE 4 - 5

In each of the following sentences, cross out the incorrect form of the demonstrative adjective.

1. (This, These) film was directed by Frank Capra.

2. Who directed (that, those) films?

3. (This, These) children are lost.

4. Kimberly is unable to eat (this, these) kind of food.

5. (That, Those) answer is only partly correct.

6. (That, Those) sand dunes are fifty feet high.

7. The space shuttle *Discovery* will land later (this, these) week.

8. Wayne owns (that, those) company's stock.

9. I doubt that (this, these) soldiers will fight.

10. Vitamin C may help to prevent (that, those) disease.

. . . .

Interrogative adjectives are used to ask a question: *which*, *what*, and *whose*.

Examples
> *Which* political party should I join?
> *What* difference is there between a revenue enhancement and a tax?
> *Whose* gloves are these?

Many words that function as indefinite pronouns can also function as **indefinite adjectives.** Some examples of indefinite adjectives are the following: *another*, *each*, *either*, *few*, *many*, *all*, *most*, *several*, and *some*.

Examples
> The treaty would ban *several* types of missles.
> The flood damaged *many* homes in Texas and Arkansas.
> Most *Germans* supported unification.

Nouns and pronouns may become **possessive adjectives** by using their possessive forms. In general, possessive forms are indicated by adding an *apostrophe* (') and *s* to nouns and to indefinite pronouns.

Examples

> I know Rafael's address.
> The bike's brakes failed.
> Pauline found somebody's umbrella.
> Nobody's money was taken.

In these examples, *Rafael's*, *bike's*, *somebody's*, and *nobody's* are **possessive adjectives.** The first two are formed from nouns; the last two are formed from indefinite pronouns.

The following basic rules apply to the formation of possessive adjectives from nouns:

1. If the noun is singular and does not end in *s* (or an *s* sound), add an apostrophe and *s* to form the possessive:

   Examples

Haiti	Haiti's poverty
volcano	volcano's eruption
Arkansas	Arkansas's farms

2. If the noun is singular and ends in an *s* sound, add an apostrophe and *s if a new syllable is formed when you pronounce the possessive.*

   Examples

   > Henry James's novels, Dallas's population, Gus's grades

   Add only an apostrophe to a singular word ending in an *s* sound *if adding an extra syllable makes the word difficult to pronounce.*

   Examples

   > Los Angeles' smog, for goodness' sake, Moses' journey

3. If the noun is plural and ends in *s*, add only an apostrophe.

   Examples

students	students' protest
victims	victims' rights

4. If the noun is plural and does not end in *s*, add an apostrophe and *s*.

   Examples

women	women's issues
children	children's toys

EXERCISE 4-6

In the blanks write the possessive form of each numbered word. The first one is done for you.

1. girls   _girls'_   clothes

2. editor   _____   job

3. plotters   _____   decisions

4. Mr. Blessings   _____   music

5. play   _____   actors

6. citizens   _____   demonstration

7. class   _____   leaders

8. flag   _____   colors

9. Latvia   _____   independence

10. actress   _____   performance

11. geese   _____   honking

12. Marx   _____   beliefs

13. eggs   _____   odor

14. Ulysses   _____   adventures

15. men   _____   basketball team

16. oxen   _____   yokes

17. heroes   _____   medals

18. wife   _____   American Express card

19. wives   _____   participation

20. New Orleans   _____   weather

· ·

As you have learned, the personal pronouns have special forms (spellings) when used as subjects and objects. The personal pronouns also have special forms when used as **possessives**:

1st person singular: my, mine
2nd person singular: your, yours
3rd person singular: his; her, hers; its
1st person plural: our, ours
2nd person plural: your, yours
3rd person plural: their, theirs

Notice that the possessive forms of the personal pronouns do not make use of the apostrophe.

My, *your*, *his*, *her*, *its*, *our*, and *their* come before the noun(s) they modify and show possession.

Examples

my home	its food
your tractor	our room
his Jaguar	your company
her Volvo 780	their mission

Mine, *yours*, *hers*, *ours*, and *theirs*, however, act differently. They may act as adjective complements following a linking verb, or they may play a role like that of a noun in a sentence.

Examples

The victory was mine.
The glory is yours.
[In these examples *mine* and *yours* act as adjective complements.]

I have theirs.
Yours is on the top shelf.
[*Theirs* acts as the direct object of *have*; the subject of the second sentence is *yours*.]

E X E R C I S E   4 - 7

Underline *all adjectives* in the following sentences.

1. Which book is hers?

2. Steve took his three final exams on the same day.

3. Greek philosophy can be difficult.

4. These shirts are mine.

5. The furious hurricane sank many small boats.

6. The jury's forewoman was calm and firm.

7. The nervous defendant got a life sentence.

8. What reply was given?

9. Happy fans applauded their victorious team.

10. Rita's early graduation pleased her parents.

11. That small bird is a wren.

12. His beliefs are hers.

13. Fernando's baseball coach demanded a positive attitude.

14. Those old warehouses contain toxic wastes.

15. Jim's personality was strong and forceful.

. . . .

ADVERBS

Another type of modifier is the adverb. In general, adverbs modify a verb, an adjective, or another adverb. Adverbs of time, manner, place and degree answer the following questions: How? When? Where? Why? Under what conditions? To what extent or degree? In the following the adverbs appear in italics.

Adverbs of Time

An adverb of time answers the questions **When?** and **How often?**

Examples
Chet will go *tomorrow*.
Janet swims *seldom*.
Leave *now*.

Adverbs of Manner

An adverb of manner answers the question **How?**

Examples
Debra moved *carefully*.
Joey wrote *hastily*.
Our cat ate *contentedly*.
She performed *well*.

Adverbs of Place

Adverbs of place simply tell **where.**

Examples
Paul went *home*.
Sheila stayed *here*.
Scott went *in*.

Adverbs of Degree

Adverbs of degree address the question **How much?**

Examples

The workers *nearly* finished the job.
She *completely* accomplished her goal.
Frank *partly* answered the question.

Following is a list of words that can function as adverbs: entirely, beautifully, usually, slowly, fast, certainly, here, below, down, really, probably, early, rapidly, under, brightly, very, not, tonight, already, once.

As the list suggests, many adverbs end in *–ly*.

Adverbs can also be used to ask questions. These **interrogative adverbs** include *how, when, where,* and *why.*

Examples

How did he do?
When do we leave?
Where are they living?
Why should we fail?

All of the adverbs used above modify predicates (main verbs). Adverbs can, however, modify adjectives or other adverbs.

Examples

Joey wrote very hastily. [*Very* is an adverb modifying the adverb *hastily.*]
John is too slow. [*Too* is an adverb modifying *slow*, an adjective complement.]
Alexandra drove quite fast. [*Quite* is an adverb modifying *fast*, another adverb.]

EXERCISE 4 - 8

Underline *all adverbs* in the following sentences.

1. Maria is leaving today.

2. Her story seemed rather unusual.

3. We enjoyed a very fine meal.

4. Ed and Dave will probably be late.

5. It was an extremely good movie.

6. His talks were always dull.

7. Chung Lee spoke English unusually well.

8. Her answer was partially correct.

9. Frank has already finished the work.

10. Where will we go?

11. We will begin shortly.

12. They arrived early.

13. Tom never went in.

14. I am not jogging Saturday.

15. How am I doing?

. . . .

E X E R C I S E   4 - 9

Each sentence in the left-hand column contains only one adjective. Underline each adjective. Write the adverb form in the blanks in the right-hand column.

Adjective	Adverb
1. He is a simple man.	1. He dresses _____.
2. It was an easy win.	2. We won _____.
3. She had a strong argument.	3. She argued_____.
4. I spent a quiet evening with Jim.	4. He spoke _____.
5. We had an equal partnership.	5. We divided it _____.
6. He was a frequent visitor.	6. He visited _____.
7. She gave a precise answer.	7. She answered _____.
8. I got a quick response.	8. He responded _____.
9. It was a random event.	9. It occurred_____.
10. She was eager.	10. She agreed _____.

. . . .

E X E R C I S E   4 - 10

Combine the following adjectives and adverbs in a single sentence.

1. Adjectives: high, difficult

   Adverbs: too, very

_____

_____

2. Adjectives: false, ridiculous

   Adverb: totally

   _____

   _____

3. Adjectives: hard, yesterday's

   Adverb: how

   _____

   _____

4. Adjective: twenty

   Adverb: exactly

   _____

   _____

5. Adjectives: long, that

   Adverb: never

   _____

   _____

. . . .

COMPARISON OF ADJECTIVES AND ADVERBS

Most adjectives and adverbs can be compared. There are three degrees of comparison:

   1. **Positive:** This test is *hard.*

   2. **Comparative:** This test is *harder* than the first one.

   3. **Superlative:** This test is the *hardest* one I have ever had.

The **positive degree** shows a positive quality, and there is no actual comparison.

   Examples
   slow   slowly
   soft   softly

The **comparative degree**, on the other hand, involves a comparison between two persons, places, or things. In general, this degree is formed by adding *–er* to the positive degree, or by using *more* or *less* as a modifier of the positive degree.

Note: All comparisons dealing with *less* use *less* for the comparative degree and *least* for the superlative degree: *hot, less hot, least hot.*

Examples

stronger	weaker
more efficiently	less important

The **superlative degree** shows that one item is greater or less than two or more other persons, places, or things. In general, it is formed by adding *–est* to the positive degree or by using *most* or *least* as a modifier of the positive degree.

Examples

softest	hardest
most significant	least slowly

Comparison of Adjectives

The comparative and superlative degrees of one-syllable adjectives are generally formed by adding *–er* and *–est* to the positive degree (for example, *cold, colder, coldest*).

Some two-syllable adjectives form their comparative and superlative degrees by adding *–er* and *–est* to the positive degree (for example: *lucky, luckier, luckiest*). Many two-syllable adjectives, however, form their comparative and superlative degrees by using *more* and *most* to modify the positive degree. (For example: *skillful, more skillful, most skillful.*)

In general, three-syllable adjectives form their comparative and superlative degrees by adding *more* and *most* to the positive degree. (For example: *significant, more significant, most significant.*)

Still other adjectives are totally irregular in their comparative and superlative degrees:

Positive	Comparative	Superlative
good	better	best
bad	worse	worst
little	less	least
many, much	more	most

When you are not sure of how to form the comparative or superlative degrees, use your dictionary. Most college dictionaries will spell out the degrees using *–er* and *–est*. If *–er* and *–est* are not indicated, use *more* and *most*.

E X E R C I S E 4 - 1 1

Complete the comparative and superlative degrees for the following adjectives. If necessary, use a dictionary.

Positive	Comparative	Superlative
1. ugly	_____	_____
2. small	_____	_____
3. beautiful	_____	_____
4. good	_____	_____
5. short	_____	_____
6. few	_____	_____
7. able	_____	_____
8. funny	_____	_____
9. lonely	_____	_____
10. removable	_____	_____

. . . .

E X E R C I S E 4 - 1 2

Write sentences using the indicated comparative or superlative degree of the adjective.

1. The comparative degree of *good*

   _____

2. The superlative degree of *tall*

   _____

3. The superlative degree of *intelligent*

   _____

4. The comparative degree of *little*

   _____

5. The superlative degree of *happy*

   _____

6. The comparative degree of *many*

_____

7. The superlative degree of *thick*

_____

8. The comparative degree of *confident*

_____

9. The superlative degree of *large*

_____

10. The superlative degree of *muddy*

_____

. . . .

Comparison of Adverbs

Some adverbs, especially one-syllable adverbs, form their comparative and superlative degrees by adding –*er* and –*est* to the positive degree. (For example: *hard, harder, hardest.*) Most adverbs, however, form their comparative and superlative degrees by using *more* and *most* to modify the positive degree. (For example: *efficiently, more efficiently, most efficiently.*) As with adjectives, *less* and *least* are used for all comparisons indicating less: *less severely, least severely.*

Some adverbs have irregular forms for the comparative and superlative degrees:

Positive	Comparative	Superlative
badly	worse	worst
little	less	least
much	more	most
well	better	best

When in doubt about the spelling of the comparative and superlative degrees of adverbs, consult a dictionary.

Notes: 1. Take care to avoid the double comparative or the double superlative (example: *most slowest*).

2. Many adjectives and adverbs do not have comparative and superlative degrees. Such words as *unique, perfect, infinite,* and *dead* do not admit of comparison. That which is perfect, for example, cannot logically be more or most perfect.

E X E R C I S E 4 - 1 3

Complete the comparative and superlative degrees for the following adverbs.
Remember: If you are unsure of an answer, use a dictionary.

Positive	Comparative	Superlative
1. quickly		
2. beautifully		
3. badly		
4. well		
5. effectively		
6. soon		
7. wildly		
8. emotionally		
9. fast		
10. brutally		

. . . .

E X E R C I S E 4 - 1 4

Write sentences using the indicated comparative or superlative degree of the adverb.

1. The comparative degree of *hastily*

   _____

2. The superlative degree of *badly*

   _____

3. The comparative degree of *well*

   _____

4. The comparative degree of *forcefully*

   _____

5. The superlative degree of *rapidly*

   _____

6. The superlative degree of *bravely*

_____

7. The comparative degree of *sincerely*

_____

8. The comparative degree of *carefully*

_____

9. The superlative degree of *fast*

_____

10. The comparative degree of *little*

_____

· ·

E X E R C I S E 4 - 1 5

The following paragraph contains errors in the usage of adjectives and adverbs. Cross out the errors and correct them.

Until more better studies are done, we will never know precise how many Americans are homeless today. However, the population is more larger today than it was thirty years ago, and the problem today is more unique. Years ago alcoholics and mentally ill persons were the likely victims of homelessness. Todays street people include a wider segment of society. These type of problem affects young people who search unsuccessful for a job. The problem affects the elderly who cannot easy afford the leastest expensive housing. Perhaps those people who are affected worse are whole families who have neither relatives nor friends to house them temporary. Of all this homeless persons, the children suffer most serious. Understanding the homeless begins with knowing that they are human beings who, in the main, are where they are because of forces over which they have little control.

· ·

Conjunctions

The largest unit of meaning within a paragraph is the sentence, and the most basic form is the simple sentence, one composed of subject, predicate, and object or complement. However, when many short simple sentences follow one after another in a paragraph, a choppy effect develops, and you may not be able to keep your reader awake. Consider the following paragraph:

> In 1849 many decent, hard-working men went to California. Gold had been discovered. Some of the Forty-Niners were not good men. They were rough, crude men. Many were not honest. Some drank too much whiskey. Some did many foolish things. They frequently got into fights in bars. Some were robbers. They stole the gold of others.

Does the following revised version seem more effective?

> In 1849 many decent, hard-working men went to California *because* gold had been discovered. *However*, some of the Forty-Niners were not good men. Some were rough, crude men, *and* many were not honest. *For example*, some of them drank too much whiskey, *and* others frequently got into fights in bars. Some were robbers *who* stole the gold of others.

In the first paragraph there are ten sentences, all of which are short, simple sentences. The effect is choppy because the ideas are not smoothly connected. The second paragraph has five sentences, only one of which is short and simple. Because the sentences are varied and because the ideas are clearly connected, the second paragraph is more coherent than the first. The reason for this smooth flow of ideas is the writer's use of connecting words: *and, because, however, for example,* and *who.* In this chapter you will study the connecting words known as **coordinating conjunctions, correlative conjunctions,** and **conjunctive adverbs;** you will learn how they function in a sentence.

What is a conjunction? **A conjunction is a word (or word group) that joins words or word groups to show how ideas are related.**

COORDINATING CONJUNCTIONS

A coordinating conjuction is a word that joins two words or word groups with similar functions and equal value.

There are only seven coooodinating conjunctions:

and	This conjunction simply shows addition. One idea is added to or strengthens another idea.
or, nor	These conjunctions choose and divide ideas. *Or* means either, and *nor* means neither.
but, yet	These conjunctions show a contrast between ideas.
for	This conjunction introduces a less direct relationship, and shows that two ideas are related as effect-to-cause or as proof for a point in question.
so	This conjunction shows that two ideas are related as action-to-result. One idea is the consequence or outcome of some other idea.

In the last chapter you learned three simple sentence patterns, each of which contained only one subject and only one predicate. Using coordinating conjunctions, you can form a fourth simple sentence pattern, one which has compound (two or more) subjects, compound predicates, compound objects, or compound complements.

Examples

Tom *or* Joan has the tickets to the Whitney Houston concert. [*Or* joins the subjects and introduces the second of two possibilities.]

The clown sang *and* danced during the party. [Two predicates are joined by *and* to form a compound predicate.]

On the beach Tim found a ring *and* a wallet. [*And* joins *ring* and *wallet* to form the compound direct object of *found.*]

Each of the simple sentence patterns has one **independent clause.** An independent clause can stand by itself as a simple sentence; that is, it has at least one subject and predicate and makes complete sense on its own:

Two Simple Sentences

The clearing of tropical rain forests for farming continues at an alarming rate. Their soil is largely unsuitable for growing crops for more than a few years.

Frequently, coordinating conjunctions are used to join two or more independent clauses to form compound units known as **compound sentences**. In the following example, *but* is used to join the two independent clauses to form a compound sentence:

A Compound Sentence

The clearing of tropical rain forests for farming continues at an alarming rate, but their soil is largely unsuitable for growing crops for more than a few years.

Study these examples:

1. **AND** shows addition:

> For the book report Laura read Anne Frank's *The Diary of a Young Girl*, and her brother Larry read John Hersey's *Hiroshima*.

The conjunction *and* adds two independent clauses together to form a compound sentence.

Note that, in general, a comma comes before the coordinating conjunction in a compound sentence. However, a comma is usually not needed before the coordinating conjunction when the independent clauses are very brief: Tom jumped and Alice laughed. A comma can serve to avoid a possible misreading: John shot Jane, and Bob shot John.

Note also that the two independent clauses are logically parallel in meaning. Put another way, they both have the same weight. Whether a sentence is composed of one independent clause or more than one, the sentence must be a single unit of meaning, one that makes unified and coherent sense. Consider the following example:

> Sylvester Stallone has made a life's work of his *Rocky* and *Rambo* movies, and he has two sons living in California.

Though this compound sentence *is* gramatically parallel, it *is not* logically parallel. Consequently, the two thoughts should not be joined; they should be in separate sentences.

2. **OR** indicates choice; **NOR** carries over a negative idea from the first clause:

> Pat did not attend class regularly, *nor* did he study for the exam. He did, however, get a 98. Perhaps the instructor was an easy grader, *or* Pat cheated on the exam, *or* Pat already knew the material. There were many possibilities.

In the first sentence the conjunction *nor* joins, and at the same time divides, the ideas found in the independent clauses. In short, *nor* joins two negative ideas. In the third sentence *or* shows an equal choice among three ideas. The conjunction *or* selects and divides ideas.

3. **BUT** and **YET** show contrast:

> According to some history books, Christopher Columbus discovered America in 1492, *but* his "discovery" was not the first one. The Norsemen discovered America five hundred years before Columbus, *and* the Indians discovered America thousands of years earlier than both of them. Some historians do give credit to the Norsemen, *yet* rarely are the Indians given adequate credit for their discovery.

In the first sentence the coordinating conjunction *but* indicates a contrast between the two ideas. In the second sentence *and* adds two related ideas together, and *yet* in the third sentence shows a strong contrast between two ideas. **Note:** Although the conjunctions *but* and *yet* show contrast between two statements, *yet* stresses the contrast more emphatically than *but* does. *But* notes the contrast without emphasizing it.

4. **FOR** shows a reason, the second clause gives a reason for the first clause:

> LeRoi Jones changed his name to Imamu Amiri Baraka, *for* he wanted a suitable name to go with his Muslim religion.

The first independent clause is the effect for the cause contained in the second independent clause. *For*, then, is an appropriate joining word here.

> Langston Hughes was a very versatile writer, *for* he wrote poetry, novels, short stories, plays, and essays.

For is appropriate in this sentence because the second independent clause is the proof for the point made in the first independent clause.

5. **SO** shows result. The first clause results in the second clause:

> Phyllis recognized the symptoms of an on-coming cold, *so* she took two aspirins and got some rest.

So is appropriate to join the two independent clauses because the idea in the second clause is the consequence of the point made in the first clause.

E X E R C I S E 5 - 1

Place commas where needed in the following sentences.

1. Joe plays baseball very well but he'll need much practice to do equally well in football.
2. Janet and Howard looked refreshed after swimming in the ocean.
3. Bill enjoyed the applause of the audience so he sang two more songs.
4. They may mail the results to you or they may notify you by telephone.
5. Ralph laughed and cried at the same time.
6. Diane did not speak quickly nor did she speak clearly.
7. Ted looked happy for he had just won a new car.
8. The dogs barked and the children screamed.
9. The laws of physics seem complicated but simple.
10. Dolores cleaned fish but she did not enjoy her job.

E X E R C I S E   5 - 2

Read each of the following sentences to understand its meaning, then supply an appropriate coordinating conjunction and proper punctuation. You must decide whether you want to show addition (*and*), an equal choice (*or*), a negative choice (*nor*), a contrast (*but*, *yet*), an effect-to-cause relationship (*for*), or a result (*so*).

1. The percentage of drug addicts in the total population is fairly constant

    _____ the percentage of addicts getting the AIDS virus

    by sharing needles is rising.

2. Language is constantly changing _____ *television* will probably be

    replaced by *TV* _____ *advertisement* will probably be replaced by *ad*.

3. During World War II a woman could serve as a WAC (Army) _____

    she could serve as a WAVE (Navy)_____ the United States

    Marines did not give women a separate identity.

4. The seasons change on the twenty-first of March, June, September, and

    December _____ changes in the climate are much less precise.

5. Gerald R. Ford was never elected vice president _____ was he

    ever elected president _____ he served in both offices.

6. Few people have ever heard of the country called Tuvalu _____ have

    they ever heard of the Republic of Vanuatu.

7. If people want to learn more about camping, they can write to the

    American Camping Association _____ they can contact the

    National Campers and Hikers Association.

. . . .

E X E R C I S E   5 - 3

Read each of the following sentences to understand its meaning, and then supply an appropriate coordinating conjunction and proper punctuation.

(1) Though born of poor African-American parents, Marian Anderson did not

let poverty hinder her success _____ did she let racial

discrimination stop her from becoming one of America's best-loved singers.

(2) In 1939, for example, the Daughters of the American Revolution kept Miss Anderson from singing in Constitution Hall _____ the group did not approve of the color of her skin. (3) Undaunted, Miss Anderson proudly performed for 75,000 people at the Lincoln Memorial _____ she later became the first African-American to sing at the White House. (4) She continued to be the victim of discrimination in America _____ her bravery, her dignity, and her talents earned her a place in the hearts of millions of Americans of all races. (5) In 1955 she became the first African-American to perform at the Metropolitan Opera in New York City _____ in 1978 President Carter awarded her a Congressional gold medal for her achievements.

. . . .

E X E R C I S E   5 - 4

Using each of the coordinating conjunctions, write seven compound sentences of your own.

1. (and) _____

_____

2. (or) _____

_____

3. (nor) _____

_____

4. (but) _____

_____

5. (yet)_____

_____

6. (for)_____

_____

7. (so) _____

_____

. . . .

CORRELATIVE CONJUNCTIONS

Like coordinating conjunctions, correlative conjunctions join words or word groups of equal status, equal weight. Among the most commonly used correlative conjunctions are the following:

either...or   neither...nor   both...and
not only...but also   not only...but   just as...so

The meanings of these conjunctions can be easily seen in the following examples:

1. *Either* John *or* Mary will help you.
   Either you do your homework, *or* you will fail.
   Either...or indicates only two alternatives. In the first sentence two subjects are joined by the conjunction; in the second sentence two independent clauses are joined. Note that, in the second sentence, a comma is needed before the conjunction *or* because the conjunction connects two independent clauses.

2. *Neither* did Dr. Moran testify at his trial, *nor* did any witnesses speak on his behalf.
   Neither...nor joins two independent clauses and shows the negation of the points made in the clauses. **Reminder:** A comma is needed before the second part of the conjunction, *nor*, because the conjunction joins two independent clauses. However, in the following example, since *neither...nor* joins only two nouns, no comma is needed:

   Neither Frank *nor* Bruce decided to enter the contest.

3. *Both* the soldiers *and* the civilians were killed by the poison gas.
   Both...and means together or equally. In the example, two nouns are joined by the correlative conjunction.

4. With the race over, the joggers were *not only* sore *but also* thirsty.
   Not only...but also (or *not only...but*) adds two ideas by showing that one of them is not alone in importance. In the example two adjectives are joined.

5. *Just as* Darnell is ready to play, *so* is Tonja.
   In this example *just as...so* joins two independent clauses. The conjunction indicates that Darnell and Tonja are each neither more nor less than ready to play.

E X E R C I S E   5 - 5

Place commas as needed in the following sentences.

1. Jennifer was neither happy nor sad on hearing of the divorce.

2. Not only did Tracy get a new job but she also got a new car.

3. Both Bill and Jim will enter the race on Saturday.

4. Either you pay your bills or you can expect to lose your credit.

5. Just as the gorilla is an endangered species so is the orangutan.

6. Tim was neither killed nor even injured in the plane crash.

7. Either Christopher or Eden will be your math tutor.

8. Neither did Dawn come in first nor did she come in second.

9. Both Michael's victory and his defeat came in the same day.

10. Not only had Toni Morrison written the novel but she had also lived it.

. . . .

EXERCISE 5 - 6

Write five compound sentences using the indicated correlative conjunctions.

1. (either...or) _____

   _____

2. (neither...nor) _____

   _____

3. (both...and) _____

   _____

4. (not only...but also) _____

   _____

5. (just as...so) _____

   _____

. . . .

CONJUNCTIVE ADVERBS

A final connecting word is the conjunctive adverb. As adverbs, these conjunctions can appear in various places in a sentence. Their purpose is to show the relationship that exists between the ideas contained in independent clauses. In other words, conjunctive adverbs function as transitional links between independent clauses.

Following is a list of commonly-used conjunctive adverbs:

accordingly	hence	next
additionally	however	nonetheless
also	incidentally	now
anyway	indeed	otherwise
besides	instead	similarly
certainly	likewise	still
consequently	meanwhile	then
finally	moreover	thereafter
further	namely	therefore
furthermore	nevertheless	thus

Certain prepositional phrases may also act as conjunctive adverbs:

after all	for instance	in other words
as a result	for example	in short
at any rate	in addition	in sum (in summary)
at the same time	in fact	on the contrary
by the way	in fine	on the other hand

Prepositional phrases used as conjunctive adverbs are also known as transitional phrases. A few examples will clarify how the conjunctive adverbs are used:

1. Tom is my brother; *furthermore*, he is my best friend.
   Tom is my brother; he is, *furthermore*, my best friend.

Similar in meaning to *additionally* or *moreover*, *furthermore* shows how the idea in the second independent clause is related to the idea in the first one, and it does so with conjunctive force or emphasis. (Compare: Tom is my brother, and he is my best friend.)

Note that *furthermore*, being an adverb, can appear in various positions in the sentence. Also note that in the first sentence, a semicolon comes before the conjunctive adverb and a comma follows it. The second example is punctuated differently because the conjunctive adverb comes in the middle of the second independent clause. Commas are placed around it; however, a semicolon must always be placed between the two independent clauses in such constructions.

2. Wendy loved Todd; however, she would not marry him.
   Wendy loved Todd; she would not, however, marry him.
   Wendy loved Todd; she would not marry him, however.

However establishes a relationship between the idea in the second independent clause and the one in the first independent clause. Note the punctuation. A semicolon must come after the first independent clause. In the first sentence a comma must come after the conjunctive adverb. When the conjunctive adverb appears elsewhere in the sentence, commas must enclose it, or a comma must come before it.

3. Hemingway wrote about what he knew; for example, he hunted wild game in Africa and fished for marlin off the coast of Cuba.

For example, a transitional phrase functioning as a conjunctive adverb, tells how the second independent clause is related to the first. Since the phrase comes immediately after the first independent clause, a semicolon precedes the phrase and a comma comes after it.

4. Frank knew that the family needed help. Nevertheless, he offered no assistance.

Conjunctive adverbs can also be used to link two separate sentences. As a result, the logical relationship between the sentences is smoothly and clearly presented to the reader.

Note: Some one-syllable conjunctive adverbs, such as *hence, now,* and *thus,* do not require a comma. For example: Paula has just earned her A.A. degree; now she's happy. Paula has just earned her A.A. degree; she's happy now. Even some multi-syllable conjunctive adverbs do not require a comma when they appear within the second independent clause, rather than at the start of it: John did not enjoy the rainy day; he was not otherwise unhappy.

EXERCISE   5-7

Assume that all of the following sentences are compound. Place semicolons and commas as needed.

1. The voters were against the plan nevertheless the governor decided to support it.

2. Most people want a larger police force therefore they should be willing to pay for a larger one.

3. Your answer makes much sense in short it solves many problems.

4. In 1961 the citizens of the District of Columbia were granted the right to vote in presidential elections moreover in 1971 Washington's citizens were granted the right to elect a non-voting member to the House of Representatives.

5. George Washington ran unopposed for president in 1789 further he ran unopposed in 1792.

6. The Mediterranean fruit flies may destroy Southern California's citrus crop nonetheless many Californians are against spraying populated areas with insecticide.

7. I will be in New York City next week I hope to see you then.

8. Many of the promises of Castro's revolution in Cuba remain unfulfilled many Cubans as a result have given up hope of a better life.

9. I had planned to order steak I have ordered turkey instead.

10. Mr. Johnson has supposedly finished the project at any rate I hope so.

. . . .

EXERCISE   5 - 8

Assume that all of the following sentences are compound. Place semicolons and commas as needed.

1. Much acid rain falls in Canada the acidity however is caused mainly by industrial emissions in the United States.

2. During the latter part of her career, Bette Davis starred in a number of films dealing with death and decay for example she had celebrated roles in *Whatever Happened to Baby Jane?* and *Dead Ringer.*

3. Bette Davis endured several unhappy marriages and many other personal griefs consequently she called her autobiography *The Lonely Life.*

4. Tony was suffering from a cold and a sore throat still he won the race.

5. The spleen cleans and stores blood cells however a person can live without one.

6. Actor Gary Cooper won three Academy Awards he nevertheless remained, on stage and off, a humble and modest man.

7. Approximately a fifth of the United States is semi-desert indeed half of the West is such.

8. Dr. Benjamin Rush, an eighteenth-century American physician, introduced the medical practice of bleeding patients in an attempt to cure them as a result many patients died from the "cure."

9. During the hearing Clarence Thomas appeared to be telling the truth similarly Anita Hill appeared truthful.

10. The French government has admitted to spying on American corporations additionally the spying has cost those corporations millions of dollars in lost sales.

. . . .

E X E R C I S E 5 - 9

Each of the numbered items has two simple sentences. Using an appropriate conjunctive adverb, make a compound sentence for each item. Punctuate each compound sentence correctly.

1. Thomas was a close friend of mine. He would not give me a loan.

   _____

2. Alex pitched a no-hit game. He hit a game-winning home run.

   _____

3. Pat missed six classes due to illness. She missed two exams.

   _____

4. Yesterday I had neither a job nor a place to stay. I have both.

   _____

5. Alice did not go to the concert. She went to Paul's graduation.

   _____

. . . .

E X E R C I S E 5 - 1 0

Construct compound sentences using the noted conjunctive adverbs or transitional phrases. Be sure to use the semicolon and comma correctly.

1. (consequently) _____

   _____

2. (hence)_____

   _____

3. (meanwhile) _____

_____

4. (in fact) _____

_____

5. (similarly) _____

_____

6. (on the contrary) _____

_____

7. (thereafter) _____

_____

8. (thus) _____

_____

9. (undoubtedly) _____

_____

10. (after all) _____

_____

. . . .

Prepositions and Prepositional Phrases

In this chapter you will learn what prepositions are and how they act in combination with other words to bring added meaning to sentences.

PREPOSITIONS

Prepositions are **relationship** words; they **connect** a noun or pronoun, called the object of the preposition, to another word (or word group). A preposition always introduces a prepositional phrase, a group of related words composed of a preposition, its object, and any modifiers (adjectives or adverbs) of that object.

The following words may be used as prepositions:

about	concerning	regarding
above	despite	respecting
across	down	round
after	during	since
against	for	through
along	from	throughout
among	in	till
around	including	to
aside	inside	toward
at	into	towards
before	like	under
behind	near	underneath
below	notwithstanding	until
beneath	of	unto
beside	off	up
besides	on	upon
between	onto	with
but (see note below)	over	within
beyond	past	without
by		

Note: Used as a preposition, *but* means *except*. Example: All of the girls *but* Jane went to the party. *But* is also used as a coordinating conjunction. Example: Jane's sisters went to the party, but Jane decided to stay home.

A preposition may be more than one word. Consider these examples:

according to   in spite of   in front of   next to   on account of

How can you tell if a word is a preposition? If a word has an object and acts as a connective, then it is a preposition. Some prepositions show relationships of time (*after, before, during, since, until*), or location (*at, beside, in, on, out, over, under, underneath*), or direction (*to, across, toward*).

PREPOSITIONAL PHRASES

Now that you have learned what a preposition is, you need to learn more about prepositional phrases. A prepositional phrase consists of a preposition, its object, and any modifiers:

> at the party   [In this phrase, *at* is the preposition; *party* is the object of the preposition; and *the* is the adjective modifier.]

> in the back yard   [Here, *in* is the preposition; *yard* is the object of the preposition; and *the* and *back* are the adjective modifiers.]

Of course, a preposition may have more than one object:

> past Mary and Tom   [In this phrase, *past* is the preposition; *Mary* and *Tom* are the objects.]

E X E R C I S E   6 - 1

Underline the prepositional phrases in the following simple sentences.

1. Tammi lives in Los Angeles.

2. I know no one like Jonathan.

3. The horse jumped over the fence and ran into the woods.

4. During the basketball game Paul lost his contact lenses.

5. There were few volunteers besides us.

6. Throughout the meeting Mr. Vincent remained silent.

7. Vivien stood beside me.

8. The woman behind Dena is my sister.

9. The decision will not be made until tomorrow.

10. Wait across the street.

EXERCISE 6 - 2

For additional practice, underline the prepositional phrases in the following simple sentences.

1. The bus from Boston will arrive at 5:15 P.M.

2. The scene before us was devastation.

3. Everyone but Ricky and Lou knew the answer.

4. Each of the defendants was found innocent.

5. Relations between Cuba and America have not improved significantly.

6. Darryl went despite Cynthia's objections.

7. The bike next to mine is Paul's.

8. I have known William since 1990.

9. Stand near me.

10. After 7 P.M. no one will be admitted.

· ·

EXERCISE 6 - 3

Using the following prepositions, write prepositional phrases:

1. above _____

2. down _____

3. below _____

4. near _____

5. during _____

6. in front of _____

7. from _____

8. over _____

9. throughout _____

10. with _____

· ·

Prepositional phrases bring added meaning to a sentence, and help make your writing more precise. Consider the differences between the following sentences:

1. The people enjoyed the music.
   The people at the party enjoyed the music.
2. The dangerous dog sleeps.
   The dangerous dog sleeps in the back yard.
3. She ran.
   She ran past Mary and Tom.

Through the use of prepositional phrases, the sentences have additional and, in at least one case, very important information. You would certainly want to know where that dangerous dog is sleeping.

E X E R C I S E   6 - 4

Use each of the prepositional phrases that you wrote for Exercise 6-3 in a short sentence.

1. _____
2. _____
3. _____
4. _____
5. _____
6. _____
7. _____
8. _____
9. _____
10. _____

· ·

FUNCTIONS OF PREPOSITIONAL PHRASES

You should now be able to recognize a preposition. Consider the sentences used previously as examples

1. The people at the party enjoyed the music. [After the word *at* you ask "What?" or "Whom?" The answer, *party*, is the object of the preposition. The prepositional phrase, *at the party*, is connected to *people* and explains which people.]

2. The dangerous dog sleeps in the back yard. [After the word *in* you ask "What?" or "Whom?" The answer, *yard*, is the object of the preposition. The adjectives *the* and *back* modify *yard*. The prepositional phrase, *in the back yard*, is connected to *sleeps* and explains where the dog sleeps.]

3. She ran past Mary and Tom [In this case, you can see that *Mary* and *Tom* are the objects of *past*. When you ask "Past whom?" your answer is *Mary* and *Tom*. The prepositional phrase, *past Mary and Tom*, is connected to *ran.*]

You can now make an added observation about prepositional phrases: they function as single parts of speech in the sentence, and can act as either adjectives or adverbs. Consider the following examples:

Adjectives

1. The man *on the motorcycle* had an accident. [In this sentence, *on the motorcycle* acts as an adjective to modify *man*, a noun.]

2. The clown *in the box* jumped up. [*In the box* functions as an adjective modifying *clown*, a noun. You may wonder what part of speech *up* is; it is, after all, on the list of prepositions. However, since *up* does not introduce a prepositional phrase, it cannot be a preposition. Actually, *up* in this sentence functions as an adverb modifying *jumped*, the predicate. When you ask the adverb question "Jumped where?" you get the adverb answer: *up*.]

3. His AIDS research was *of great importance*. [*Of great importance* is the prepositional phrase, but how does it function in this sentence? The phrase is an adjective complement. Since *of great importance* follows a linking verb (*to be*: *am*, *is*, *are*, *was*, *were*, *being*, *been*) and since the phrase describes the research, the phrase acts as an adjective.]

Adverbs

An adverb can modify a verb, another adverb, or an adjective. Adverbs answer the following questions: How? When? Where? Why? To what extent? Under what conditions?

1. Fred ran *into the field*. [*Into the field* follows the predicate *ran*. When you ask the question, "Ran where?" you get the adverb answer: *into the field*. The phrase acts as an adverb modifying the predicate *ran*.]

2. Rita is happy *at her job*. [In this sentence *happy* is an adjective complement, and *at her job* modifies *happy*. The

phrase answers the question, "Happy where?" Thus, *at her job* acts as an adverb.]

3. The apartment is large enough *for Tom's family.* [Here, *for Tom's family* modifies *enough*, which is an adverb modifying the adjective complement *large.*]

In some cases, a prepositional phrase may modify an entire sentence: For example, Patricia, Don, and Scott bought new Fords. A prepositional phrase such as *for example*, which modifies the entire sentence, is considered an adverb. In rare cases, a prepositional phrase may act as a noun: *After lunch* is best. *After lunch* functions as the subject of the sentence and hence is a noun.

EXERCISE   6 - 5

Underline the prepositional phrases in the following simple sentences. In the blanks tell how each phrase functions: *adjective*, *adverb*, or *noun*.

1. _____ John left at five o'clock.

2. _____ The cover of my book is torn.

3. _____ In right field is fine.

4. _____ A baby like Wendy is a joy.

5. _____ Every student but Mark passed the test.

6. _____ Alisa walked toward the door.

7. _____ I bought this ring for you.

8. _____ The *Queen Elizabeth II* docked in spite of the strike.

9. _____ In fact, Jennifer joined the United States Navy.

10. _____ Who saw the man with the white jacket?

EXERCISE   6 - 6

For additional practice, underline the prepositional phrases in the following simple sentences. In the blanks tell how each phrase functions: *adjective*, *adverb*, or *noun*.

1. _____ Ruth was at peace.

2. _____ Donna ran round the track.

3. _____ She is fast on her feet.

4. _____ Across the Atlantic Ocean is too far.

5. _____ On the contrary, the customer was right.

6. _____ The cat in the tree will not come down.

7. _____ I will visit Japan during my vacation.

8. _____ Todd was within his rights.

9. _____ Carol jumped from the car.

10. _____ She came between you and me.

. . . .

E X E R C I S E   6 - 7

Sentences can, of course, contain more than one prepositional phrase. Underline the prepositional phrases in the following sentences. In the blanks write the function of each prepositional phrase: *adjective*, *adverb*, or *noun*.

1. The house next to mine on Elm Street is for sale.

(a)_____   (b)_____   (c)_____

2. The pig ran through the house and into the field.

(a)_____   (b)_____   (c)_____

3. For instance, in the morning or in the afternoon will be fine.

(a)_____   (b)_____   (c)_____

4. The woman in the red dress is the love of my life.

(a)_____   (b)_____   (c)_____

5. I found it under the old books in the shed.

(a)_____   (b)_____   (c)_____

. . . .

E X E R C I S E   6 - 8

Write sentences using the following prepositional phrases.

1. of toxic waste

_____

2. inside the tunnel

_____

3. along the road

_____

4. before breakfast

_____

5. upon the desk

_____

6. behind the mask

_____

7. beneath the rug

_____

8. beyond the mountains

_____

9. within the burning building

_____

10. in spite of Joan's objections

_____

. . . .

SPECIAL USAGE PROBLEMS

Certain prepositions present special usage problems. A list of key problems is shown below.

1. **among**	is used with three or more persons, places, things.
	Cynthia was *among the guests* at the party.
between	is used with two persons, places, things.
	I must choose *between Fitz and Lex.*
2. **beside**	means at the side of or next to.
	Angie stood *beside her husband* as he was awarded the Congressional Medal of Honor.
besides	means in addition to or futhermore.
	Scott has many admirers *besides Amy.*
3. **in**	means within some person, place, thing.
	She is *in the house.*
into	implies motion from without to within.
	She walked *into the house.*
	Not: She is into music. **But:** She enjoys music.

4. **as**   means in the role or capacity of.

She acted *as president* during my absence.

like   expresses similarity between persons, places, things.

Your brother talks *like me.*

Note: Though both *as* and *like* can function as subordinate conjunctions, many writers prefer using *as* rather than using *like.* Subordinate conjunctions are followed by a subject and a predicate.

Prefer: The audience responded as I had predicted.

Not: The audience responded like I had predicted.

5. **on**   shows position or placement.

She is *on the roof.*

Put the money *on the table.*

onto   shows motion toward the upper surface of something.

The cat jumped *onto the table.*

Not: Sid is onto our plans.

But: Sid knows our plans.

E X E R C I S E   6 - 9

Some of the following sentences contain errors in the use of prepositions. Cross out any errors that you find, and make appropriate revisions. Write *C* next to any sentence that is correct.

1. Frank answered like I thought he would.

2. Stay beside me during the meeting.

3. Alice is onto our schemes.

4. I saw little difference among the two cars.

5. The dog ran in to the street.

6. Mr. Andrews accepted my offer, like I knew he would.

7. He demanded my rings and my watch, beside demanding my money.

8. Pablo, like Carlos, lives in New York City.

9. Kirk jumped onto the platform as the train was leaving.

10. Sandra is in the room on your left.

11. The Seeing Eye dog sat besides Danny during dinner.

12. Larry is into sports.

13. Between the five job candidates, only two were qualified.

14. As I had expected, Barbara arrived late.

15. A choice between war and peace is not an easy one.

. . . .

E X E R C I S E 6 - 1 0

Cross out the incorrect word or words in the parentheses in each of the following sentences.

1. A strong friendship exists (among, between) Jeanine and Angela.

2. Jim is (onto, aware of) our schemes.

3. (As, Like) Dr. Quillen had suspected, Darius had pneumonia.

4. (Beside, Besides) his regular job Scott has two part-time jobs.

5. The fans leaped (on, onto) the stage and surrounded Axel Rose.

6. The bishop walked (among, between) the assembled thousands of people and blessed them.

7. Jim sat (beside, besides) his wife and children during the hearing.

8. Ms. Bostic responded to the man's urgent call for help, (as, like) any professional nurse would.

9. Senator James seemed uncomfortable (among, between) the demonstrators.

10. (Beside, Besides) his house and its contents, Paul's car was destroyed by the fire.

. . . .

. . . .

Verbals and Verbal Phrases

A phrase is a group of grammatically related words that lacks a subject and predicate.

Examples

> *Eighty students* [This is a **noun phrase**: it has a noun modified by the adjective *eighty*. This phrase might form the subject of a sentence, but without a predicate there is no sentence.]

> *will graduate* [This is a **verb phrase**: it is composed of the main verb *graduate* and the helping verb *will*. For *will graduate* to function as a predicate in a sentence, a subject is needed.]

Clearly, both of the phrases above are something less than a sentence. However, when joined, they make a sentence:

> *Eighty students will graduate.*

> *on June 20* [Here is a prepositional phrase introduced by the preposition *on* and followed by the object *June 20*.] Here, again, the phrases can be joined to make a complete and meaningful sentence:

> *Eighty students will graduate on June 20.*

Being able to recognize phrases and understand their roles in a sentence can help you avoid a host of errors, such as sentence fragments, dangling modifiers, and misplaced modifiers, to name a few.

In this chapter you will learn to recognize a verbal phrase and use it effectively. To do so, you need to know the difference between a **finite verb** and a **nonfinite verb**.

A verb that is the predicate of a clause or a sentence is called a finite verb. A finite verb (predicate) makes a statement about its subject.

Example

Mrs. Benjamin slapped a police officer. [The finite verb (predicate) is *slapped*; it makes an assertion about the subject of the sentence, *Mrs. Benjamin.*]

A nonfinite verb, on the other hand, is called a verbal. Even though these are verbs, they function as nouns, adjectives, or adverbs in a clause or sentence. A nonfinite verb cannot, by itself, be the predicate of a clause or sentence. There are three types of verbals: **gerunds, participles,** and **infinitives.** In a clause or sentence these nonfinite verb forms may function alone or as part of a verbal phrase. (Note: A clause is a group of related words that contains a subject and a predicate.)

GERUNDS AND GERUND PHRASES

A gerund is the –ing verb form and functions as a noun. As a noun, the gerund can function as a subject, an object, a complement, or an appositive.

Examples

Jogging can be excellent exercise. [*Jogging* functions as the subject of the sentence.]

Marie and George enjoyed jogging. [The direct object of this sentence is *jogging.*]

My favorite exercise is jogging. [*Jogging* follows the linking verb *is* and is thus the subject complement of the sentence.]

Alex improved his physical fitness by jogging. [In this sentence *jogging* functions as the object of the preposition *by.*]

My favorite afternoon exercise, jogging, keeps me fit. [*Jogging* is the appositive (noun explaining another noun, in this case) for *exercise.* Note that a comma must precede and follow the appositive.]

Gerunds can have several verb forms, but only two are commonly used, the present (e.g., *walking*), and the present perfect (e.g., *having walked*). The important point to remember is that the gerund is the *-ing* form of the verb and functions as a noun in a clause or sentence. Also remember that, since gerunds are nouns, they can be preceded by possessive pronouns and nouns.

Examples

my love (noun)
my loving (gerund)
Edward's success (noun)
Edward's succeeding (gerund)

E X E R C I S E   7 - 1

Underline the gerunds in the following sentences. **Note:** Not all words ending in –*ing* are gerunds.

1. A good exercise is walking.

2. I enjoy wrestling.

3. The tree was damaged by lightning.

4. Susan likes fishing.

5. Tom's single aim, winning, was also his obsession.

6. Alice enjoyed being chosen.

7. The police officer arrested Arnold for stealing.

8. Sailing is relaxing.

9. The meeting is on Tuesday.

10. Having won did not excite her.

· ·

E X E R C I S E   7 - 2

For additional practice underline the gerunds in the following sentences. Remember that not all words ending in -*ing* are gerunds.

1. Drew's favorite hobby was reading.

2. Studying can be hard and enjoyable work.

3. Having been loved made Tonya happy.

4. Writing can be a pleasure.

5. George hit a home run in the fifth inning.

6. His running surprised me.

7. A fire destroyed the priceless painting of George Washington.

8. Graduating was Hank's goal.

9. Her leaving upset everyone.

10. Andy enjoys swimming.

· ·

Frequently, gerunds appear as part of a phrase in a clause or a sentence. Since a gerund is a verb, it can have a subject as well as an object or complement and modifiers. **Thus, a gerund phrase is a group of related words composed of a gerund and any subjects, objects, complements, or modifiers (adjectives or adverbs).**

Examples

Winning the race was a thrill. [The subject of the sentence is *winning the race*, a gerund phrase. *Race* is the direct object of the gerund *winning*, and *the* is an adjective modifying *race*, a noun.]

Tina enjoyed reading Swift's **Gulliver's Travels.** [The direct object of this sentence is *reading Swift's* **Gulliver's Travels**, a gerund phrase. **Gulliver's Travels** is itself the direct object of *reading*, and *Swift's* is a possessive adjective modifying **Gulliver's Travels.**]

Sam's hobby was collecting rare coins. [*Collecting rare coins* is the subject complement of the linking verb *was. Rare* is an adjective modifying the gerund's direct object, *coins.*]

In a Tennessee public school in 1925, John Scopes broke a state law by teaching Darwin's theory of evolution. [*Teaching Darwin's theory of evolution* is a gerund phrase that functions as the object of the preposition *by. Theory* is the direct object of the gerund *teaching*, and *Darwin's* is a possessive adjective modifying *theory.* The prepositional phrase *of evolution* acts as an adjective modifying the noun *theory.*]

The manager's task, preparing the yearly budget, took nearly three weeks. [*Preparing the yearly budget* is a gerund phrase that acts as an appositive. The gerund phrase explains the noun *task*, which is the subject of the sentence. In the phrase, *the* and *yearly* are adjectives modifying the gerund's direct object, *budget.*]

John did not like his grade being lowered for spelling errors. [*His grade being lowered for spelling errors* is the gerund phrase. The gerund, *being lowered*, has a subject, *grade*; *for spelling errors* is a prepositional phrase used as an adverb to modify the gerund.]

E X E R C I S E   7 - 3

Underline the gerund phrases in the following sentences.

1. Al's favorite winter sport is skiing on the mountains of Maine.

2. Saving money for the vacation was difficult.

3. Driving under the influence of drugs or alcohol endangers one's own life and the lives of others.

4. Winning the war in the Persian Gulf required the courage and dedication of men and women of many nations.

5. I enjoyed being selected for the team.

6. Having lost his legs in the Vietnam War did not stop him from having success in his private and public life.

7. Brett finds happiness in helping less fortunate people.

8. The assignment, writing a thousand word essay, took me many hours.

9. Elizabeth enjoyed hearing Dr. Bush's lecture on Camelot.

10. Tony was fired for drinking vodka during office hours.

. . . .

E X E R C I S E   7 - 4

For additional practice, underline the gerund phrases in the following sentences.

1. Saving the ozone layer is one of humanity's greatest challenges.

2. Becoming a teacher was her goal in life.

3. Speaking well and writing well require much patience.

4. Being red or yellow was Kermit the Frog's dream.

5. Thompson admitted leaving the scene of the accident.

6. Capturing the lion was not an easy task.

7. His objective, earning a degree in biology, took only three years to reach.

8. Ronald was fined for giving false testimony at the trial.

9. After waiting sixteen years Natalie Cole recorded her father's songs.

10. Christina challenged its having occurred.

. . . .

E X E R C I S E   7 - 5

Write sentences using the following verbal phrases as gerunds.

1. getting a good education

_____

2. walking to school

_____

3. gambling at a horse race

_____

4. sleeping on the job

_____

5. writing a long essay

_____

. . . .

E X E R C I S E 7 - 6

Combining ideas is one way to avoid the choppy effect of a series of short, simple sentences. Given each pair of simple sentences below, convert one sentence into a gerund phrase, and combine that phrase with the other sentence.

Example
> **From:** I flunked the exam. I got upset.
> **To:** Flunking the exam upset me.
> **Or:** After flunking the exam I got upset.

1. I work on a farm. I enjoy the job very much.

_____

2. I ate the entire pizza. I got very sick.

_____

3. I swim before breakfast. Exercise gives me a good appetite.

_____

4. I won a new automobile. The taxes cost me $3,000.

_____

5. Sally supervises fifty employees. She has no time to relax.

_____

6. I read mystery novels. I want to be a detective.

_____

7. I lift weights at the gym. I feel and look better.

_____

8. George played tennis well. He earned a position on the team.

_____

9. I solved the puzzle. The task took me two hours.

_____

10. Peter collects rare stamps. The hobby is an expensive one.

_____

· ·

PARTICIPLES AND PARTICIPIAL PHRASES

A participle is any form of the verb that is used as an adjective.

Examples

We saw a falling meteor. [*Falling* is a participle modifying *meteor*, a noun that functions as the direct object. In general, like most adjectives, the participle immediately precedes the noun it modifies.]

Falling meteors burn brightly in the night. [*Falling*, the participle, modifies *meteors*, a noun that functions as the subject of the sentence.]

Crying, Tom and Mary left the funeral home. [Note that in this example a comma comes between *crying* and *Tom and Mary*. If the adjective is restrictive (limits or confines the meaning of the noun or pronoun), use no comma. However, if the adjective is non restrictive (not essential to the basic meaning of the sentence), use a comma.]

The girl running is my sister. [In this case the participle *running* comes after the *girl* and states *which girl*. The modifier is restrictive.]

Sir Edmund Hillary, having succeeded, celebrated on the top of Mount Everest. [*Having succeeded* is a participle that is non restrictive and is thus set off by commas.]

She seemed exhausted. [The participle *exhausted* is an adjective complement coming after *seemed*, a linking verb. Remember that the most common linking verb is *to be* (*am, is are, was, were, being, been*) and that *appear, become, grow, look*, and *sound* are among the verbs that can be used as linking verbs (see Chapter 2).]

Participles have several verb forms: the present (e.g., *playing*), the past (e.g., *played*), the present perfect (*having played*), and a progressive form (e.g., *having been playing*).

Take care not to confuse the passive voice verb with a true participle. Consider this sentence:

> The fish was tagged.

Was tagged can be considered the passive voice predicate of this sentence. If your meaning is that at some point in the past the fish *was tagged by someone*, then you are using a passive voice predicate. However, if your meaning is that at some point in the past the fish was *in a tagged condition*, the word *was* is a linking verb, and *tagged* is an adjective complement, a participle.

E X E R C I S E   7 - 7

Draw one line under the participles in the following sentences. Draw two lines under the word(s) that the participle modifies.

1. Barking dogs greeted us at the gate.

2. The disappointed fans booed the band.

3. Exhausted, the mountain climbers rested for several hours.

4. The car came to a screeching halt.

5. The marching soldiers appeared proud.

6. Rampaging floodwaters devasted Arkansas and Texas.

7. John, having been fired, simply got up and left the building.

8. The impoverished masses of Eastern Europe want democracy and economic growth.

9. Wounded, the police officer fell to the ground.

10. I enjoyed the fried chicken.

. . . .

E X E R C I S E   7 - 8

For additional practice draw one line under the participles in the following sentences. Draw two lines under the word(s) that the participle modifies.

1. The soaring stock market pleases investors.

2. Having overslept, Cynthia was late for class.

3. The FDA wants more exact labeling requirements for the nation's processed foods.

4. In general, married men live longer than single men.

5. The excited contestants waited anxiously for the announcement.

6. Tired and defeated, the players left the field.

7. Fortunately, no workers were injured by the falling debris.

8. Having been selected, the members of the panel took their seats.

9. The captured documents contained much useful information.

10. The man talking is my brother Jason.

. . . .

E X E R C I S E   7 - 9

Write sentences using the following participles to modify nouns or pronouns.

1. running

_____

2. having fallen

_____

3. surging

_____

4. aching

_____

5. having been nominated

_____

6. stolen

_____

7. having rested

_____

8. collected

_____

9. speeding

_____

10. burned

_____

11. rising

_____

12. smiling

_____

13. Having stumbled

_____

14. losing

_____

15. coming

_____

· ·

A participle can be part of a longer construction called a participial phrase. **A participial phrase consists of a participle along with its subject (if any), objects or complements, and any modifiers.** Like the participle, the participial phrase acts as an adjective modifying a noun or pronoun.

Examples

Having landed on the moon, the astronauts displayed the American flag. [_Having landed on the moon_ is a participial phrase modifying _astronauts. On the moon_ is a prepositional phrase acting as an _adverb_ modifying _having landed._]

Manuel Noriega, slowly telling his sad tale, began to cry. [_Slowly telling his sad tale_ is a participial phrase modifying _Manuel Noriega_, the subject of the sentence. In the phrase _slowly_ is an adverb modifying _telling_, and _tale_ is the direct object of _telling. His_ and _sad_ are adjectives modifying _tale._]

The changes sweeping the countries of the former Soviet Union promise hope for millions of people in Europe. [_Sweeping the countries of the former Soviet Union_ is a participial phrase modifying _changes_, the subject of the sentence. _Of the former Soviet Union_ is a prepositional phrase acting as an adjective modifying _countries,_ the direct object of _sweeping._]

The preacher, appearing ill, left her pulpit. _Appearing ill_ is the participial phrase modifying _preacher_, the subject of the sentence. _Ill_ is an adjective complement modifying _appearing_, a linking verb.

E X E R C I S E 7 - 1 0

Underline the participial phrases in the following sentences. Draw two lines under the noun(s) or pronoun(s) that each participial phrase modifies.

1. Announced at the morning press conference, her plan was warmly received by her supporters.

2. Called a "shocking experience" by the warden, the execution took place at midnight.

3. Joan joined the students taking part in the play.

4. Bugs Bunny, having turned fifty years old, announced no retirement plans.

5. Appearing quite discouraged by the judge's decision, the defendant looked somber.

6. The student standing next to the teacher is my sister Ruth.

7. Selling for nearly one hundred million dollars, the yacht is for those people who do not need to float a loan.

8. Alex, seeming greatly upset, abruptly left the courtroom.

9. Having received their independence, the Baltic republics look to a brighter future.

10. The man kissing the babies is Senator Bounder.

. . . .

E X E R C I S E 7 - 1 1

For additional practice, underline the participial phrases in the following sentences. Draw two lines under the noun(s) or pronoun(s) that each participial phrase modifies.

1. Having paid the largest fine ($600 million) in the history of the United States, Michael Milken is still a multimillionaire.

2. Surging twenty feet high, the waves pounded the coastal resorts from Maryland to New York.

3. The marlin, leaping ten feet into the air, landed on the deck of the boat.

4. Filled with exciting episodes, *Huckleberry Finn* is doubtless Mark Twain's best novel.

5. The elderly woman, having hurt herself in the fall, required medical assistance.

6. The Twawan Sugu Company produces edible plates made from wheat.

7. Addressing the crowd, President Yeltsin called for resistance to dictatorship.

8. Suffering from a 10% drop in ads, America's magazines are seeking new sources of income.

9. Having become extinct sixty-five million years ago, dinosaurs continue to fascinate people of all ages.

10. Ninety-six Americans, each possessing more than $1 billion, comprise a third of the world's billionaires.

. . . .

E X E R C I S E   7 - 1 2

Write sentences using the following as participial phrases to modify nouns or pronouns.

1. appearing very happy

   _____

2. having hastily studied for the exam

   _____

3. having been feeling unhappy

   _____

4. kissing my wife

   _____

5. needing $500

   _____

6. filled with mystery

   _____

7. attracting a great deal of attention

_____

8. astounded by the turn of events

_____

9. having grown up in a poor family

_____

10. going at full speed

_____

11. using their new computer

_____

12. falling victim to a burgler

_____

13. having walked over fifty miles

_____

14. standing next to my sister

_____

15. sleeping on the front porch

_____

. . . .

INFINITIVES AND INFINITIVE PHRASES

An infinitive is a verb form that functions as a noun, an adjective, or an adverb. The infinitive is easy to recognize because it is usually preceded by *to*, which is called **the sign of the infinitive.**

Examples

To join is Tom's intention. [*To join* is the subject of the sentence.]

Sonya wants to run. [*To run* is the direct object of the sentence.]

Randy's desire was to win. [*To win* is the subject complement.]

I have no choice except to resign. [*To resign* is the object of the preposition *except*.]

We went to play. [*To play* is an adverb modifying the predicate *went*.]

Vinnie was quick to speak. [*To speak* is an adverb modifying the adjective complement *quick*.]

The students to be honored were happy. [*To be honored* is an adjective modifying *students*, the subject of the sentence.]

Kathy looked for a house to buy. [*To buy* is an adjective modifying *house*, the object of the preposition *for*.]

The infinitive has the following verb forms: the present (e.g., *to buy*), the present perfect (e.g., *to have bought*), the present progressive (e.g., *to be buying*), and the present perfect progressive (e.g., *to have been buying*).

The present perfect infinitive, progressive form, may be used with some linking verbs. For example: Marie seemed to be growing sad.

As was noted earlier, the infinitive is usually easy to recognize because it is preceded by *to*, the sign of the infinitive: *to run, to jump, to go, to be, to be going, to have been selected*, etc. For some verbs, however, the *to* is not always used. Such verbs as *bid, do, dare* (not), *feel, make*, and *see* may be followed by infinitives with the sign *to* omitted. For example: She bid me go. He dare not leave.

In addition, the sign of the infinitive may not appear after the prepositions *but* and *except*. For example: The mule did nothing except sit.

You will notice that these infinitives do not require punctuation. However, a comma (or commas) is needed when an infinitive acts as an adverb and comes before the word (or words) it modifies.

Examples

To be heard, he shouted. [*To be heard* is an adverb modifying *shouted*.]

An athlete, to be successful, must practice daily. [*To be successful* is an adverb modifying *must practice*, the predicate of the sentence.]

E X E R C I S E 7 - 1 3

Most of the following sentences contain infinitives. In the blank, indicate whether the infinitive functions as a *noun*, an *adjective*, or an *adverb*. Remember that *to* can also be used to introduce a prepositional phrase.

_____1. To succeed is my plan.

_____2. Norman was happy to win.

_____3. Professor Pass is the teacher to get.

_____4. I have a map to use.

_____5. Lynn went to the store.

_____6. Simon did nothing but complain.

_____7. I want to dream.

_____8. Please let go.

_____9. My trip to Boston took three hours.

_____10.I was happy to have been loved.

. . . .

E X E R C I S E 7 - 1 4

Most of the following sentences contain infinitives. In the blank, indicate whether the infinitive(s) functions as a _noun_, an _adjective_, or an _adverb_. Remember that _to_ can also be used to introduce a prepositional phrase.

_____1. They offered to listen, to talk, and to negotiate.

_____2. Maria's rise to power was swift.

_____3. Mike had other battles to fight.

_____4. To worry is not part of Joan's makeup.

_____5. Stefan has ten dollars to spend.

_____6. The right to vote has been hard won by some
American citizens.

_____7. Isaac plans to run.

_____8. The children had no food to eat and no clothes
to wear.

_____9. The prisoner to be executed died peacefully in
his sleep.

_____10.Earl is quick to argue.

. . . .

E X E R C I S E 7 - 1 5

Write sentences using the following infinitives.

1. to jog

_____

2. to go

_____

3. to find

_____

4. to live

_____

5. to eat

_____

6. to do

_____

7. to work

_____

8. to build

_____

9. to pick

_____

10. to talk

_____

· ·

An infinitive can be part of a longer construction called an **infinitive phrase**. *An infinitive phrase consists of an infinitive along with its subject (if any), objects or complements, or any modifiers.*

Examples

Tom liked to swim in the ocean. [*To swim in the ocean* is the infinitive phrase and functions as the direct object of *liked*. *In the ocean* is a prepositional phrase that functions as an adverb modifying *to swim*.]

To write clearly was her goal. [*To write clearly* is the infinitive phrase and acts as the subject of *was*. *Clearly* is an adverb modifying *to write*.]

Dan hated to lose the race. [*To lose the race* is the infinitive phrase and acts as the direct object of *hated*. *Race* is the direct object of *to lose*.]

I know her to be a capable worker. [The infinitive phrase, *her to be a capable worker*, acts as the direct object of *know*. *Her* is the subject of the infinitive, and *worker* is the subject complement of *to be*. Note that you use the same pronoun for the subject of an infinitve as you would use for the direct object of the sentence.]

This is the perfect movie to watch on Halloween. [*To watch on Halloween* is the infinitive phrase and acts as a adjective modifying the noun *movie*. *On Halloween* is a prepositional phrase that acts as an adverb to modify *to watch*.]

Paula attended to learn English well. [*To learn English well* is the infinitive phrase and acts as an adverb to modify *attended*. *English* is the direct object of *to learn*, and *well* is an adverb modifying *to learn*.]

He was tall enough to play basketball. [*To play basketball* is the infinitive phrase and acts as an adverb to modify *enough*. *Basketball* is the direct object of *to play*.]

E X E R C I S E 7 - 1 6

Underline the infinitive phrases in the following sentences. Above each phrase write *N* for *noun*, *ADJ* for *adjective*, and *ADV* for *adverb*. Remember that *to* can introduce a prepositional phrase.

1. We went to catch some fish for lunch.

2. The time to go home is now.

3. To find good employees and to keep them is most important.

4. Do you want to have success?

5. They were ready to begin the race.

6. The director of the band expected Elizabeth to sing.

7. She studied to do well on the test.

8. To play tennis was not to my liking.

9. Players who need to take batting practice should line up.

10. Her story seems, at least to me, too strange to be true.

EXERCISE 7-17

For additional practice, underline the infinitive phrases in the following sentences. Above each phrase write *N* for *noun*, *ADJ* for *adjective*, and *ADV* for *adverb*. Remember that *to* can introduce a prepositional phrase.

1. Al left to seek a new life in Canada.

2. Her mother made her leave home.

3. To be victorious meant a fight to the death.

4. To drive with care should be the goal of all motorists.

5. He appears to have been treated well during his captivity.

6. To surf on high ocean waves can be dangerous.

7. Look to your left as you enter the room.

8. To construct the house took only one week.

9. Roberto had the knowledge and the skills to survive in the jungle.

10. She wished them to be on time.

· ·

EXERCISE 7-18

Write sentences using the following infinitive phrases *as nouns*.

Example
>   to write about famous people
>   Like Kitty Kelley, I want to write about famous people.

1. to travel at night on that street

_____

2. to read all of *War and Peace*

_____

3. to become a lawyer

_____

4. to find the lost treasure

_____

5. to visit Japan

_____

. . . .

E X E R C I S E 7 - 1 9

Write sentences using the following infinitive phrases as modifiers (_adjectives_ or _adverbs_).

Example
> to take Paul to lunch
> The cost to take Paul to lunch was thirty dollars.

1. to go for good fishing

_____

2. to register for class

_____

3. to pay for the vacation

_____

4. to feed the cats

_____

5. to solve the problem of world hunger

_____

. . . .

. . . .

Subordinating Conjunctions, Relative Pronouns, and Subordinate Clauses

The meaning that you want your reader to gain can be expressed in a variety of sentence patterns (or structures). As we have seen in previous chapters, the first and most basic of these patterns is the **simple sentence**, which expresses one main idea contained in one independent clause composed of at least a subject and a predicate:

Examples

1. Subject/Predicate

   Ted loves. Ted is loved.

2. Subject/Predicate/Object

   Ted loves Joan.

   Ted gave Joan the ring.

   [The first sentence has only a direct object (Joan); the second sentence has both an indirect (Joan) and a direct object (ring).]

3. Subject/Predicate (linking verb)/Complement

   Ted is a doctor.

   Ted is happy.

   [The complement may be a noun (doctor) or a pronoun (Ted is somebody.) or an adjective (happy).]

4. Compound Subject/Compound Predicate/Compound Object or Complement

   Ted and Joan buy and sell stocks and bonds.

   Ted and Joan are friendly and helpful.

Of course, simple sentences can have meaning added to them through the use of modifiers: adjectives modifying nouns or pronouns, as well as adverbs modifying verbs, adjectives, or other adverbs.

Though the simple sentence has its place in writing, especially to express one idea with force, effective writing is usually not composed of a string of simple sentences. Independent clauses can be combined to form another sentence pattern, one which has two or more independent clauses joined by coordinating conjunctions (*and, or, for, nor, so, yet, but*), or correlative conjunctions (*either...or, neither...nor*, etc.), or by conjunctive adverbs (*however, moreover, therefore*, etc.), or by only a semicolon or, in special cases, a colon. These sentences are called **compound sentences**. For example:

> Twenty-two years were needed to construct India's Taj Mahal, but only eight years were required to construct Donald Trump's Taj Mahal. India's Taj is a tomb; however, Trump's is a gambling casino and hotel. According to Trump, "It's a billion-dollar hotel, and it looks it."

These compound sentences are examples of parallel structure. The ideas that are so joined (independent clause joined to independent clause) must be logically parallel in meaning. They must carry equal weight.

Just as effective paragraphs are rarely composed of only simple sentences, so are they rarely composed of only compound sentences. Consider, for example, the following paragraph. The first sentence is the topic sentence: it introduces the main idea of the paragraph. In this case, the main idea is *many hardships*.

Topic sentence: During their trip across the ocean on the *Mayflower*, the Pilgrims suffered many hardships.

The ship was a very small craft, and the decks were crowded. The cabins were packed beyond capacity. There were 149 people on board. The ship was slow, and the winds were not always favorable. The crossing took two painful months. Frequently, the tiny *Mayflower* was tossed about on the waves, and it rolled like a loose barrel upon raging waters. The Pilgrims suffered from seasickness, and their food supplies ran low. There was only one fire on board for cooking, and it was built on a flat hearth on the open deck. In November 1620 the Pilgrims reached land, but most of the weary Pilgrims had to suffer on board for three more difficult weeks. Some men had to find a safe place for a settlement.

The purpose of this paragraph is to discuss *the Pilgrims* in terms of the *hardships they suffered*, but are the sentences composed so that the emphasis is on the Pilgrims' hardships? Are all of the ideas of equal weight? No. The paragraph is not unified because not all of the ideas are of equal weight, and yet all of the ideas are expressed in independent clauses forming simple or compound sentences, *as if* they were of equal weight. Now consider this revision of the sample paragraph:

Topic sentence: During their trip across the ocean on the *Mayflower*, the Pilgrims suffered many hardships.

Since the ship was a very small craft with 149 people on board, the Pilgrims crowded the decks and packed their cabins beyond capacity. *Because* the winds were not always favorable, the Pilgrims suffered a slow and painful crossing of two months. Frequently, they were tossed about on the ship *because* it rolled like a loose barrel upon raging waters. As a result, the Pilgrims suffered from seasickness. *Though* they did have a hearth on deck for cooking, they had precious little food to cook. *When* they did reach land in November 1620, most of the weary Pilgrims had to suffer on board for three more difficult weeks *until* a safe place to settle could be found.

This second paragraph is more unified and coherent than the first version. Why? One reason is the use of **subordination**. Some of the ideas in the original paragraph have been put in subordinate clauses introduced by subordinating conjunctions such as *since*, *because*, *though*, *when*, and *until*. These clauses contain ideas that are helpful to the paragraph, but which are not the main ideas. Only main ideas should be in independent clauses. Notice also that, since the subject of the paragraph is *Pilgrims*, the independent clauses emphasize that subject either by repetition of the word or through the use of a pronoun (*they*). The effective use of subordination shows which ideas are of major importance and which are of minor, and helps you to write with brevity and greater variety.

COMPLEX SENTENCES

A sentence that contains an independent clause and one or more subordinate clauses is called a complex sentence. The subordinate clauses in a complex sentence are introduced by **subordinating conjunctions** and **relative pronouns**, and can function as an adverb, adjective, or noun.

SUBORDINATING CONJUNCTIONS AND RELATIVE PRONOUNS

The words used to introduce subordinate clauses form three groups that correspond to the function of each clause in a sentence.

Introducing Adjectival Clauses

The following relative pronouns may be used to introduce adjectival clauses:

>   that which who whom whose

In addition, *when*, *where*, and *why* may introduce adjectival clauses.

Introducing Adverb Clauses

The subordinating conjunctions commonly used to introduce adverb clauses include the following:

To show time relationships:	after, until, as soon as, when, before, whenever, since, while
To show place relationships:	everywhere, where, wherever
To show manner relationships:	as, as if, as though
To show comparison relationships:	as...as, than, less (more) than
To show contrast or concession relationships:	
	although, even if, though, even though
To show conditional relationships:	if, even if, unless
To show causal relationships:	as, since, because, that
To show purpose relationships:	in order that, so that

Introducing Noun Clauses

The following relative pronouns, adjectives, and adverbs can be used to introduce noun clauses:

how	where	whom (ever)	that
whether	whose	what (ever)	which (ever)
why	when	who (ever)	

RECOGNIZING SUBORDINATE AND INDEPENDENT CLAUSES

Examples

1. **Independent clause:** Winston Churchill won the Nobel Prize for Literature.

   Subordinate clause: *Although* Winston Churchill won the Nobel Prize for Literature...

   [Placing the subordinate conjunction in front of the independent clause changes the clause to a subordinate one.]

   Complex sentence: *Although Winston Churchill won the Nobel Prize for Literature*, his true love was not writing but painting. [This complex sentence starts with a subordinate clause (italicized) and is followed by an independent clause. The idea in the independent clause is thus given emphasis.]

2. **Independent clauses:** Mayor Black's press conference was most informative. It lasted over three hours.

   Subordinate clause: *which* lasted over three hours.

Complex sentence: Mayor Black's press conference, *which lasted over three hours*, was most informative. [The main emphasis is on the informative nature of the press conference. Thus, that idea makes up the independent clause. How long the conference lasted is not the major point, and so the less important idea is placed in a subordinate clause.]

3. **Independent clauses:** President Nixon resigned. This action can be easily explained.

Subordinate clause: *Why* President Nixon resigned...

Complex sentence: *Why President Nixon resigned* can be easily explained. [In this complex sentence the italicized subordinate clause is different from those contained in examples 1 and 2. In example 3 the subordinate clause functions as the subject of the sentence. You will learn more about the functions of subordinate clauses as adverbs, adjectives, or nouns in the next section of this chapter.]

E X E R C I S E   8 - 1

Indicate whether each of the clauses below is independent by writing *I* in the blank, or subordinate by writing *S* in the blank.

_____ 1. Until John receives the offer of employment.

_____ 2. Whomever you want to help you on the project.

_____ 3. Third National Bank has low interest rates on car loans.

_____ 4. So that he might find happiness in his marriage.

_____ 5. As soon as the semester is completed.

_____ 6. If you find the treasure in the sunken ship.

_____ 7. Before he had learned to swim.

_____ 8. Life in America seems more complicated these days.

_____ 9. Which lasted for over three months.

_____10. How often they went.

. . . .

EXERCISE 8 - 2

For additional practice, indicate whether each of the clauses below is independent by writing *I* in the blank, or subordinate by writing *S* in the blank.

_____ 1. Although Judge Thomas was confirmed by the United States
Senate.

_____ 2. Why more political reform is needed in the Russian Republic.

_____ 3. Jimmy Connors proves that there is tennis, as well as life, after
forty.

_____ 4. Since yesterday, I have not caught one fish.

_____ 5. Everywhere Madonna goes.

_____ 6. What Americans want most from their government.

_____ 7. Whenever *It's a Wonderful Life* is shown on television.

_____ 8. Even though the Dead Sea Scrolls were found.

_____ 9. More than $40 million was earned by Woody Allen's *Hannah
and Her Sisters.*

_____10. Much less than what was hoped for.

. . . .

EXERCISE 8 - 3

In the following complex sentences underline each subordinate clause one time and the main clause two times. Circle the subordinating conjunction or the relative pronoun that introduces each subordinate clause.

1. When the Exxon *Valdez* spilled oil into Alaska's waters in March 1989,
the nation was shocked and angry.

2. Many citizens of Quebec, which is largely composed of French-speaking
Canadians, have called for independence.

3. Today's strikers often fear that they will not be able to get their jobs back.

4. Although the Sierra Club advocates protecting the nation's wilderness
areas, some members criticized their club because it did not print its 1990
calendar on recycled paper.

5. Since the population of America's racial and ethnic minority groups continues to grow rapidly, white Americans will be a minority in a little over fifty years.

6. As soon as President Roosevelt took office, he called for the repeal of the Eighteenth Amendment so that Americans could once again legally drink liquor.

7. Sandra Day O'Connor, who was the first woman appointed to the United States Supreme Court, has earned the admiration of her fellow justices.

8. Unless a cure is found for AIDS, currently-infected people must live with both hope and fear.

9. The Panama Canal was constructed so that a ship sailing from San Francisco to New York could cut three weeks from its travel time.

10. Irving Berlin, whose songs inspired Americans for decades, gave a large portion of his earnings to the Boy Scouts and Girl Scouts.

. . . .

E X E R C I S E 8 - 4

Using the subordinate clauses below, construct complex sentences.

1. although the river had overflowed its banks

   _____

2. who got the highest mark on the test

   _____

3. whenever the instructor calls on me in class

   _____

4. so that I may win the race

   _____

5. less than I had wanted

   _____

6. after the party was over

   _____

7. as happy as my parents were

_____

8. whom they had seen

_____

9. even if it rains

_____

10. whatever the reason might be

_____

. . . .

THE FUNCTIONS OF SUBORDINATE CLAUSES

The subordinate clause functions in a sentence as a single part of speech: an adverb, an adjective, or a noun.

The Adjectival Clause

Subordinate clauses that function as adjectives modify nouns or pronouns. In general, the adjectival clause comes right after the word(s) it modifies, and is introduced by *that*, *which*, *who*, *whom*, *whose*, *when*, *where*, and *why*.

Note: The relative pronoun *that* is sometimes omitted before an adjectival clause: I know the type of clothes [that] you like.

Examples

The neighbors *who have four dogs* live next to me. [In this example, *who have four dogs* modifies neighbors, the subject of the independent clause.]

Rocky knows the lake *where the fishing is good*. [*Where the fishing is good* modifies lake, the direct object of the independent clause.]

I am looking for the student *whose book was left in the classroom*. [In this example, *whose book was left in the classroom* is an adjectival clause modifying *student*, which is the object of the preposition *for*.]

All of the adjectival clauses in these examples are called **restrictive**; that is, they are absolutely necessary to fix the identity of the noun or pronoun modified. Ask yourself this question: *which one?* The answer will give you a restrictive adjectival clause. As a result, no comma is used to set the restrictive adjectival clause apart from the rest of the sentence. However, not all adjectival clauses are restrictive; some contain helpful, but not necessary, information. The word(s) modified in such cases is already adequately identified. Such non-essential adjectival clauses are termed **non restrictive**, and commas must be used to set them apart.

Examples

Dr. Murphy, *who teaches French and Spanish*, has just been named Teacher of the Year. [*Who teaches French and Spanish* is helpful but not essential to the meaning of the sentence. Thus, commas should be placed around this adjectival clause.]

But consider this sentence:

The woman *who teaches French and Spanish* has just been named Teacher of the Year. [In this example, no commas are used because the adjectival clause identifies which woman. The modifying clause is absolutely necessary to fix the identity of the *woman*.]

Congress voted to increase federal spending for research to help AIDS victims, *whose numbers now surpass the 200,000 mark in the United States*. [Since the subordinate clause is inessential to the meaning to the sentence, a comma must precede that clause.]

EXERCISE 8 - 5

Underline the adjectival clauses in the following sentences. For non restrictive adjectival clauses insert commas as appropriate.

1. I know the man who won the new Toyota.

2. Many Americans enjoy jogging which is an excellent exercise for the heart and lungs.

3. Arizona which is one of the fastest-growing states in America boasts the Grand Canyon, the Painted Desert, and the Petrified Forest as tourist attractions.

4. Darryl knows the time when we must leave.

5. Do you know the spot where the fish are biting?

6. Dr. King was a man whom most people naturally liked.

7. I know the reason why he was fired.

8. The letter Joan wrote never reached its destination.

9. Students that study hard will usually do well on tests.

10. The tiger which could once be found throughout the world's forests and jungles is now nearly extinct in the wild.

. . . .

E X E R C I S E   8 - 6

Write complex sentences of your own using **restrictive** adjective clauses introduced by the following subordinating words:

1. (that) _____

_____

2. (which) _____

_____

3. (who) _____

_____

4. (whom) _____

_____

5. (whose) _____

_____

. . . .

E X E R C I S E   8 - 7

Write complex sentences using **non restrictive** adjective clauses introduced by the following subordinating words:

1. (that) _____

_____

2. (which) _____

_____

3. (who) _____

_____

4. (whom)_____

_____

5. (whose)_____

_____

. . . .

The Adverbial Clause

A subordinate clause functions as an adverb when it modifies a verb, an adjective, or another adverb. Like single-word adverbs, the adverb clause may come at the start of a sentence, at the end of one, or somewhere in the middle. If the adverb clause comes at the start of the sentence, it is followed by a comma unless it is very brief and no misunderstanding occurs if the comma is omitted:

Examples

When we attended the lastest edition of Ringling Brothers and Barnum & Bailey Circus, we truly experienced the Greatest Show on Earth.

After I had come to know the Bible, I wanted to visit the Holy Land.

While I talked they laughed. [Since the introductory adverb clause is very short, the comma may be omitted.]

In general, if the adverb clause comes at the end of the independent clause, no comma is used:

Examples

Albania declares itself an atheist nation because the practice of any religion is forbidden.
The 1919 World Series really had no winner since eight Chicago players conspired to lose to Cincinnati.

If the adverb clause comes in the middle of the independent clause, commas precede and follow it.

Examples

The celebration, since it was scheduled for Thursday, had to be postponed due to the funeral.
The accident victim, after he had awakened from his coma, could not remember any details of the plane crash.

Following is a list of the several kinds of adverb clauses:

Relationships of	Introduced by	Examples
Time (when?)	after, as soon as, before, since, until, when, whenever, while	I will speak when Tom arrives. When you have packed your bags, we'll go.
Place (where?)	everywhere, where, wherever	I know where the gold is buried. Paul was unhappy everywhere he went.
Manner (how?)	as, as if, as though	He looked as though he had seen a ghost. They talked as if they were excited.
Comparison (to what degree?)	as...as, less than, more than, than	She has more money than he has. I am faster than he [is].
Contrast or Concession (under what conditions? admitting what?)*	although, though, even if, even though	Although the test was difficult, I still did very well on it. I will go to the party, even though my friends won't go.
Condition (under what conditions?)	if, even if, unless	If it should rain today, be sure to close the windows.
Cause (why?)	as, because, since, that	He went because he was needed. Are we children that we behave in this way?
Purpose (why?)	in order that, so that	I will study so that I will pass the test.

*Special note on punctuation: When an adverb clause of concession, such as that in the example in the table, comes at the end of a sentence, a comma usually separates the adverb clause from the independent clause.

Example

John passed the exam, although he did not study for it. [*Although he did not study for it* is a non restrictive clause; that is, it does not restrict the meaning of the independent clause. The writer could have omitted the subordinate clause completely and still have communicated his essential thought.]

E X E R C I S E   8 - 8

Underline the adverb clauses in the following sentences.

1. Rita ran faster than Joan ran.

2. When you are ready, Bob and I will join you.

3. Even though George had a bad cold, he still played tennis.

4. I will not leave unless you tell me to do so.

5. Because our car got a flat tire, we were two hours late.

6. Paula went on a strict diet so that she would not have to take insulin shots.

7. Since Alec worked hard, he was tired.

8. While I was waiting for Carla, Tim and Fred arrived.

9. The concert, whenever it takes place, will be exciting.

10. After you have washed the car, please cut the grass.

. . . .

E X E R C I S E   8 - 9

Write complex sentences of your own introduced by adverb clauses that start with the following subordinating conjunctions:

1. As soon as _____

_____

2. If_____

_____

3. As _____

_____

4. Since_____

_____

5. Until _____

_____

. . . .

E X E R C I S E 8 - 1 0

Write complex sentences that end with adverb clauses which are introduced by the following subordinating conjunctions:

1. _____

   after _____

2. _____

   in order that _____

3. _____

   as though_____

4. _____

   where _____

5. _____

   while _____

· ·

The Noun Clause

Subordinate clauses that act as nouns can fulfill any of the standard roles that a noun can have in a sentence: subject, direct or indirect object, complement, object of a preposition, appositive, or the object of a verbal. Remember that noun clauses can be introduced by *how, that, what, whatever, when, where, whether, which, whichever, who, whoever, whom, whomever, whose, and why.*

Examples

Subject: *Where he went* was not known. *What she wanted* was clear.

Direct Object: I know *why they left early.* Show me *how he managed to escape.* I believe [*that*] *he is right.* [Sometimes *that* is omitted from the subordinate clause.]

Indirect Object: Give *whoever is selected* your support.

Subject Complement: Your answer is *what I want.* My reason is *that I want the money.*

Object of a Preposition: I know nothing except *that he will arrive this evening.* I do not know from *where he is coming.*

Appositive: His demand—*that he be granted immunity from prosecution*—surprised all of us.

Object of a Verbal: Knowing *which is correct* is impossible. [*Which is correct* is the object of the gerund *knowing.*] Suspecting *that he would be caught*, the convict crossed into Mexico. [*That he would be caught* is the object of the participle *suspecting.*] I want you to know *what I think.* [*What I think* is the object of the infinitive *to know.*]

A noun clause may also be a delayed subject after the expletive *it*: It became clear *that she would win*. In effect, *it* merely introduces the sentence; *that she would win* is the actual subject.

E X E R C I S E 8 - 1 1

Underline the noun clauses in the following sentences. In the blank space, indicate the function of the noun clause: *subject, direct object, indirect object, subject complement, appositive, object of a preposition, object of a verbal*, or a *delayed subject after it*.

_____1. I know that you want to join us.

_____2. Why he decided to enter the race is a mystery.

_____3. Do not be concerned about what he said.

_____4. This is how I solved the puzzle.

_____5. It is obvious he is loved by his fans.

_____6. Do you agree with what I think?

_____7. I do not know whom I can believe.

_____8. I asked whether he could be trusted.

_____9. Thinking that he was coming late, I delayed the start of the meeting.

_____10. She gave whoever entered a kiss.

_____11. Knowing when you need to act is important.

_____12. I hope to find what I need.

_____13. Give whoever comes what is requested.

_____14. The problem is that we have a flat tire.

_____15. What was reported was what I knew.

. . . .

E X E R C I S E 8 - 1 2

Write complex sentences using the following relative pronouns, adjectives, and adverbs to introduce *noun* clauses.

1. (who) _____

_____

2. (whose) _____

_____

3. (whatever)_____

_____

4. (whether)_____

_____

5. (that)_____

_____

6. (how) _____

_____

7. (what)_____

_____

8. (which) _____

_____

9. (whom) _____

_____

10. (when) _____

_____

· ·

E X E R C I S E 8 - 1 3

Underline the subordinate clauses in the following sentences. In the blank, indicate *ADJ* for adjective clause, *ADV* for adverb clause, and *NOUN* for noun clause.

_____ 1. The timber industry claims that saving the spotted owl will

cost 30,000 men and women their jobs.

_____ 2. Giant Douglas firs, trees which were old when Washington and Jefferson were alive, can be cut down in less than two minutes.

_____ 3. A year after the *Exxon Valdez* catastrophe, while Congress still pondered reform legislation, the *Mega Borg* spilled millions of gallons of crude oil off Galveston, Texas.

_____ 4. Although both William Faulkner and Ernest Hemingway wrote poetry, they preferred to write fiction.

_____ 5. Japanese investment in the United States means that nearly 300,000 Americans now work in Japanese-owned companies.

_____ 6. By the time that Operation Desert Storm ended, more than 228,500 National Guard members and reservists had been called to active duty.

_____ 7. The places that fully half of the residents of Bombay, India, call home are either shanties or sidewalks.

_____ 8. There are some Bombay slums where there is neither water nor electricity.

_____ 9. Some residents who do, in fact, have a "roof" over their heads live in sewage pipes.

_____ 10. When a social worker was asked what was needed, he spoke of a relief effort of massive proportions.

. . . .

E X E R C I S E 8 - 1 4

The following paragraph contains a series of short, simple sentences. On your own paper, rewrite the paragraph using subordinate conjunctions. Combine pairs of sentences, but keep some simple sentences for variety. Keep in mind that the main idea of the paragraph is "disaster."

Topic sentence: My son's room is a disaster.

(1) The pine floor is not even visible. (2) Clothing is scattered everywhere. (3) His baseball shirt and pants protrude from under the bed. (4) This bed is covered with dirty socks and underwear. (5) The dresser overflows with shirt sleeves. (6) His dresser is missing one drawer. (7) A baseball glove and three bats lie among the items of clothing. (8) On the night table is an over-

turned Pepsi can. (9) This can slowly drips its contents to the floor. (10) From the partly opened closet comes the odor of week-old pizza. (11) The closet door has an "ENTER AND DIE" sign on it. (12) I have placed a sign on the entrance door: "ENTER AND CLEAN—OR DIE."

· ·

EXERCISE 8-15

Like the one in the exercise above, the following paragraph contains a series of short, simple sentences, and the effect is choppy. On your own paper, rewrite the paragraph using subordinate conjunctions. Combine pairs of sentences, but keep some simple sentences for variety. Keep in mind that the main idea of the paragraph is "talented man."

Topic sentence: Benjamin Franklin was a talented man.

(1) He published the *Pennsylvania Gazette*. (2) This was noted for its quality and wide readership. (3) Another success was a series of almanacs called *Poor Richard's*. (4) These were printed from 1732 to 1757. (5) Franklin was also a celebrated inventor. (6) He was interested in helping others. (7) He invented a stove. (8) It heated a room better than a fireplace did. (9) The lightning rod and bifocal eyeglasses were his inventions. (10) From one of his proposals came the Academy of Philadelphia. (11) This eventually grew into the University of Pennsylvania. (12) Perhaps his greatest talent was political. (13) He was an ambassador to France in 1776. (14) He secured men and money for Washington's army. (15) He was a member of the Constitutional Convention of 1787. (16) He was decisive in getting the Constitution approved. (17) Of Franklin's life, one Frenchman wrote: "He snatched the lightning from the skies and the sceptre from tyrants."

· ·

Types and Classes of Sentences

In this chapter we will review the three types of sentence structures studied earlier (simple, compound, and complex), and learn about a fourth type, the **compound-complex sentence.** In addition to studying these sentence structures and practicing how to use them effectively, you will learn that a sentence can be identifed and classified by its purpose. A sentence can make a statement (*John hit Fred*), ask a question (*Did John hit Fred?*), voice a command (*John, hit Fred*), or express strong emotion (*John hit Fred!*).

TYPES OF CLAUSES AND SENTENCES

Types of Clauses

There are two types of clauses:

An independent clause is a group of related words having a subject and a predicate and expressing a complete thought.

Examples
The kiwi is native to New Zealand.
Explorer 1 was the first American satellite to orbit the earth.
The Gold Rush of 1849 increased California's population by hundreds of thousands of people.

As these examples show, an independent clause can stand alone as a sentence.

A subordinate clause is a group of related words having a subject and a predicate but not expressing a complete thought. Unlike the independent clause, the subordinate clause cannot stand alone. It is made dependent by the subordinating conjunction (*after, although, as, because, before, how, since, unless, until, when, where, while, why,* etc.) or the relative pronoun (*that, which, who, whom, whose*) that introduces it.

Examples
> Although *Explorer 1* was the first American satellite to orbit the earth.
> When the Gold Rush of 1849 increased California's population by hundreds of thousands of people. [The use of subordinating conjunctions *although* and *when* changes what were independent clauses into subordinate clauses.]

In the following sentence, the subordinate clause modifying *kiwi* is introduced by the relative pronoun *which*:

> The kiwi, which is native to New Zealand, cannot fly.

The subordinate clause introduced by *that* in the following sentence is the direct object of *know*:

> I know that the kiwi cannot fly.

Types of Sentences

Using independent and subordinate clauses, four types of sentences can be formed: **simple, compound, complex**, and **compound-complex.**

The Simple Sentence   The simple sentence contains one independent clause and has several patterns:
- Subject/Predicate (Alex writes.)
- Subject/Predicate/Object (Alex is writing a letter.)
- Subject/Predicate (linking verb)-Complement (Alex is a letter carrier.)
- Compound Subject/Compound Predicate/Compound Object or Complement (Alex and Maria are writing a letter. Alex and Maria are happy and content.)

Of course, the simple sentence can have single-word modifiers or phrase modifiers in it.

Examples
> Bob and I celebrated Earth Day by planting fifty trees. [*By planting fifty trees* is a prepositional phrase that functions as an adverb. It modifies the predicate *celebrated* and answers the question, "*how?*"]
>
> Most of the Hispanics living in the United States lived previously in Mexico. [*Of the Hispanics* is a prepositional phrase that modifies *most* and acts as an adjective. *Living in the United States* is a participial phrase modifying *Hispanics*. *In Mexico* is a prepositional phrase modifying *lived* and answering the question, "*where?*" The phrase functions as an adverb.]
>
> The Republic of Nauru, a small Pacific island, has one marketable product: phosphates. [The subject of this simple sentence is *The Republic of Nauru*, the predicate is *has*, and the

direct object is *product. A, small,* and *Pacific* are adjectives that modify *island. A small Pacific island* is a phrase that acts as a noun to more fully identify *The Republic of Nauru. One* and *marketable* are adjectives modifying *product,* and *phosphates* is a noun that acts to identify *product.*]

Note: A noun or noun phrase coming next to or near another noun or noun phrase and identifying it more fully is an **appositive.** For example, *phosphates* is an appositive for *product.*

Simple sentences are very effective vehicles of a single meaning or intention; however, a long series of simple sentences in a paragraph can create a choppy effect and bother your reader. (See the paragraph on the Forty-Niners at the start of chapter 5.)

The Compound Sentence   The compound sentence is composed of two or more independent clauses. These clauses can be be joined in several ways to express ideas that are parallel in form and content.

Examples

Tim enjoyed New Wave music, but Tom preferred the classics. [In this example the independent clauses are joined by the coordinating conjunction *but.* (The other coordinating conjunctions are *and, or, so, for, nor,* and *yet.*)]

Either you pay your rent, or you will be evicted. [In this example the two independent clauses are joined by the correlative conjunction *either...or.* (Other correlative conjunctions are *not only...but also, neither...nor, not only...but, both...and,* and *just...so.*)]

Tim enjoyed New Wave music; however, Tom preferred the classics. [In this case the two independent clauses are joined by the conjunctive adverb *however.* (Examples of other conjunctive adverbs are *also, further, similarly, meanwhile, therefore, thus, hence, likewise, additionally, still, then, instead.*)]

Tim enjoyed New Wave music; Tom preferred the classics. [Only a semicolon joins the clauses.]

Tim sang, Christina danced, Tom left. [In this instance, since the independent clauses are very short, commas may be used to join them.]

You may want to review the detailed discussion of the compound sentence in chapter 5.

The Complex Sentence   A complex sentence is composed of one independent clause and at least one subordinate clause. As you saw at the start of this chapter, a subordinate clause is introduced by a subordinating conjunction or a relative pronoun.

Examples

> Amnesia, which is usually caused by a sudden shock or blow to the head, means a loss of memory. [In this complex sentence the clause introduced by *which* is an adjective modifying the subject *amnesia.*]

> When the environmental movement began in the 60s, it concerned itself with legislative issues. [In this example the introductory subordinate clause is an adverb modifying the predicate *concerned.*]

> What Charles Darwin presented in *Origin of Species* in 1859 was evidence for his theory of evolution. [In this case the introductory subordinate clause, which begins with the relative pronoun *what*, is a noun, the subject of the predicate *was.*]

The Compound-Complex Sentence   The last type of sentence, the compound-complex sentence, has at least two independent clauses and at least one subordinate clause. Like the compound sentence, the compound-complex sentence displays thoughts in parallel structure:

> Independent clause: The world will little note nor long remember
> Subordinate clause: what we say here,
> Independent clause: but it can never forget
> Subordinate clause: what they did here.

In this sentence (taken from Lincoln's Gettysburg Address), the two independent clauses and two subordinate clauses are parallel.

In the following example, independent and subordinate clauses are parallel and form a compound-complex sentence:

> Introductory phrase: According to Thomas Malthus,
> Subordinate clause: when population is unchecked,
> Independent clause: it increases at a rate of 2, 4, 8, 16, etc.;
> Subordinate clause: when food production is maximized,
> Independent clause: it increases at a rate of 1, 2, 3, etc.

E X E R C I S E   9 - 1

Identify each of the following sentences by writing *simple, compound, complex,* or *compound-complex* in the blank. Underline each subordinate clause.

_____1.   One of the most serious problems in the United States is that of the homeless.

_____2.   About half of the Puerto Ricans called for statehood, and about half of them preferred independence.

_____3. Though Andrew Jackson, Millard Fillmore, and Abraham Lincoln were born in log cabins, each man became president of the United States.

_____4. Polygamy, which is practiced in several cultures today, means having two or more husbands or wives at the same time; monogamy, which is the standard practice in the United States, means being married to only one person at a time.

_____5. According to British Lord Acton, "Power corrupts, and absolute power corrupts absolutely."

_____6. Risk of heart disease is increased with a cholesterol count of 240 or more; a count between 200 and 239 may mean increased risk; a count below 200 is generally considered safe.

_____7. The catfish of Mississippi continues to grow in importance as part of the American diet.

_____8. Many environmentalists are fond of pointing out that 200 years ago a squirrel could travel from New York to California without ever having to leave the treetops.

_____9. Since the Soviet Union no longer exists, the Castro government has lost a major financial backer.

_____10. Chimpanzees routinely eat leaves and seeds, but these animals occasionally kill and eat small baboons and colobus monkeys.

. . . .

E X E R C I S E   9 - 2

For additional practice, identify each of the following sentences by writing *simple*, *compound*, *complex*, or *compound-complex* in the blank. Underline each subordinate clause.

_____1. I enjoyed seeing the film version of *Billy Budd*; however, I enjoyed reading the novel even more.

_____2. The Panama Canal, which is fifty miles long, connects the Atlantic and Pacific oceans.

_____3. Gettysburg was the site of a famous battle during the Civil War and of a famous address by President Abraham Lincoln.

_____4. When the United States signed the Paris peace accords in 1973, the Vietnam War officially ended, but the fighting continued.

_____5. Noted for helping the poor and teaching children the Bible, Jimmy Carter has gained new respect.

_____6. Passover, which lasts seven days, celebrates the exodus of the Hebrews from Egypt around 1300 B.C.

_____7. After reading Homer's *Iliad*, I realized that human nature has remained constant for centuries.

_____8. In Botswana the vast majority of the population is engaged in herding or farming.

_____9. After North Vietnam defeated South Vietnam, Saigon became Ho Chi Minh City.

_____10. Most people know the stock market as Wall Street.

· ·

E X E R C I S E   9 - 3

Write five simple sentences of your own.

Example
I enjoy freshwater fishing in the summer.

1. _____
2. _____
3. _____
4. _____
5. _____

. . . .

E X E R C I S E   9 - 4

Take each of the five simple sentences that you have written for Exercise 9-3 and add an independent clause to that simple sentence so that you form a compound sentence. Remember that the independent clauses should be parallel in meaning as well as in structure.

Example
I enjoy freshwater fishing in the summer, but I prefer saltwater fishing in the fall.

1. _____

   _____

2. _____

   _____

3. _____

   _____

4. _____

   _____

5. _____

   _____

. . . .

E X E R C I S E   9 - 5

Take the sentences that you have written for Exercise 9-4 and convert them into complex sentences. Your purpose is to emphasize one idea.

Example

Although I enjoy freshwater fishing in the summer, I prefer saltwater fishing in the fall.

1. _____

_____

2. _____

_____

3. _____

_____

4. _____

_____

5. _____

_____

. . . .

E X E R C I S E   9 - 6

Combine each of the following groups of clauses into a compound-complex sentence.

1. I will go with you
   if you want to go
   and we can enjoy the game together.

   _____

   _____

2. it is rather ordinary
   when the sun is compared with other stars
   scientists call it a "yellow dwarf"

   _____

   _____

3. it is composed of the House of Commons and the House of Lords
   Parliament is the British legislative body
   Congress is the American legislative body
   it consists of the House of Representatives and the Senate

   _____

   _____

   _____

4. he was one of America's most popular comedians
   Redd Foxx began his career in vaudeville
   and he later became a celebrated television star

   _____

   _____

   _____

5. he is known as Larry the Liquidator
   in *Other People's Money* Danny DeVito plays a selfish and ruthless man
   in his private life, however, DeVito is a mild-mannered and charitable
   man

   _____

   _____

   _____

. . . .

CLASSES OF SENTENCES

In addition to being classified according to structure, sentences can be classified according to purpose as **declarative, interrogative, imperative,** or **exclamatory.**

The Declarative Sentence

The declarative sentence is one that makes a statement.

Example

The 1991 eruption of Mount Pinatubo in the Philippines hurled ash twenty miles into the sky.

The Interrogative Sentence

The interrogative sentence asks a question.

Example

Exactly how many points does the Star of David have?

The Imperative Sentence

The imperative sentence makes a request or voices a command.

Examples

> Please come here.
> Leave at once.

The Exclamatory Sentence

The exclamatory sentence voices surprise, determination, or strong emotion or passion.

Examples

> I've won!
> We will not fail!
> He's been shot!

Note: Do not use a series of exclamation points at the end of a sentence to increase emphasis. *Not:* The volcano has exploded!!!! *But:* The volcano has exploded! In a paragraph, avoid writing sentence after sentence ending with exclamation points. Exclamatory sentences should be used sparingly, or they lose their effect.

What is important about the types of sentences (simple, compound, complex, and compound-complex) and the classes of sentences (declarative, interrogative, imperative, and exclamatory) is the way they are used in writing paragraphs. While it is important for you to know what the types and classes are, you must also be able to use them effectively.

As you know, a long string of simple sentences can result in dull reading. Similarly, a long string of compound sentences (especially when *and* joins the independent clauses) can be boring. What is needed is sentence variety. Place main ideas in independent clauses, and place subordinate ideas in subordinate structures, such as modifying phrases and clauses. Vary, as appropriate, the classes of sentences you use. Starting a paragraph with a question or an exclamation can help to increase the interest of your reader. Following several long sentences with a short one provides variety and allows you to emphasize the idea in the short sentence. Above all, you want to emphasize the exact relationship of ideas through the proper use of coordination and subordination.

E X E R C I S E   9 - 7

The following paragraph contains five compound sentences. However, the sentences show faulty coordination because they contain ideas that are not equal in importance. Rewrite the sentences so that subordinate ideas are placed in modifying phrases or clauses. The main idea in the paragraph is "huge."

Topic sentence: Among mammals the blue whale epitomizes the word *huge.*

1. The blue whale is a member of the order Cetacea, and it grows to about one hundred feet in length.

   _____

   _____

2. The blue whale eats small fish and shrimplike animals, and at maturity it can weigh from 130 to 150 tons.

   _____

   _____

3. The time from conception to birth is similar to that for humans, but the newborn blue whale must be measured in yards and tons instead of inches and pounds.

   _____

   _____

4. The blue whale is able to produce sounds with a very low pitch; however, the whale can project those sounds at the ear-splitting level of over 180 decibels.

   _____

   _____

5. The blue whale seems to have a rather small vocabulary of sounds, yet its enormous lungs and vocal cords can propel those sounds many hundreds of miles.

   _____

   _____

. . . .

E X E R C I S E   9 - 8

In the following paragraph each of the numbered sentences shows faulty subordination. Rewrite the the sentences so that the main ideas receive emphasis in independent clauses. Put all minor or supporting ideas in subordinate phrases or clauses. The main idea of the topic sentence is "curious origins."

Topic Sentence: Many words in the English language have curious origins.

1. Although the word *acre* meant any plot of land in Anglo-Saxon England, today the word means exactly 4,840 square yards.

2. *Dunces* are stupid people, though many of the followers of John Duns Scotus (*Duns men*) in the 1200s were highly educated.

3. *Lawn*, which once meant land filled with trees and shrubs, now means a plot of grass.

4. *Mess*, a word that basically meant food from the 1300s to the 1800s, is today a disorderly or dirty condition, though the term retains its original meaning in *mess hall*.

5. A natural or learned ability is *talent*, which once meant a measurement of weight or money.

. . . .

E X E R C I S E   9 - 9

A topic sentence and several numbered sentences follow and form a paragraph. The main idea of the topic sentence is "kept many facts about his life secret...or nearly so." However, some of the numbered sentences contain faulty subordination or faulty coordination. Rewrite the sentences so that the main ideas form independent clauses and the minor ideas are placed in subordinate phrases or clauses. (Some sentences are correct and do not need to be rewritten.)

Topic Sentence: Throughout his life, Dr. James kept many facts about his life secret...or nearly so.

1. Although few people knew that Dr. James had once managed a chain of car washes, many people knew his work as a physician.

2. Many people knew that he was a religious man, but few people knew that he had once studied to be a monk in Japan.

_____

_____

3. Even fewer people knew that he had been married four times.

_____

4. On a wall of his office at Cutler Hospital, Dr. James displayed pictures of his award-winning cats, although locked in his desk were pictures of his four wives and fifteen children.

_____

_____

_____

5. His neighbors in Hidden Valley knew that he was collecting their folklore; what they did not know was that he had published their stories under an assumed name and had earned ten thousand dollars.

_____

_____

_____

6. What was almost unknown in James's lifetime was his knowledge of wrestling.

_____

_____

7. True, he had organized a charity event featuring the World Wrestling Federation; however, he kept his involvement hidden from all but a few people.

_____

_____

8. Though he had secretly worked for years on an unpublished book titled _Wrestling in America_, his colleagues at the hospital knew that he had published little of significance to medicine.

_____

_____

_____

9. After he left medicine for a career as a professional wrestler, his neighbors and his former patients and colleagues never knew the man behind the mask, the man called "Cutthroat Jim."

_____

_____

_____

. . . .

Fragments and Run-On Sentences

A sentence is unified and coherent when it states its meaning clearly, completely, and smoothly. In this chapter you will learn about two errors which result in disunified and incoherent sentences, the sentence fragment and the run-on sentence, and how to avoid these errors.

FRAGMENTS

As you know, every sentence must contain a subject and a predicate. A sentence fragment, however, is an incomplete sentence, for a fragment is missing a subject or a predicate or both, or the fragment is a subordinate clause written as a sentence. Although you might sometimes want to use fragments for a special effect or to answer a question, you should use them cautiously and deliberately. Rather than obscure meaning, a fragment, if used effectively, should enhance meaning.

There are several kinds of fragments:

A subject without a predicate

Example
> The Constitution of the United States.

A predicate without a subject

Example
> Contains ten amendments known as the Bill of Rights.

A prepositional phrase

Example
> In the woods and valleys.

A verbal phrase

Example
> To go home. Going home.

A subordinate clause

Example

> Since the Constitution of the United States contains ten amendments known as the Bill of Rights.

Note: When a subordinate conjunction is placed at the start of a sentence, that sentence becomes a fragment. However, a clause beginning with *how, who, which, where, when,* or *why* and asking a question is a sentence.

Examples

> Where are you going?
> What are you doing today?

To change fragments into unified and coherent sentences:

Add a predicate to the subject

> From: A large and vicious dog.
> To: A large and vicious dog attacked the baby.

Add a subject to the predicate

> From: Welcomed the sight of land.
> To: The weary Pilgrims welcomed the sight of land.

Attach the prepositional phrase to a sentence

> From: From the beauty and richness of the island of San Salvador.
> To: From the beauty and richness of the island of San Salvador, Columbus thought that he had discovered the land that Marco Polo had written about.

Attach the verbal phrase to a sentence or convert the verbal phrase into a sentence

> From: Called the core.
> To: Called the core, the innermost layers of the earth are probably composed of iron and nickel.
> Or: The innermost layers of the earth are called the core and are probably composed of iron and nickel.

Remove the subordinate conjunction from the subordinate clause, or attach the subordinate clause to an independent clause (thus forming a complex sentence).

> From: Which starred Boris Karloff.
> To: The Hollywood movie *Frankenstein*, which starred Boris Karloff, was based on a novel by Mary Shelley.
> Or: The Hollywood movie *Frankenstein* was based on a novel by Mary Shelley. The movie starred Boris Karloff.

EXERCISE 10-1

Make a complete sentence by adding predicates (and objects) to the following subjects.

1. The stormy weather during last December _____.

2. The students attending the demonstration _____.

3. Many large cities in the United States _____.

4. My main purpose in going to college _____.

5. The rock concert featuring Paul Simon _____.

· ·

EXERCISE 10-2

Make a complete sentence by adding subjects to the following predicates.

1. _____ enjoyed the party.

2. _____ hardly believe it.

3. _____ bit the boy.

4. _____ is protected by the skull.

5. _____ continues rainy.

· ·

EXERCISE 10-3

Use each of these prepositional phrases in a sentence.

1. around the world

_____

2. of unknown origin

_____

3. in the United States Air Force

_____

4. for thirty years

_____

5. but John

_____

. . . .

E X E R C I S E 10-4

Use each of the following verbal phrases in a sentence, or convert the verbal
phrase into a sentence by adding a subject and changing the *-ing* or *to* form of
the verb into a predicate.

Example
> From: Falling on my face.
> To: I disliked falling on my face.
> Or: I fell on my face.

1. enjoying the vacation.

_____

2. To visit Washington, D. C.

_____

3. Changing fragments.

_____

4. Breaking a leg.

_____

5. To earn much money.

_____

. . . .

E X E R C I S E 10-5

Convert the following subordinate clauses into independent clauses (sentences), or attach the subordinate clauses to independent clauses (thus forming complex sentences).

1. If the Cold War has ended.

_____

_____

2. Which upset Darryl very much.

_____

_____

3. Although Eva arrived late.

_____

_____

4. Who she is.

_____

_____

5. After I fell asleep on the beach.

_____

_____

· ·

E X E R C I S E 10-6

Some of the following groups of words are complete sentences, and some are not. If the group of words is a sentence, write *S* in the blank. If the group of words is a fragment, write *F*, and convert the fragment into a sentence.

_____ 1. When Wendy returned home after a long day of work.

_____

_____

_____ 2. Running through the woods to avoid the hunters.

_____

_____

_____ 3. After the battle was over, the troops rested.

_____

_____

_____ 4. Since Debby liked everybody.

_____

_____

_____ 5. Which students are going to the game?

_____

_____

_____ 6. In newspapers, in magazines, and on television.

_____

_____

_____ 7. Although I knew that the job would be difficult.

_____

_____

_____ 8. Whatever Matt wanted was unclear.

_____

_____

_____ 9. For Marie to do well on her test.

_____

_____

_____10. Such as the Fourth of July and Memorial Day.

_____

_____

· ·

RUN-ON SENTENCES

Another way to make a meaning unclear is to write a run-on sentence. **A run-on sentence simply means that one independent clause runs into another one—without having the appropriate punctuation or the right conjunction between those independent clauses.** Two kinds of errors can result: the comma splice and the fused sentence.

Avoiding the Comma Splice

When only a comma joins two independent clauses, a comma splice results. In such a case, you have done one of two things. You may have left out a needed coordinating conjunction (_and, or, so, but, for, nor, yet_), or you may have placed a comma before a conjunctive adverb (_however, on the contrary, accordingly, nevertheless_, etc.) that joins two independent clauses. A few examples will clarify these points:

1. The poorest state in America, Mississippi, is in the Old South, California, the richest state, is in the West. [This sentence has the "classic" comma splice error. Two independent clauses are incorrectly joined by nothing but a comma after *Old South*. Placing a semicolon after *Old South* is one of several ways to correct the error.]

2. Fort Sumter was attacked on April 12, 1861, as a result, President Lincoln asked for 75,000 volunteers to fight the rebels. [In this sentence, *as a result* functions as a conjunctive adverb phrase joining two independent clauses. A semicolon (not a comma) is needed after *1861*.]

3. In the North as in the South, Frederick Douglass was often the victim of racist words and acts, however he always retained his sense of self-confidence and self-respect. [*However* is a conjunctive adverb. Rather than use a comma between the two independent clauses, you need a semicolon before *however* and a comma after it.]

There are four ways to correct comma splices:

Make two sentences.

Change: Published in 1852, Harriet Beecher Stowe's *Uncle Tom's Cabin* showed the severe hardships endured by the slaves, years later President Lincoln said that Stowe was "the little lady" who started the Civil War.

To: Published in 1852, Harriet Beecher Stowe's *Uncle Tom's Cabin* showed the severe hardships endured by the slaves. Years later President Lincoln said that Stowe was "the little lady" who started the Civil War.

This method of correcting a comma splice is probably not the best one to use if the clauses are short and are closely related. The result may be two weak sentences when one strong one is needed. The example above has two independent clauses of equal value or significance, but they are not so closely related that they should be made into one sentence. In any case, try to avoid a series of short sentences to compose a paragraph, for such a series results in abrupt starts and stops, and creates a disjointed effect.

Add a coordinating conjunction after the comma.

Change: Each year Queen Elizabeth II receives a tax-free income of $35 million from investments, the British government still gives her about $15 million yearly for "expenses."

To: Each year Queen Elizabeth II receives a tax-free income of $35 million from investments, but the British government still gives her about $15 million yearly for "expenses."

To use a comma and a coordinating conjunction between two independent clauses requires that the two clauses be of parallel value. Remember that *and* adds ideas, that *nor* and *or* divide ideas, that *for* and *so* show cause-effect relationships, and that *but* and *yet* indicate contrast. If you find that one of the clauses contains a less important idea, you may want to put that idea in a subordinate clause and thus form a complex sentence rather than a compound one.

Use a semicolon in place of the comma, or a semicolon and a conjunctive adverb followed by a comma.

Change: The capital of Thailand is Bangkok, the city is also known as "Venice of the Orient."

To: The capital of Thailand is Bangkok; the city is also known as "Venice of the Orient."

Change: Lafayette was only nineteen years old when he came to America, Congress made him a major general in Washington's army.

To: Lafayette was only nineteen years old when he came to America; however, Congress made him a major general in Washington's army.

Use subordination as appropriate.

Coordination is appropriate when ideas are of equal value; however, subordination is appropriate when one idea is more important than another.

Change: The northern spotted owl has been declared an endangered species, its preservation may cost loggers thirty thousand jobs over the next ten years.

To: The preservation of the northern spotted owl, which has been declared an endangered species, may cost loggers thirty thousand jobs over the next ten years.

Of course, this revision is subject to dispute. An environmentalist might consider the placement of the bird on the endangered species list as the main idea. If so, the revision might read:

Although the preservation of the northern spotted owl may cost loggers thirty thousand jobs, the bird and the woods it inhabits have been saved from destruction.

In the following sentence, what is of major importance and what is of minor importance are not in doubt:

Change: Cambodia is one of the world's poorest nations. It is in Southeast Asia.

To: Cambodia, which is in Southeast Asia, is one of the world's poorest nations.

E X E R C I S E   1 0 - 7

Some of the following sentences are correctly punctuated; other sentences contain a comma splice. If the sentence is correct, write *C* in the blank. If the sentence is incorrect, write *X* in the blank and rewrite the sentence using any two of the methods you have learned; however, in some cases, you may want to use the subordination method only.

_____ 1. A dollar bill lasts only eighteen months before it must be destroyed, a dollar coin lasts twenty years.

a. _____

_____

b. _____

_____

_____ 2. The Susan B. Anthony dollar never became popular because of its quarter size and its silver color, a gold-colored coin, when minted, might spell the end of the paper dollar.

a. _____

_____

b. _____

_____

_____ 3. Each year the Treasury Department must spend hundreds of millions of dollars to replace worn-out dollar bills, the cost of replacing dollar coins would be only a fraction of that sum.

a. _____

_____

b. _____

_____

_____ 4. The spy plane known as the SR-71 Blackbird was retired from service in December 1989, its work is being done by spy satellites.

a. _____

_____

b. _____

_____

_____ 5. The SR-71 could fly at an altitude of 100,000 feet, and it could travel at a speed of 3,000 miles per hour.

a. _____

_____

b. _____

_____

_____ 6. Rumors persist that the Air Force is building a super SR-71, the Air Force will not discuss the matter.

a. _____

_____

b. _____

_____

_____ 7. According to rumors, the new SR-71 will have no pilot, it will fly at speeds in excess of 4,000 miles per hour.

a. _____

_____

b. _____

_____

_____ 8. Daily newspaper circulation in the United States grew by 1.5 million in the 1970s, but it grew by only 500,000 in the 1980s.

a. _____

_____

b. _____

_____

_____ 9. Steven Spielberg's _Star Wars_ amazed audiences through the use of 545 special effects, its sequel, _The Empire Strikes Back_, had a sensational 942.

a. _____

_____

b. _____

_____

_____10. Toward the end of Operation Desert Storm, Iraqi troops set the oil fields of Kuwait ablaze, as a result perhaps $15 billion will be the final cost to restore the fields.

a. _____

_____

b. _____

_____

. . . .

Avoiding the Fused Sentence

A fused sentence is one in which two or more independent clauses have collided. **When two (or more) independent clauses are joined without proper punctuation or a suitable conjunction, a fused sentence results.** For example:

1. In the 1950s Elvis Presley made his hometown of Tupelo, Mississippi, famous in England the Beatles made Liverpool second only to London in fame during the 1960s. [As you can see, such a fused sentence leads to a misreading and should be avoided. The error can be corrected by adding a semicolon or a period after *famous*.]

2. The state with the largest population is California Wyoming is the state with the smallest one. [After *California*, you could add a comma and an *and*, or you could add just a semicolon.]

Most fused sentences can be corrected in ways similar to those you use to correct a sentence with a comma splice:

- Make two sentences.
- Add a comma and a suitable coordinating conjunction.
- Use a semicolon, or a semicolon and a conjunctive adverb followed by a comma.
- Use subordination as appropriate.

Note: Some "fused" sentences do not fit neatly into any category. Consider this example:

One of America's greatest entertainers was Sammy Davis, Jr., sang and danced in nightclubs, recorded many hit songs, and starred on Broadway and in movies. [Confusion results because *Sammy Davis, Jr.*, cannot be both the complement of *was* and the subject of the predicate beginning with *sang and danced*.]

You can probably think of several ways to revise the sentence. One obvious way is to make two sentences by ending the first one with *Jr.* and starting the next one with *He*:

> One of America's greatest entertainers was Sammy Davis, Jr. He sang and danced in nightclubs, recorded many hit songs, and starred on Broadway and in movies.

EXERCISE 10-8

Some of the following sentences are correctly punctuated; other sentences are fused. If the sentence is correct, write *C* in the blank. If the sentence is incorrect, write *X* in the blank and rewrite the sentence using any two of the methods noted above. In some cases, however, you may want to use the subordination method only.

_____ 1. The human tongue has a significant function in speech its essential function is the movement of food in the mouth and down the throat.

a. _____

_____

b. _____

_____

_____ 2. A human being can survive without a spleen a person cannot live without a liver.

a. _____

_____

b. _____

_____

_____ 3. In biology, the largest class of beings is known as a *kingdom* within this category the *species* is the smallest class of beings.

a. _____

_____

b. _____

_____

_____ 4. For example, human beings belong to the animal kingdom, and they belong to the species known as *Homo sapiens*, meaning wise man.

a. _____

_____

b. _____

_____

_____ 5. In Greek mythology Zeus was the ruler of gods and human beings his sister-wife Hera was the goddess of marriage and the home.

a. _____

_____

b. _____

_____

_____ 6. For war, the Greeks had Ares for love, the Greeks had Aphrodite.

a. _____

_____

b. _____

_____

_____ 7. Apollo was a god with many responsibilities for example he concerned himself with prophecy, law, medicine, painting, and sculpture.

a. _____

_____

b. _____

_____

_____ 8. The chief shrine of Apollo was located on the island of Delos; therefore, Apollo came to be known as the Delian god.

a. _____

_____

b. _____

_____

_____ 9. "Know thyself" was written above one door of Apollo's shrine above the other door was written "Nothing in excess."

a. _____

_____

b. _____

_____

_____10. Apollo is often thought of as being the Greek god of light and of the sun that association actually occurred much later in history.

a. _____

_____

b. _____

_____

. . . .

EXERCISE 10-9

The following paragraphs contain comma splices and fused sentences. Correct each error by using whatever method of the several that you have learned seems most suitable. Write the revised paragraphs on separate paper.

A. Henry Armstrong was one of the most celebrated boxers in American history, he was born in Columbus, Mississippi, on December 12, 1912. He fought as an amateur from 1929 to 1932, he fought as a professional from 1932 to 1945. During his professional career, he held three world championships at the same time specifically he held the titles of featherweight, lightweight, and welterweight champion. Professionally, he fought 175 bouts and he won nearly one hundred of them by knockouts. His boxing career ended in 1945, he studied to be a minister, he was ordained a Baptist minister six years later.

B. An aircraft carrier is essentially both a floating airfield and a small town. For its crew a carrier has living quarters however it also has stores, a post office, and recreational facilities, such as a gym and a theater. The carrier's airfield, the flight deck, has catapults to help launch planes it also has wires attached to hooks to help stop landing aircraft. Known as the "island," the control tower maintains radio contact with the pilots and crew members on the deck use hand signals to assist pilots in takeoffs and landings. An aircraft carrier is a major and often decisive weapon in war the recent conflict in the Persian Gulf proves this point well.

. . . .

. . . .

Agreement of Subject and Predicate

In this chapter you will learn that a subject must agree with its predicate in number (singular or plural) and person (first, second, or third). If the subject of the sentence is singular, then the predicate must be singular. This is called agreement in number.

Examples

Singular Subject	Singular Predicate	
Marky Mark	enjoys	great popularity as a rap singer.
The *Arizona*	was sunk	by Japanese planes at Pearl Harbor on December 7, 1941.

Similarly, a plural subject agrees with a plural predicate.

Examples

Plural Subject	Plural Predicate	
Musk oxen	live	in arctic America and Greenland.
The investors	expect	to recoup their losses.

The subject and predicate must also agree in person:

1st person, singular number:	I walk,	am,	have
2nd person, singular number:	You walk,	are,	have
3rd person, singular number:	He, she, it walks,	is,	has
1st person, plural number:	We walk,	are,	have
2nd person, plural number:	You walk,	are,	have
3rd person, plural number:	They walk,	are,	have

With the exception of the verbs *to be* and *to have* (see above), all present tense predicates in the third person singular add *–s* or *–es*. Examples of third-person singular subjects include the following:

Nouns: John sings.
          The dog barks.

Pronouns: He jogs. She swims. It flies.
Each talks.
Nobody wins.

In general, getting a subject to agree with its predicate is not difficult. But there are some problem areas:

The predicate must agree with its subject regardless of what phrases come between the subject and predicate.

Consider the prepositional phrase:

Examples

An account of the bank failures is in the report.
This article on Poe's poems explains his genius.
This book about birds has beautiful illustrations.

In these examples, *of the bank failures*, *on Poe's poems*, and *about birds* are not the subjects of the sentences. The simple subjects and predicates are the following: *account...is, article...explains, book...has.*

Next, when phrases come between the subject and the predicate and are introduced by words such as those in the following list, the subject and predicate must agree:

accompanied by	including
along with	like
as well as	no less than
besides	together with
in addition to	with
included with	

Examples

The captain, as well as the crew members, knows the evacuation procedures.
Fred, together with Dale and June, is absent.
These newspaper accounts, along with the taped interview, give added information.

Note that commas precede and follow the phrases.

The simple subjects and predicates of the above sentences are the following: *captain...knows, Fred...is, accounts...give.*

E X E R C I S E 11-1

Cross out the incorrect predicate in each of the following sentences.

1. The chairperson, no less than the committee members, (agree, agrees) with me.

2. The story of the two wars (are, is) fascinating.

3. The risks of such an investment (seem, seems) high.

4. Inflation, like deflation, (cause, causes) financial problems.

5. Our victories, including the recent one, (has, have) not been without losses.

6. Alice, accompanied by Jim and Craig, (are, is) going to the play.

7. The facts in this book (are, is) disturbing to me.

8. The sailors, as well as the captain, (are prepared, is prepared) to abandon the ship.

9. The students, in addition to their teacher, (enjoy, enjoys) writing poetry.

10. The cost of these souvenirs (seem, seems) very high.

. . . .

In general, a compound subject joined by and ***agrees with a plural predicate.***

Examples
> Brazil and Argentina are in South America.
> Satchel Paige and Ray Dandridge were among the famous baseball players admitted to the Baseball Hall of Fame on the basis of their excellence in the old Negro Leagues.

Exceptions: If the compound subject is really a singular idea or person, then the subject agrees with a singular predicate.

Examples
> My friend and lover is my wife Tina.
> Rock 'n' roll is the music I like.

Use a singular predicate when *each* or *every* comes before a compound subject connected by *and*.

Examples
> Each cat, dog, and monkey was taken from the lab.
> Every bush, tree, and animal was destroyed by the forest fire.

When a compound subject is joined by or, nor, either...or, neither...nor, or not only...but also, ***the predicate agrees with the nearer subject.***

Examples
> The cats or the dogs have messed up the room.
> Either you or your sisters are responsible for cleaning the room.
> Neither the enlisted men nor the lieutenant was aware of the order.

Either he or you are needed in the emergency room.
Either you or he is needed in the emergency room.
Not only Paula but also her parents were happy about the results of the test.

E X E R C I S E 11-2

Cross out the incorrect predicate in each of the following sentences.

1. Neither the campers nor their guide (was, were) prepared for the snow.

2. Not only the fire fighters but also the police officers (seem, seems) anxious about the pay raise being approved.

3. Macaroni and cheese (are, is) Ted's favorite meal.

4. Either Roger or his sisters (has, have) the key.

5. Nixon, Ford, and Reagan (was, were) the three Republican presidents immediately prior to Bush.

6. My best friend and confidant (are, is) going to marry my sister.

7. Each man, woman, and child (was, were) required to get the flu shot.

8. Ham and cheese (are, is) the sandwich I always have for lunch.

9. Either Tom or I (am, is) willing to help you.

10. Neither my brothers nor I (want, wants) to go to the party.

. . . .

E X E R C I S E 11-3

Complete each of the following sentences using only present tense predicates.

1. Darryl, like his parents, _____

_____.

2. Neither WJZ-TV nor WBAL-TV _____

_____.

3. Neither the cab driver nor the passengers _____

_____.

4. Each book, magazine, and newspaper _____

_____.

5. The children, along with their grandmother, _____

_____.

6. The teacher, together with his students, _____

_____.

7. My dog or my cats_____

_____.

8. The president and chief executive officer_____

_____.

9. The nails and hammer _____

_____.

10. Either the committee members or the chairperson _____

_____.

. . . .

Indefinite pronouns do not refer to specific persons, places, or things. Some indefinite pronouns are clearly singular and take a singular predicate; others are clearly plural. Still others may be singular or plural, depending on the nouns or pronouns they refer to.

Study the following lists:

Always Singular

another	each	everything	nothing
anybody	either	neither	one
anyone	everybody	nobody	somebody
anything	everyone	no one	someone
something			

Examples

Each is able to play tennis well.
Nobody seems unhappy about the results.
Someone hits a home run at nearly every game.

Always Plural

both	few	many	others	several

Examples

Both enjoy the sport of fishing.
Several were selected.
Others remain at home.

Singular or Plural

all	any	more	most	none	some	such

Examples

Most of the students were pleased with their scores on the second test.

Most of the grain in storage was eaten by rodents. [In the first example, *most* is clearly intended to be plural; in the second example, *most* refers to a single quantity and is thus singular.]

Some of the gold coins were recovered from the wreck.

Some of the gold dust was stolen from the jeweler. [*Some* in the first example is plural since it refers to coins, itself a plural noun; *some* in the second case is singular since it refers to a single amount, sum, or mass.]

E X E R C I S E 11-4

Cross out the incorrect predicate in each of the following sentences.

1. All of the employees (was, were) pleased with the new contract.

2. Such (are, is) my goal in life.

3. Neither (know, knows) the correct answer.

4. Many in the Cuban population (long, longs) for more economic opportunities.

5. (Are, Is) any of the flour spoiled?

6. Either (seem, seems) right to me.

7. I think that everyone (enjoy, enjoys) bright and sunny days.

8. Some of the members of the jury (was, were) in disagreement.

9. Captain Rodriquez says that nothing (go, goes) wrong on her ship.

10. Each (are, is) going on the trip to Canada.

E X E R C I S E 11-5

Write brief sentences using the subjects that are provided. Use the present tense only.

1. Some of the customers _____.

2. Everyone _____.

3. Both_____.

4. None of the reports _____.

5. Either _____.

6. Nothing_____.

7. Nobody_____.

8. All of the crop_____.

9. Everybody _____.

10. Each_____.

· ·

A collective noun names a group.

Examples

army	crew	flock
band	crowd	group
class	enemy	jury
committee	faculty	navy
company	family	team

In general, collective nouns may be singular or plural depending on how they are used. If one unit is intended, use a singular predicate; if the members of the unit are intended, use a plural predicate.

Examples

The jury is chosen.
The jury have taken their seats. [In the first example *jury* is considered as one body; in the second example the members of the *jury* are referred to.]

In general, you should consider a collective noun as singular unless you want to stress the members of the body.

Examples

The committee is meeting in its assigned room.
The committee have left for their individual fact-gathering missions in Burma, India, and Pakistan. [The stress in the first

sentence is on the unity of the body; the stress in the second is on the various members having separate tasks in several nations.]

To avoid sounding awkward, you may want to rewrite a sentence:

Examples

The members of the committee have left for their individual fact-gathering missions in Burma, India, and Pakistan.
The jury members have taken their seats.

EXERCISE 11-6

Write sentences using the following collective nouns.

1. Use *enemy* as singular

_____

2. Use *enemy* as plural

_____

3. Use *faculty* as singular

_____

4. Use *faculty* as plural

_____

5. Use *band* as singular

_____

6. Use *band* as plural

_____

7. Use *flock* as singular

_____

8. Use *flock* as plural

_____

9. Use *rest* as singular

_____

10. Use *rest* as plural

_____

E X E R C I S E 11-7

List other collective nouns you know.

1. _____   2. _____   3. _____

4. _____   5. _____   6. _____

7. _____   8. _____   9. _____

10. _____

. . . .

A subject agrees with its predicate and not with its subject complement.

Examples

My concern is the people.
The best section in the stadium is the bottom rows.

If the subjects and subject complements are reversed, then the predicates must change as well.

Examples

The people are my concern.
The bottom rows are the best section in the stadium.

When you refer to a single item, use there is/was; when you refer to a plural noun or nouns, use there are/were.

There alone is considered an expletive, a word that is without meaning in the sentence. An expletive is like a pointer used by a teacher to draw attention to something on the chalk board.

Examples

There is a snake in the grass!
There are snakes in the grass!
There was a goose on the loose.
There were many geese near the pond.
There are a chair, a desk, and a bed in the room.

After *it* (as an expletive), the predicate is always singular.

Examples

It is you, Erik, whom I want.
It is both of you whom I want.
I suspect that it was Tom who took the money.
I know that it is Sal and Deb who are coming.

You should avoid overusing the expletive. In many cases, by removing the expletive and rewriting the sentence, you can achieve brevity and directness.

Examples

From: There was a goose on the loose.
To: A goose was loose.
From: I suspect that it was Tom who took the money.
To: I suspect that Tom took the money.

E X E R C I S E   1 1 - 8

Five of the following sentences involve the use of subject complements; five sentences use *there* and *it* as expletives. Cross out the incorrect predicate in each of the sentences. In the space below the exercise, rewrite the five sentences with expletives so that those sentences are brief and direct.

1. The movie's best part (are, is) the last three scenes.

2. There (was, were) several cars involved in the accident.

3. It (was, were) the boys who won the cooking contest.

4. The segment that I liked (was titled, were titled) "New Worlds."

5. Men (are, is) a minority in the nursing profession.

6. I think that it (are, is) Mark, Janice, and Lee who have to go.

7. The subject of Alice's talks (was, were) spiders.

8. A large part of most grammar textbooks (are, is) exercises.

9. I believe that it (are, is) Evan and Mark who have to work tonight.

10. There (was, were) many gifts under the Christmas tree.

_____

_____

_____

_____

_____

With a subject that is the name of a book, a play, a short story, a poem, a newspaper, etc., use a singular predicate.

Examples

The *Los Angeles Times* has won several Pulitzer Prizes for excellence in journalism.

Fences was given a Tony Award for the best Broadway play in 1987.

The Satanic Verses continues to stir controversy, especially among readers who follow Islam.

In general, nouns that end in –s but are singular in meaning agree with singular predicates.

Examples of such nouns are:

athletics	mathematics	news
billiards	measles	politics
economics	mumps	physics

Examples

Measles is not a disease contracted only by children.

The news was good.

Politics has been defined as the art of compromise.

Sums of money, figures, measurements that end in –s, and multiples of numbers are usually considered singular and require a singular predicate.

Examples

Five dollars is the cost of admission.

Ten yards is what I want.

Two-thirds of the forest was burned.

Ten and twelve equals twenty-two.

Five times eight is forty.

In these examples, you can see that the writer's intention is singular, and that such words as *politics*, *ten yards*, and *two-thirds* should be considered as whole units. However, some of the words and sums could be given a plural meaning if they refer to two or more individual units.

Examples

Her politics are different from mine in two key ways.

The dollars are in five piles.

Two-thirds of these patients have AIDS.

Certain words ending in -s, such as *pants* and *scissors*, are considered plural and require a plural predicate.

Examples

> The pants are on the table.
> The scissors were lost.

The number is singular; a number is plural.

Examples

> The number of passenger pigeons in the United States was once in the billions; now there is not one such bird alive.
> A small number of these pigeons were housed in zoos and thus were safe from the hunters' guns; however, the last passenger pigeon died on September 1, 1914, in an Ohio zoo.

Exception: A number is listed for Fred Jones on Main Street.

E X E R C I S E   1 1 - 9

Cross out the incorrect predicate in each sentence.

1. There (are, is) the rare coins that you want.

2. Saul's greatest joy (are, is) his wife and children.

3. There (was, were) something wrong with the rocket.

4. Nine-tenths of an iceberg (are, is) under water.

5. John's trousers (was, were) left in the dryer.

6. The number of cars on the road (increase, increases) every year.

7. Six times six (are, is) thirty-six.

8. Mathematics (require, requires) logical thinking.

9. The acoustics in this concert hall (leave, leaves) something to be desired.

10. *Twice Told Tales* (was written, were written) by Nathaniel Hawthorne.

11. I think it (was, were) Guns 'n' Roses that I most enjoyed at the concert.

12. The pliers (are, is) broken.

13. Fifty dollars (are, is) more than I care to pay for this shirt.

14. The statistics (show, shows) that buying a home is becoming increasingly difficult for many Americans.

15. Electronics (are, is) what Kathy will study in college.

16. There (are, is) four deer in the yard.

17. With every passing second, gallons of oil (was spilling, were spilling) from the broken pipe.

18. Chemicals (are, is) an industry that seems to be prospering in the United States.

19. Cuba's politics (are, is) very different from those of the United States.

20. *Roots* (continue, continues) to be enjoyed by thousands of readers each year.

21. There (was, were) only some paper and pencils on the desk.

22. A number of police officers (was, were) wounded by the robber.

23. Twenty-four inches (are, is) two-thirds of a yard.

24. "Bette Davis Eyes" (was, were) the winner of a Grammy for the best song of 1981.

25. The *Chicago Daily News* (has, have) won several Pulitzer Prizes.

. . . .

Finally, a relative pronoun (who, which, and that) that refers to a singular antecedent agrees with a singular predicate; a relative pronoun that refers to a plural antecedent requires a plural predicate.

Note: An antecedent is a word (or group of words) to which a pronoun refers.

Examples

Chang is the only student who swims.
Chang is one of the students who swim. [In the first sentence *who* refers to a single *student*; consequently, *swims* must be used. In the second sentence *swim* must be used because *who* refers to *students*, a plural noun.]

E X E R C I S E 11-10

Cross out the incorrect predicate in each sentence.

1. It is I who (am, is) going.

2. Caroline Gordon's *Collected Stories* (was, were) published in 1981.

3. The driver, as well as his passengers, (seem, seems) drunk.

4. The tweezers (appear, appears) just right for this job.

5. There (are, is) termite problems in the neighborhood.

6. This movie, containing scenes of both violence and sex, (seem, seems) suited for adults only.

7. The conclusion of these reports (are, is) alarming.

8. A family from the Marshall Islands (has, have) moved next door.

9. This is one of the dogs that (bite, bites) strangers.

10. Athletics (has, have) become the single concern of his life.

11. Neither Paul nor his sisters (seem, seems) amused.

12. Gin and tonic (are, is) what Alex usually orders.

13. Some of the stolen cars (was, were) recovered.

14. Every mother and father (has, have) a serious commitment with respect to raising children well.

15. The Stars and Stripes (fly, flies) both day and night at Fort McHenry in Baltimore.

16. Each of these stamps (are, is) old and rare.

17. A number of passengers (was, were) injured when Flight 341 crashed.

18. None of the food (was, were) spoiled because of the hot weather.

19. Tonya or Monique (are, is) traveling with Carlos.

20. Two quarts (are, is) all that this jar holds.

21. Two members of the committee (has, have) disagreed with each other.

22. Billiards (require, requires) great skill and poise.

23. The best student and athlete in the three counties (was, were) Luis Rivero.

24. Neither (want, wants) to be the last in line.

25. Three-fourths of the membership (desire, desires) a change in leadership.

. . . .

E X E R C I S E **11-11**

The following paragraph contains errors in the agreement of subject and predicate. Cross out the incorrect predicates and make corrections.

In India, perhaps the most powerful medium of mass communications are

movies. The number of movies produced each year are in excess of 800, far beyond the nearly 400 movies which is produced yearly in the United States. Thirteen cents buy a seat in one of nearly 13,000 movie theaters. Every city, town, and major village are home to at least one theater. In a country where the per capita income is about $250 a year, few in the population seems unable to find the money to see a favorite star perform. Neither the cost of a seat nor the limited availability of seats keep people away. In fact, there is five showings a day at some theaters. Romantic love, along with physical violence of various kinds, are the main ingredient of many of the films, and this combination stir the interest of large numbers of people.

. . . .

. . . .

Pronoun Case

Case refers to the form (spelling) that a pronoun or noun takes to show its function in a sentence. In English there are three cases: **subjective** (or **nominative**), **objective**, and **possessive**.

The **subjective case** indicates the topic(s) being considered (*History 101* is my most difficult course, and *it* is my most enjoyable one.), or the person(s) or thing(s) performing an action. (*Presidents Bush and Gorbachev* signed a historic trade agreement on June 1, 1990. *They* spoke of signing an arms limitation agreement at a future meeting.)

The **objective case** indicates the person or thing receiving the action. (After the two leaders signed the *agreement*, the audience applauded *them*.) The **objective case** is also used for the object of a preposition. (The people placed their trust in *them*.)

The **possessive case** indicates ownership. The person(s) or thing(s) that owns or possesses something is said to be in the possessive case. (Presidents Bush and Gorbachev called the agreement a victory for *their* nations.)

A noun changes its form only in the possessive case:

Subjective Case	Objective Case	Possessive Case
dog	dog	dog's
Fred	Fred	Fred's
airplane	airplane	airplane's
Mexico	Mexico	Mexico's
boys	boys	boys'

In effect, a noun has only two case-forms: subjective and possessive, for a noun does not change its form when used as a subject or an object.

The pronouns, however, are another story. In particular, the personal pronouns *I*, *we*, *he*, *she*, and *they* change their form in all three cases. For example, while you can write "Russell loves Anne" and "Anne loves Russell," you should not write "He loves she" or "Her loves him." You must write "He loves her" and "She loves him." Although the nouns do not change their form when they are used as subjects or objects, some pronouns do have different forms for subjective and objective case.

THE PERSONAL PRONOUNS

The personal pronouns in the three cases are the following:

	Subjective Case	Objective Case	Possessive Case
1st person singular	I	me	my, mine
2nd person singular	you	you	your, yours
3rd person singular	he	him	his
	she	her	her, hers
	it	it	its
1st person plural	we	us	our, ours
2nd person plural	you	you	your, yours
3rd person plural	they	them	their, theirs

As you can see, only the pronous *it* and *you* stay the same in the subjective and objective case. When are these pronouns used?

Subjective Case

Use the subjective case for the subject of a sentence.

Examples
I enjoyed the movie.
She may stay here.
They played well.

In these examples *I, She,* and *They* are all subjective case forms of the personal pronoun; each pronoun is the subject of its sentence.

Use the subjective case after the linking verb be (am, is, are, was, were, being, been).

The linking verb is like an equal sign (=). The verb links the subject to its complement, a word (or words) that defines, identifies, or describes the subject of the sentence. The linking verb shows that the subject and its complement are the same; as a result, the complement is in the subjective case.

Examples
The winner is she.
The new employees are they.
The last head of the company was he.

In these sentences the personal pronouns *she, they,* and *he* follow the linking verbs *is, are,* and *was,* respectively. Though the three sample sentences are technically correct, they express their meanings in rather stiff and formal ways. The following revisions sound more natural and direct:
She is the winner.
They are the new employees.
He was the last head of the company.

In informal writing, most people prefer *It's me* or *It's her*, for example, instead of the stiff-sounding *It is I* or *It is she*. In certain sentences, however, using the subjective case seems more natural and can serve to emphasize the pronoun:

>It was *I* who found the money.
>
>Dennis and Alex are certain it was *she* who killed their father.

Use the subjective case when the pronoun is an appositive identifying the subject.

Note: An appositive is a noun or noun phrase placed close to another noun or noun phrase to further identify it.

Example

>Three women—Alice, you, and I—will make the decision.
>[In effect, *Alice, you*, and *I* share as the subject of the sentence with *women*.]

In general, use the subjective case when the predicate is implied rather than expressly stated after the conjunctions than and as.

Examples

>Pedro is taller than he [is].
>Lois is as strong as she [is].

In some sentences, however, depending on your intended meaning, you will use either the objective or the subjective case:

Examples

>My mother loves my sister more than [she loves] me.
>My mother loves my sister more than I [do *or* love her].

As you can see, two quite different meanings result from the use of the objective case (*me*) in the first sentence and of the subjective case (*I*) in the second one.

Objective Case

Use the objective case for the direct or indirect object of a verb.

Examples

>Rosa joined us at the picnic.
>Coretta gave me the ball.

Us in the first sentence is the direct object; *me* in the second one is the indirect object; both pronouns are thus in the objective case.

Use the objective case for the object of a preposition.

Examples

This fight is between him and me.

The two of us wrote the report.

The objective case of the personal pronouns (*him*, *me*, and *us*) is used because the pronouns are objects of prepositions (*between* and *of*).

Use the objective case when the pronoun is an appositive identifying an object.

Example

Phyllis prevented two people—Paul and me—from being injured.

[Since *Paul* and *me* are in apposition to the direct object of this sentence (*people*), the objective case is used.]

Use the objective case when the pronoun is the object of a verbal or the subject of an infinitive.

Examples

Telling him was not easy. [*Him* is the object of the gerund *telling.*]

Dawn wanted to help Jon and me. [*Jon* and *me* are the objects of the infinitive *to help.*]

Having fired him, the manager then gave him a final paycheck. [The first *him* is the object of the participle *having fired*, and the second *him* is the indirect object of *gave.*]

Robert wanted me to join her. [*Me* is the subject of the infinitive *to join*, and *her* is the object of the infinitive. The subject of the infinitive, as well as the object of the infinitive, is in the objective case.]

Possessive Case

Use the possessive case before a noun.

Examples

My cards are on the table.

I do not have your keys.

Lynette enjoyed their performance.

My, *your*, and *their* are all possessive pronouns modifying nouns.

Use the possessive case before the gerund.

Examples

His moving to Florida surprised us.
The teacher disliked my leaving the class early. [In the first sentence *His* is the possessive before the gerund *moving*; in the second sentence *my* is the possessive before the gerund *leaving*.]

Mine, yours, his, hers, ours, *and* theirs *are possessive pronouns that may take the place of a noun in a subject or object position in a sentence.*

Examples

I have mine. Do you have yours?
The victory was ours, and the defeat was theirs.

EXERCISE 12-1

Underline the pronouns in the following sentences. Indicate the case of each pronoun as *SUB* (subjective), *OBJ* (objective), or *POS* (possessive).

1. I gave her the money.

2. We will join you at his meeting.

3. He and I were the supervisors of the project.

4. Her dispute was with us.

5. Three students—Paul, Lee, and I—will accompany you.

6. They comforted me during my illness.

7. We students liked the lecture.

8. Paula asked me to help her.

9. His dating her surprised us.

10. The win is for you and me to enjoy.

11. The general awarded both Drew and me Silver Stars.

12. Mine was located below theirs.

13. He told her to leave John.

14. Did you receive my check?

15. Loving her was easy for me.

. . . .

E X E R C I S E 12 - 2

In the following sentences change the italicized words to pronouns.

1. Howard gave the *baseball* to Todd.

   _____

2. The *players* celebrated the victory.

   _____

3. Alisa bought the *books*.

   _____

4. The girls enjoyed the *picnic*.

   _____

5. The *boys* helped Julie and Cynthia.

   _____

6. *Samantha* won the prize.

   _____

7. Mrs. Holton told the *students* to buy the textbook.

   _____

8. *Mary's* telling the truth was important to her *sisters*.

   _____

9. *Mike* watched Mary flying the kite.

   _____

10. *Tom's* not going to the party surprised Melanie.

   _____

11. Betty, Steve, and Ed liked the Mexican *food*.

_____

12. Cheryl came between *Jeffrey* and *Sue*.

_____

13. Kirk and Ken are taller than *Sue*.

_____

14. Sherry loves her sister better than her *brothers*.

_____

15. John asked *Mary* to give the *money* to Tim and Joyce.

_____

· ·

E X E R C I S E   1 2 - 3

Cross out the incorrect pronoun in the parentheses. Above each correct pronoun write *SUB* for subjective case, *OBJ* for objective case, and *POS* for possessive case.

1. (She, Her) and (I, Me) did very well on the test.

2. (They, Them) expected (she, her) to win the race.

3. (She, Her) knowing the answer did not surprise (we, us).

4. (We, Us) wanted (they, them) to come.

5. The baton was passed from Tim to (I, me).

6. Three of us—Chuck, Chou Lee, and (I, me)—arrived late.

7. Neither (he, him) nor (I, me) read James's novels.

8. After capturing (he, him), (we, us) questioned (he, him).

9. Rose likes (he, him) more than she likes (I, me).

10. Mary, Tim, and (I, me) stood before (he, him).

11. Lawrence spotted Kate before (I, me) saw her.

12. Senator Horn gave Rhonda, Laurie, and (I, me) an invitation.

13. It was (she, her) who made (we, us) lose the game.

14. (We, Us) three girls—Edna, Pauline, and (I, me)—got the Joneses out of the smoke-filled apartment.

15. A group of (we, us) bystanders decided to aid (she, her) and (he, him).

· ·

RELATIVE AND INTERROGATIVE PRONOUNS

A relative pronoun (*who, whom, that, what, which*) is one that introduces a relative or adjectival clause. An interrogative pronoun (*who, whom, whose, which, what*) asks a question. The relative and interrogative pronouns have the following case forms:

Subjective Case	Objective Case	Possessive Case
who	whom	whose
whoever	whomever	whosever
what, which, that, etc.	what, which, that, etc.	————

The major concern is with the use of *who* and *whom*, for they change their form to show the different cases. Use the subjective or objective form according to how the word functions in the sentence; the possessive form presents less difficulty.

Subjective and Objective Case

Use *who* and *whoever* to function as subjects. (An exception is the use of *whom* as the subject of an infinitive.) Use *whom* and *whomever* in objective positions.

Examples

Who is the winner of the writing contest? [*Who* functions as the subject of the sentence. An easy way to tell whether to use *who* or *whom* is to answer the question above: He is the winner. Since *he* is in the subjective case, *who* must be used in the question.]

Whom did she know at the party? [*Whom* is the object of this sentence. Why? Answer the question: She knew them. Since *them* is in the objective case, *whom* must be used in the question. You could also reverse the wording of the sentence: She did know whom at the party? *Whom* is then seen as the object of *did know*.]

Who came remains uncertain. [In this example, *who came* is a subordinate noun clause that is the subject of *remains*, the predicate. *Who* is the subject of the noun clause. **Note:** You may want to review noun clauses in chapter 8.]

Whom Luis wanted was uncertain. [*Whom Luis wanted* is a subordinate noun clause that is the subject of *was*. In the noun clause *whom* is the direct object of *wanted*. By changing the word order, you get this clause: Luis wanted whom. *Whom*, then, is clearly the object.]

Send the brochures to whoever is on the list. [*Whoever is on the list* is a subordinate noun clause that is the object of the preposition *to*. *Whoever* is the subject of the noun clause.]

Mario knew whom he wanted. [*Whom he wanted* is a subordinate noun clause that is the direct object of *knew*. *Whom* is the direct object of *wanted* in the noun clause. This fact is clear through reverse order: He wanted whom.]

Possessive Case

The possessive case, *whose*, presents little difficulty.

Examples

Whose books are these? I know whose books these are.
[In both examples *whose* modifies *books*.]

E X E R C I S E 12-4

Cross out the incorrect form of the pronoun *who* or *whom* in the parentheses:

1. (Who, Whom) are you traveling with?

2. Anne is a woman (who, whom) knows what happiness is.

3. (Whoever, Whomever) David chooses will have a difficult time.

4. Mr. Rodriquez gives money to (whoever, whomever) asks for it.

5. Nickie told me (who, whom) is needed.

6. The woman (who, whom) Phil is talking with is my sister.

7. I am pleased to know (who, whom) you are.

8. (Who, Whom) did she say Janet had called?

9. I do not know (who, whom) is coming to the party.

10. Russell addressed an audience of over seventy-five people, most of (who, whom) he had never seen before.

11. It was I, George, (who, whom) slew the dragon.

12. She is the student (who, whom) won the scholarship.

13. Al knew that (whoever, whomever) he chose could not help Eric.

14. (Who, Whom) is the better teacher of the two?

15. Point out five people (who, whom) are blameless.

· ·

INDEFINITE AND RECIPROCAL PRONOUNS

The indefinite pronouns (*another, anybody, anyone, everybody, everyone,* etc.) and the reciprocal pronouns (*each other, one another*) use the apostrophe and *s* (*'s*) to form the possessive case.

Examples

another's	one's
anyone's	each other's
no one's	something's

EXERCISE 12-5

The following paragraph contains errors in the use of pronoun and noun case. Cross out the errors and make corrections above them. Be able to explain why your revisions are correct.

Art and me approached the huge, circular spaceship with caution. The

ground glowed red on the otherwise pitch-black night at Mr. Johnsons farm.

Suddenly, a door opened; out came three green men no more than four feet tall. Us teenagers shook with fear. One of the men, who I took to be the leader, walked to we fearful boys. Myself and Art did not dare move. The green man held up its arm in a sign of peace and began speaking, but he spoke in Spanish. Between Art and I we could understand little of what he said. He spoke of him leaving Havana and wanting to teach Spanish to whoever he met in America. He wanted us to know Spanish as well as him. In my poor Spanish I said: "Who needs it?" He got very angry and began yelling at Art and I. Then I knew for certain it was him. *Profesor* Castro, my Spanish teacher! At that moment, I awoke from my nightmare and began studying hard for the test.

• •

. . . .

Agreement of Pronoun and Antecedent

In this chapter you will learn about the agreement of a pronoun and its antecedent. A pronoun must agree with its antecedent in person, number, and gender. (You may want to review the detailed discussion of person, number, and gender in chapter 2.) Having a pronoun agree in person, number, and gender with its antecedent helps to keep a sentence smooth-flowing and logical.

First, what is an antecedent? It is the word (or group of words) that the pronoun refers back to.

Examples

The students said that they enjoyed the class. [The pronoun *they* refers back to *students*. In other words, *students* is the antecedent of *they*. Both the pronoun and its antecedent are in the third person and are plural in number. The gender is unspecified.]

Rita took her cat on the trip to Ocean City. [The possessive pronoun *her* refers back to the antecedent *Rita*. Both the pronoun and its antecedent are in the third person and are singular in number. Both have the same gender.]

E X E R C I S E **13-1**

In each of the following sentences, underline the pronoun(s) and antecedent(s). Write *P* above each pronoun and *A* above each antecedent.

1. Though Native Americans probably numbered about five million in 1492, they numbered about 250,000 in 1900.

2. On Halloween in 1938, when Orson Welles told radio listeners of Martians landing in New Jersey and battling United States troops, he caused a national panic.

3. In the early 1960s Andy Warhol's art was denounced by numerous art critics; now it is held in high regard and can be found in major museums.

4. Born into slavery, Sojourner Truth became a tireless campaigner in the abolition and women's rights movements; at the White House in 1864 President Lincoln personally thanked her for her efforts in support of liberty and equality.

5. For Hindus the Ganges River is sacred because it has the spiritual power to cleanse them of sins.

6. Perhaps the worst printing error in publishing history is found in the so-called Wicked Bible; printed in 1631, this Bible tells its readers that they "shalt commit adultery."

7. The United States and the Soviet Union, fearful of each other, began a Cold War in the 1950s; prior to the breakup of the Soviet Union in 1991, however, both had entered an era of cooperation.

8. When New York City police raided a gay bar, the Stonewall Inn, on June 28, 1969, they encountered resistance from the patrons.

9. Instead of quietly accepting eviction, the patrons refused to move, and many fought a hand-to-hand battle with the police.

10. As a result, militant gay protests followed, and out of them emerged the gay rights movement.

. . . .

There are five rules for ensuring pronoun/antecedent agreement:

When two or more antecedents are joined by the coordinating conjunction **and,** *the plural pronoun is generally used.*

Examples

John and Tom enjoyed their flight to London.
Heather and I lost our money at the casino.

[In the first example *their* refers back to *John* and *Tom*; the third person plural pronoun is needed. *Our* refers back to *Heather* and *I* in the second example; here a first person plural pronoun is needed.]

Note: When the compound antecedent is preceded by *every* or *each*, use a singular pronoun.

Example

Every man and boy took his place on the stage.

When antecedents are joined by or, either...or, or neither...nor, the pronoun agrees with the nearer antecedent.

Examples

Neither Tina nor her parents sent their best wishes. [The pronoun *their* refers back to *parents*, the nearer antecedent joined by *neither...nor.*]

Either my Siamese cats or Rex, my German shepherd, will have to make his home on the back porch. [*His* refers back to *Rex*, the nearer antecedent joined by *either...or.*]

While both of the previous examples are technically correct, you may want to revise the sentences to avoid sounding awkward.

Examples

Neither Tina nor her parents sent best wishes.

Either my Siamese cats or Rex, my German shepherd, will have to sleep on the back porch.

Occasionally, observing the rule above results in a sentence which does not seem to make good sense:

Monika or Earl will sell his car.

Rewrite such a sentence to make your thoughts flow smoothly:

Earl will sell his car, or Monika will sell hers.

Use a singular pronoun to refer back to the indefinite singular pronouns **each, either, neither, one, no one, someone, somebody, anyone, somebody, everyone, everybody, nobody,** *etc.*

Examples

One of the men lost his arm in the accident. [*His* refers back to *one*; from the text of the sentence you know that the masculine gender is intended.]

Neither of the women paid her taxes on time. [*Her* refers back to *neither*, and from context you know that the feminine gender is intended.]

Each of the movies won its place in cinema history. [*Its* refers back to *each*; the gender is neuter.]

Caution: An awkward-sounding sentence results when you use a singular pronoun to refer back to an indefinite pronoun that is singular in form but plural in intention.

Example

Everybody brought his food with him. [Rewrite such a sentence by using plural pronouns: They brought their food with them.]

There is another problem with having *his* and *him* refer back to *everybody*. You would assume that some of the people were male and that some were female. To refer to *everybody* as *he*, or to refer to such indefinite words as *person*, *officer*, *child*, and *student* as automatically being masculine in gender is termed *gender bias*. You should avoid such bias in your writing.

Change: A person needs to keep his attention on the road when he is driving.

To: People need to keep their attention on the road when they are driving.

Change: Unless threatened with deadly force, a police officer should not fire his gun at a suspected criminal.

To: Unless threatened with deadly force, police officers should not fire their guns at suspected criminals.

Since collective nouns (nouns that name a group of persons, places, and things) may be either singular or plural according to their intended meaning in the sentence, use the appropriate singular or plural pronoun to refer back to them.

Examples of collective nouns are the following: *army*, *band*, *class*, *committee*, *company*, *flock*, *jury*, *navy*, and *team*. When you refer to such a word as a unit acting as one, use the singular pronoun. When you refer to the members of the group as acting individually, use the plural pronoun.

Examples

The team went to its assigned locker room. [*Its* is appropriate here because the team is considered as one unit, one body.]

The team argued among themselves and later resolved their differences. [*Team* in this sentence refers to members acting individually. The members argued with one another. *Their* is thus the appropriate pronoun to use.]

The family took its traditional summer vacation during the last two weeks of July. [*Its* refers to the *family* as one unit.]

The family fastened their safety belts as the plane taxied down the runway. [*Their* is appropriate because the members of the *family* are acting as individuals.]

In general, nouns that are plural in form (end in -s) but are singular in meaning agree with a singular pronoun.

Example

Politics is a fascinating subject to study, and it has gained many new students in recent years. [*It* is appropriate because *politics* is considered as a single *subject to study.*]

Jefferson's politics found their best expression in the Declaration of Independence. [Here *politics* refers to political opinions and principles; thus, the plural pronoun *their* is used.]

E X E R C I S E 13-2

Cross out the incorrect pronoun in each of the following sentences.

1. Robin and I lost (my, our) way in the dense forest.
2. Daniel or Victor should have brought (his, their) keys.
3. Loyal employees are those who are dedicated to (his, their) work.
4. The radio is broken, but (it, they) can be repaired.
5. The Kennedy family was united behind the campaigns of (its, their) sons John and Robert for president of the United States.
6. Did Anne or Christina lose (her, their) self-confidence in the debate?
7. Every cat at the show had (its, their) registration papers.
8. My wife Carol and my best friend Woody never fail to give me (his, their) best advice.
9. Each woman and girl took (her, their) turn at speaking.
10. Economics may be a boring subject for some students, but (it, they) can stimulate (his, their) thinking abilities.
11. Everyone on the girls' basketball team had (her, their) own style of play.
12. If one of the boys arrives, send (him, them) to the auditorium.
13. Neither of the automobiles had (its, their) brakes in working order.
14. The members of the jury took (its, their) seats.

15. George Bell's statistics were at (its, their) best during his 1987 season with the Toronto Blue Jays.

16. Neither the teacher nor the students knew that (his, their) classes had been canceled.

17. Every defective machine in the factory had (its, their) motor replaced.

18. All of the trees had (its, their) limbs trimmed.

19. Neither the crew nor the passengers abandoned (its, their) ship.

20. Either of the two drugs will have (its, their) effect felt in less than five minutes.

· ·

E X E R C I S E   1 3 - 3

Rewrite the following sentences to remove awkwardness of pronoun reference or gender bias.

1. Every student was given his assignment as he entered the class.

   _____

2. Either Ken or Janice will take her leave of absence after the baby is born.

   _____

3. Everyone should be concerned about his government's relations with foreign nations.

   _____

4. The average married person is concerned about the welfare of his spouse.

   _____

5. We wanted to find the best man to manage the company's Baltimore branch, and we hoped that he could assume his duties in August.

   _____

· ·

E X E R C I S E   13 - 4

The following paragraph has subject-predicate and pronoun-antecedent agreement problems. Cross out the problems and make revisions above them. You may have to change some pronouns into nouns, or some nouns into pronouns.

Everyone has his opinion about bird watchers. If they are a man, he has beady eyes and thin legs. If they are a woman, they have gray hair and a matronly appearance. Neither of them find his name listed in the Best-Personality-of-the-Month Club. I had these opinions when Mr. and Mrs. Rock moved next door in late August. Their nicknames for one another sounded the same; however, each nickname had their own distinct spelling. Hers was *Rockie*, and his was *Rocky*. Under the deck in the back yard the Rocks set up all kinds of weightlifting equipment. They told me that they worked in a gym but that they would not start working until September. Each day, either Rocky or Rockie could be seen straining her muscles on the equipment. After exercising together, they would practice posing. The team made their movements as one body. I was certain that each of them were getting ready for the Mr. and Mrs. America Contest, which was being sponsored by the National Bodybuilding and Weightlifting Association (NBWA). Being friendly people, he invited me to the next NBWA contest. Each of them told me that his statistics was the best in the country and that victory was certain to be his at the contest being held on September 1. Imagine my surprise when I found myself with the Newark Bird Watchers Association on that fateful Saturday in September. Neither of the Rocks lost his chance to get into the record books once again. The pair spotted more birds than any other members or me spotted. I had fun on that trip, and later in the month I enjoyed seeing the Rocks win the other NBWA contest. I now have a different opinion of bird watchers—and a better understanding of the meanings of NBWA.

. . . .

. . . .

Vague, General, and Unclear Pronoun Reference

To maintain a smooth flow of thought, you want to be sure that a pronoun agrees with its antecedent in person, number, and gender. You also want a pronoun to clearly and exactly refer to its stated antecedent. **Consequently, you want to avoid vague, general, and unclear pronoun references.** The following guidelines should help you to do so.

VAGUE AND GENERAL PRONOUN REFERENCE

This, *that*, *these*, *those*, *which*, *they*, *it* and *you* are the pronouns most often found in vague and general reference problems. You can correct these reference problems by adding a specific antecedent or by removing the pronoun and using a noun in its place. Study the following examples:

1. The fish are plentiful in this lake, and they also say that the woods are full of deer. [Exactly, who are *they*? You cannot tell because there is no stated antecedent for the pronoun. Certainly, the fish are not talking.] You could correct this sentence in a couple of ways; in each case, you tell who *they* are:

    The game wardens say that the fish are plentiful in this lake and that the woods are full of deer.

    or According to the game wardens, the fish are plentiful in this lake, and the woods are full of deer.

2. Frederick helped me to plan the party, which was a surprise. [Exactly what does the relative pronoun *which* refer to? You do not know because *which* has no stated antecedent, save for the vague idea of "helping." Then again, perhaps the *party* was the *surprise*.] You can correct this problem by rewriting the sentence:

    Frederick's helping me to plan the party was a surprise.

    or Frederick helped me to plan the surprise party.

    Note: Many readers do not object to the use of *this*, *that*, and *which* in what may *seem* a general sense as long as the meaning is clear:

The dogs barked constantly, and this upset the neighbors. [In this example *this* refers to the whole concept of the dogs' constant barking (rather than to a specific noun); however, the meaning is clear.]

3. California is the state with the most windmills to generate electricity; however, it has several disadvantages. [What, precisely, does *it* refer to? The reference is a vague one. Most probably, *it* means *using wind power*.] In this sentence you can remove the vagueness by stating the antecedent:

California is the state with the most windmills to generate electricity; however, using wind power has several disadvantages.

Note: The use of *it says* to introduce a sentence such as the following one should be avoided:

It says in *Time* magazine that the residents of Leningrad have restored their city's former name, St. Petersburg.

A more precise sentence might read:

An article in *Time* magazine reports that the residents of Leningrad have restored their city's former name, St. Petersburg.

Note, as well, that the use of the indefinite *it* is fully acceptable in some standard constructions or expressions (especially concerning time, weather, or distance):

I cannot find it in my heart to believe him.

It is 2 A.M.

It rained this morning.

4. Before President Franklin Roosevelt began his economic reform programs, you saw little cause for optimism. [The use of *you* and *they* in an indefinite or general sense is not unusual in informal writing or speech; however, such use should be avoided in more formal writing. (The use of *you* is, of course, appropriate when you have a definite audience in mind. *You* is also appropriate for giving directions or instructions.) In example #4, however, *you* is used in a vague or general sense.] You can correct the error by identifying the *you*:

Before President Franklin Roosevelt began his economic reform programs, jobless people saw little cause for optimism.

or Before President Franklin Roosevelt began his economic reform programs, the poor saw little cause for optimism.

UNCLEAR PRONOUN REFERENCE

Again, remember that your readers must be able to understand clearly what a pronoun refers to. In vague and general reference, you force your readers to create an antecedent; the problem is that they may come up with the wrong one. In unclear pronoun reference, you force your readers to make a choice between two or more possible antecedents. As with vague and general reference problems, unclear pronoun reference problems will usually require you to rewrite the sentence to correct the faulty pronoun reference. Consider these examples of unclear reference:

1. Don Quixote tells his companion that he has an adventuresome spirit. [Exactly who has the *adventuresome spirit*, *Don Quixote* or the *companion*?] Often, the best way to correct such a problem is to use a direct quotation:

   Don Quixote tells his companion, "You have an adventuresome spirit."

   or "I have an adventuresome spirit," Don Quixote tells his companion.

2. After the first meeting between Frost and Sandburg, he wrote some unfriendly words about him. [Did Frost write the words? Did Sandburg? You do not know because the reference is unclear. In fact, Sandburg wrote that Frost was a great poet; Frost, on the other hand, had some very unkind words for Sandburg.] The sentence needs to be rewritten so that the reference is unmistakably apparent:

   Frost wrote some unfriendly words about Sandburg after their first meeting.

3. After Tim and Ray got home, we told him the sad news. [Who got the news, Tim or Ray? The reference is unclear.] All you need to do in this instance is to repeat the correct noun:

   After Tim and Ray got home, we told Tim the sad news.

The basic point is this: pronouns merely stand for some person, place, thing, or idea. Pronouns do not themselves name the person, place, thing, or idea. Consequently, you must make certain in your writing that the antecedent of a pronoun is identified clearly.

E X E R C I S E 14-1

Some of the following sentences contain vague, general, or unclear pronoun reference; others do not. If the sentence is correct, write *C* in the blank. Write *X* if the sentence is incorrect, and then rewrite the sentence so that the pronoun reference problem is removed.

_____1. It is approximately 3,000 miles from New York to California.

_____2. Mr. Harper said that he was proud to be a teacher and that he always did it in an informal and humorous way.

_____3. A great long-distance runner must have strong legs and lungs, and this is why Johnson never won.

_____4. Our ambassador reviewed the South African situation with Mr. Mandela; he said he knew that racial harmony could be achieved.

_____5. Marco enjoys both the arts and the sciences; however, he gets better grades in the one rather than in the other.

_____6. In the game shows on television, they jump up and down and scream whenever they win a prize.

_____7. I told my teachers that I was going to join the United States Air Force, which my parents disliked.

_____8. They say that the states with the largest gains in popula-
tion are California, Florida, and Texas.

_____

_____

_____9. Iran is no stranger to earthquakes, and they say that it will
happen again.

_____

_____

_____10. In the United States you find many different ways to
fund public education.

_____

_____

_____11. It is fascinating to observe the dolphins at play.

_____

_____

_____12. Alex yelled to Francisco as he left the ship.

_____

_____

_____13. It says in the book that the most populous state in
America is California.

_____

_____

_____14. During the vacation, I spent over 200 dollars for sou-
venirs, which greatly upset my mother.

_____

_____

_____15. Peg enjoys reading novels and poetry. This will be her
major in college.

_____

_____

· ·

E X E R C I S E   1 4 - 2

The following paragraph contains errors in pronoun reference. Rewrite the paragraph on your own paper so that all such errors are removed.

(1) It says in these books that giant pandas are most unusual animals. (2) They have studied it, but they have not determined if they are relatives of the raccoon, the bear, or some other animal. (3) In fact, giant pandas can make sounds resembling that of a bear, a lamb, and a dog. (4) Unlike those, however, it has a "thumb" on each of their front feet. (5) Outside of zoos, giant pandas are found only in a few bamboo forests in mountain ranges in China and Tibet, which are difficult to explore. (6) Except during the mating season, giant pandas are gentle, solitary animals that spend most of its time searching for and eating bamboo leaves and small animals. (7) However, they much prefer eating the one rather than the other, even though it is very low in nutritional value. (8) Each day, they must eat twenty-five or more pounds of it just to survive. (9) During the spring mating season, one male will ferociously battle another one for the right to mate; the two shove and claw one another until they run away. (10) A female giant panda can conceive only during a two- to three-day period each year, and this means that, if successful mating does not occur, she is unable to reproduce for another year. (11) After a gestation period of three to five months (they do not know the precise length), they usually give birth to one or two cubs. (12) If two are born, she may neglect one and give the other special care. (13) The result is that one of the cubs is likely to die. (14) Because they take a year and a half to raise their young, it means that female giant pandas will probably raise only five or six cubs in their lifetime.

. . . .

. . . .

Misplaced and Dangling Modifiers

Modifiers limit or make more exact the meaning of a word or words in a sentence. As you learned in chapter 4, **adjectives** modify a noun or pronoun; **adverbs** modify a verb, an adjective, or another adverb.

In this chapter, you will learn to avoid two key problems: **misplaced modifiers** and **dangling modifiers.** Effective modification shows how ideas are related, and it provides your readers with a fuller and more exact understanding of the point you want to make in a sentence. Faulty modification, on the other hand, makes relationships unclear.

MISPLACED MODIFIERS

In general, a modifier should be placed as close as possible to the word or word group modified. You need to be certain how words function and where they belong in a sentence to get your meaning across to the reader. In each of the following sentences a modifier has not been placed correctly. The sentences do not say what the writer intended, and the result is confusion and unwanted humor.

1. Landing on a nearby tree, John watched the eagle. [The verbal phrase, *landing on a nearby tree*, should be *placed* after the noun *eagle* so that the thought flows smoothly and clearly.]

    The sentence should read:

    John watched the eagle landing on a nearby tree.

2. The human heart pumps blood through miles of blood vessels in the body, which is a powerful muscle. [In this sentence the adjectival subordinate clause, *which is a powerful muscle*, has been misplaced. It needs to be placed next to *human heart*.]

    The sentence should read:

    The human heart, which is a powerful muscle, pumps blood through miles of blood vessels in the body.

3. Paul almost revealed all of the secrets.

    Paul revealed almost all of the secrets. [Note that these sentences are not the same in meaning. The first sentence says that Paul did not reveal the secrets, but the second one says that Paul revealed most of them. Modifiers such as *almost, even, hardly, just, only, nearly, often,* and *simply* require care in placement. Be certain that you place them before the word they actually modify.]

    Notice how the placement of *just* in the following sentences changes the meanings:

    Carl just shot a rabbit.

    Just Carl shot a rabbit.

    Carl shot just a rabbit.

4. Because I worked so hard last month my boss gave me a raise. [What exactly does the writer intend? The problem is that *last month* could apply to either the subordinate clause or to the independent clause. Did the hard work occur last month? Was the raise given last month? You do not know. *Last month* looks both backward and forward because of where it is placed. It is a **squinting modifier.**]

    One easy way to correct the problem in this sentence is to provide a comma after the introductory subordinate clause:

    Because I worked so hard last month, my boss gave me a raise.

    or Because I worked so hard, last month my boss gave me a raise.

    Another way to make the meaning clear would be to move *last month*:

    Because last month I worked so hard, my boss gave me a raise.

    or Because I worked so hard, my boss gave me a raise last month. [In any case, unless an introductory adverbial clause is very short and no misunderstanding would result from the omission of a comma, place a comma after it.]

E X E R C I S E 15-1

In the following sentences, if the modifiers are correctly placed, write *C* in the blank. If you find that a modifier or modifiers have been misplaced, write *M* and rewrite the sentence. Every modifier should refer clearly to the word (or words) it modifies.

_____ 1. The Smithsonian Institution is in Washington, D.C., which has a collection of over one hundred million items.

_____

_____   2. Tom said in June we will visit our relatives in Jamaica.

_____   3. Armed with camcorders, the fans eagerly awaited the arrival of Guns 'n' Roses.

_____   4. A survivor of the Holocaust in 1986 Elie Wiesel won the Nobel Peace Prize.

_____   5. Our instructor told us that the tiger will soon become extinct in class.

_____   6. Fighting to escape capture, she watched as the trout leaped high into the air.

_____   7. Christopher Columbus told his father when just six years old that sailing was the good life.

_____   8. The second largest organ in the body, fat is digested by bile from the liver.

_____   9. The old clothes filled the trunk of my new Cadillac, which I had saved for the Salvation Army.

_____

_____

_____   10.   I spotted a flight of ducks concealed in my duck blind on the Wye River.

_____

_____

_____   11.   Wanting to preserve a distinctly French culture, the people of France are concerned about the increasing influence of America on their way of life.

_____

_____

_____   12.   Albert Einstein visited the United States in 1921 greeted by thousands of New Yorkers.

_____

_____

· ·

EXERCISE 15-2

For each listed modifier, write two brief sentences whose only difference in word choice and order is the placement of the modifer. Next to your sentences, briefly explain what effect the placement of the modifier has on the meaning of the sentence.

Example

Tony enjoyed _only_ Italian food.

Explanation: He enjoyed no other food.

Only Tony enjoyed Italian food.

Explanation: Tony was the one person who liked the food.

1. even

_____

_____

2. hardly

_____

_____

3. nearly

_____

_____

4. often

_____

_____

5. simply

_____

_____

. . . .

DANGLING MODIFIERS

A dangling modifier is one that has nothing to modify in the sentence. This problem develops when you fail to edit your sentences so that they clearly and sensibly say exactly what you want them to say. What is obvious to you may not be so obvious to your reader.

Example

> Flying over New York City on a bright, sunny day, the buildings, cars, and people looked like a Christmas garden. [Were the *buildings, cars, and people* flying? Probably not. *Who* was flying needs to be indicated.]

One way to do so is to change the introductory participial phrase into a subordinate clause:

> As I was flying over New York City on a bright, sunny day, the buildings, cars, and people looked like a Christmas garden.

Since this revision is still somewhat awkward, a better revision adds something that the phrase can modify:

> Flying over New York City on a bright, sunny day, I noticed that the buildings, cars, and people looked like a Christmas garden.

An equally good revision places the doer in the subordinate as well as the independent clause:

As I was flying over New York City on a bright, sunny day, I noticed that the buildings, cars, and people looked like a Christmas garden.

The problem of the dangling modifier arises when the word or word group modified is implied rather than expressed. Though a dangling modifier can appear in various locations in a sentence (including the end), the problem is most often found at the start of a sentence and involves dangling phrases and clauses:

Dangling Participial Phrases

Example

Failing to pop out correctly, the Coca-Cola Company abandoned its "MagiCan" campaign. [The introductory participial phrase, *failing to pop out correctly*, has nothing to modify.]

This sentence needs to be rewritten so that the meaning is clear to the reader; a subject (doer) needs to be added:

When the cash in some cans failed to pop out correctly, the Coca-Cola Company abandoned its "MagiCan" campaign.

Dangling Gerund and Prepositional Phrases

Example

After spilling 19,500 gallons of a weed killer into the Sacramento River in July 1991, an ecological disaster followed. [The gerund phrase, *spilling 19,500 gallons of a weed killer into the Sacramento River*, is the object of the preposition *after*. The whole phrase has nothing to modify because of the omission of a key fact.]

One way to correct the problem is to make the phrase into a subordinate clause by adding the omitted fact:

After a derailed Southern Pacific tank car spilled 19,500 gallons of a weed killer into the Sacramento River in July 1991, an ecological disaster followed.

Of course, the phrase could be followed by a noun that it can modify:

After spilling 19,500 gallons of a weed killer into the Sacramento River in July 1991, a derailed Southern Pacific tank car caused an ecological disaster.

Dangling Infinitive Phrase

Example

To learn the numbers of the foreign bank accounts of the Rumanian dictator, his execution was delayed. [The infinitive phrase, *to learn the numbers of his foreign bank accounts*, cannot logically modify *execution*.]

The sentence can be corrected with the addition of a noun to be modified:

> To learn the numbers of the foreign bank accounts of the Rumanian dictator, several soldiers delayed his execution.

Dangling Subordinate Clauses

When a subject and a predicate are omitted from a subordinate clause, an elliptical clause results. If the implied subject of the elliptical clause is the same as the subject stated in the independent clause, there is no problem:

Example

> When tortured, the Rumanian dictator still refused to talk. [This sentence has a clear meaning because the introductory elliptical clause is understood to refer to *dictator*, the subject of the independent clause.]

Sometimes, however, the meaning is not clearly stated. If the omitted subject of the elliptical clause is not the same as the subject that immediately follows in the independent clause, confusion results. A dangling elliptical clause is created.

Example

> While watching *The Simpsons* on television, lightning struck our house. [Obviously, the lightning was not enjoying Bart's performance in the TV cartoon known as *The Simpsons*.]

One way to correct the problem is to add a subject to the elliptical clause:

> While Joan and I were watching *The Simpsons* on television, lightning struck our house.

E X E R C I S E 15 - 3

In the following sentences, if you find no modification problem, write *C* in the blank. If you find that a sentence has a dangling modification problem, write *D* in the blank and rewrite the sentence to achieve a smooth flow of thought.

_____ 1. While addressing the students, the subject of abortion was introduced.

_____

_____

_____ 2. To climb to the summit, the shoes must be specially designed.

_____

_____

_____ 3. Walking through the forest, the trees showed the effects of acid rain.

_____

_____

_____ 4. Although only nine, my father taught me how to hunt.

_____

_____

_____ 5. After reading about the famine in Ethiopia, a contribution to the World Food Program of the United Nations was made.

_____

_____

_____ 6. Entering the room, the victims of the fire lay dead on the floor.

_____

_____

_____ 7. To play baseball well, a person needs keen eyes and quick reflexes.

_____

_____

_____ 8. Hoping for a bite, a severe thunderstorm broke over the bay.

_____

_____

_____ 9. After sitting for fifty minutes, an announcement was made that the play had to be canceled.

_____

_____

_____ 10. Staying awake, the hours seemed like days.

_____

_____

_____   11.   To arrive on time, you will need to leave by 7:00 P.M.

_____

_____

_____   12.   While eating my picnic lunch, a snake slithered out of a nearby rotten log.

_____

_____

· ·

E X E R C I S E 15-4

Some of the following sentences are unified and coherent. Others have misplaced or dangling modifiers. If the sentence is correct, write *C* in the blank.
If the sentence has a modification problem, in the blank write *M* for misplaced modifier and *D* for dangling modifier. Then rewrite the sentence so
that the thought flows smoothly.

_____   1. After sailing for several months, land was sighted.

_____

_____

_____   2. With one mile left to run in the marathon, exhaustion   best
described the runners.

_____

_____

_____   3. Condemned to die in the electric chair, execution was scheduled
for June 1 at 9 A.M.

_____

_____

_____   4. Because Thelma ate too many chocolates this morning she had
indigestion.

_____

_____

_____ 5. Blazing in the night sky, we nearly counted a dozen shooting stars.

_____

_____

_____ 6. Lost in the Sahara, Hadji had only enough water for two days.

_____

_____

_____ 7. You will enjoy seeing the home videos that you made years later.

_____

_____

_____ 8. Grilled over an open fire, Paula served the steaks to the hungry guests.

_____

_____

_____ 9. When jogging through the park, the scenery was enjoyed by Frank and Joyce.

_____

_____

_____ 10. His gold coins were stored in a safe which he had collected over many years.

_____

_____

_____ 11. Having studied the evidence, it was clear who the robbers were.

_____

_____

_____ 12. While looking for the hammer and nails, a bird flew through the shop's open window and landed on the drill press.

_____

_____

_____   13. To earn a degree, a student needs to follow the prescribed program of study.

_____

_____

_____   14. Praying often results in a peaceful state of mind.

_____

_____

_____   15. I bought the table at Bob's Discount Center which cost only $10.00.

_____

_____

. . . .

E X E R C I S E 15 - 5

Underline the misplaced and dangling modifiers in the following letter. On your own paper, rewrite the letter so that all modification problems are eliminated.

Dear Miss Etiquette: Being unmarried, I want you to know that my husband and I resent your remarks about the handling of our daughter's wedding by the _Zenith Gazette._ Specially engraved invitations were sent out to all the guests in gold envelopes. Our daughter wore the wedding dress of my mother that had been carefully stored in a closet almost for sixty years. Walking down the aisle, the pews were nearly decorated with every shade of carnation imaginable. At the reception a lavish amount of food was available for the guests on three large tables. Wearing my mother's treasured dress, my husband danced proudly with his daughter. The band, Modified Confusion, played some excellent music, which had interrupted its tour of America for this performance. After the reception, the newlyweds did not leave for their honeymoon on the _African Queen_! My husband and I personally waved to them as they sailed on the _Love Boat_ high up on the Golden Gate Bridge. I hope that you will print this letter in the next issue of the _Gazette_ so that the people of Zenith will know the truth. Hastily, (Mrs.) Amanda Bristles

. . . .

. . . .

Parallel Structure

This chapter introduces the importance of expressing parallel thoughts—thoughts that are equal in value—in parallel (or similar) grammatical form. **Form simply refers to the structure of the idea: an idea can be found in a word, a phrase, a subordinate clause, or an independent clause.**

Parallel thoughts can be two or more nouns used as subjects:

> *Wendy* or *John* will help you.

Or they can be two adjectives modifying a noun, as is the case with *warm* and *sunny* in the following sentence:

> The vacationers enjoyed a *warm* and *sunny* day at the beach.

Parallel thoughts are expressed in parallel prepositional phrases (*into the house* and *up the stairs*) in the following sentence:

> My sister ran *into the house* and *up the stairs*.

And they are expressed in parallel subordinate clauses in the following sentence:

> *What Tom said* and *what he meant* were not the same.

What Tom said and *what he meant* are parallel subordinate noun clauses that form a compound subject.

ACHIEVING PARALLEL STRUCTURE

In general, parallel elements are joined by coordinating conjunctions: *and, or, nor, so, but, yet,* and *for.* Correlative conjunctions also join parallel elements: *both...and, either...or, neither...nor, not only...but also,* and *whether...or.*

In short, ideas of equal value should be expressed in parallel grammatical forms. The following chart illustrates parallel words, phrases, and clauses:

Noun parallel with noun
> I bought *shirts* and *pants.*

Verb parallel with verb
> During the 1920s many American artists *lived* and *worked* in France.

Adjective parallel with adjective
> Sue's boyfriend is neither *tall* nor *lean.*

Adverb parallel with adverb
> Al's batting average improved *slowly* but *steadily.*

Prepositional phrase parallel with prepositional phrase
> Sam walked across the lawn and into the woods.

Verbal phrase parallel with verbal phrase
> Neither *eating hot peppers* nor *drinking sour milk* upset Paul's stomach.

Independent clause parallel with independent clause (also subordinate noun clause parallel with subordinate noun clause)
> *Ask not what your country can do for you; ask what you can do for your country.* (President Kennedy's Inaugural Address)

E X E R C I S E 16-1

Maintain parallel structure in each the following sentences by supplying a *noun* parallel with the underlined noun(s).

Example
> *Parents, teachers,* and ____*students*____ attended the meeting.

1. Both valuable *antiques* and worthless _____ were for sale at the auction.

2. Either *Jacqueline* _____ or will assist you.

3. For dessert we had *cookies, cupcakes,* and _____.

4. I would not want to move to *Albania, to Tibet,* or to _____.

5. The people demanded *freedom, equality,* and _____.

. . . .

E X E R C I S E   1 6 - 2

Maintain parallel structure in each of the following sentences by supplying the appropriate form of the underlined verb(s).

Example

A fine baseball player, Rob *ran*, *hit*, and ____*fielded*____ well.
(field)

1. Mr. Sturgis *designed*, *built*, and _____ the house.
(sell)

2. Our organization *will buy* the forest and _____ it
   for future generations of Americans.   (preserve)

3. Though we *felt* the flames' heat and _____ an explosion,
(fear)
   we ran into the burning house and _____ the family.
(rescue)

4. Each day I *cleaned* my room, *walked* the dog, and _____
   out the trash.   (take)

5. Becky *invented*, *produced*, and _____ several perfumes.
(market)

. . . .

E X E R C I S E   1 6 - 3

Maintain parallel structure in each of the following sentences by supplying an *adjective* parallel with the underlined adjective(s).

Example

A *large*, *strong*, and _____*mean*_____ bulldog was in the yard.

1. A *long*, *slow*, and _____ journey lay before us.

2. As an employee, Howard was neither *loyal* nor _____.

3. That snake has *short*, *sharp*, and _____ fangs.

4. Christine is both *intelligent* and _____.

5. I enjoy *cold*, *windy*, and _____ days.

. . . .

E X E R C I S E   16-4

Maintain parallel structure in each of the following sentences by supplying an *adverb* parallel with the underlined adverb(s).

Example

The robber worked *quickly* and _____*silently*_____.

1. The soldiers *carefully* and _____ walked through the minefield.

2. Lance was *extremely* handsome and _____ rich.

3. Carolyn will leave for Mexico *today* or _____.

4. He told us to write *simply* and _____.

5. Amanda looked *lovingly* and _____ at her mother.

. . . .

E X E R C I S E   16-5

Maintain parallel structure in the following sentences by supplying a *prepositional phrase* parallel with the underlined prepositional phrase.

Example

The mouse ran across the floor and   __*into a shoe*__ .

1. Wally jumped *over the fence* and ran _____.

2. I will expect to see you either *in the morning* or _____.

3. The rocket soared *above the clouds* and headed _____.

4. The jet landed *off the runway* and _____.

5. With little help from me and _____ , Jack won support for his business venture.

. . . .

E X E R C I S E   16-6

Maintain parallel structure in the following sentences by supplying a *verbal phrase* parallel with the underlined verbal phrase. Use the suggested verb under the blank, but remember to use the proper form of the verb.

Example

To play poker or   _*to watch television*_ is my choice.
(watch)

1. The doctors know how *to prevent the disease* but not how_____

   _____.

      (cure)

2. After *driving from the airport* and _____,

      (arrive)

   we decided to take a nap.

3. After graduating, Alice hopes *to find a good job* and _____

   _____.

      (earn)

4. *Exploring foreign countries* and _____ were Al's

      (meet)

   principal joys during his summer vacation.

5. *Demanding money* but not _____ caused the bank

      (get)

   robber to shoot the teller.

· ·

E X E R C I S E   16 - 7

Maintain parallel structure in the following sentences by supplying a *subordinate clause* parallel with the underlined subordinate clause. You should use the subordinating conjunction or relative pronoun under the blank.

   Example
         When he began his speech, people applauded;
         when he finished it, people booed.
         (when)

1. I do not know *why you came here* or _____.

      (what)

2. Peter got less *than he expected* but more_____.

      (than)

3. The man *who planned the murder of Mr. Kane*, and the woman

   _____ , were Kane's brother and sister.

      (who)

4. Let's have a talk *after Max has left the room* but _____ .

                                                                    (before)

5. Lois knew *that Alan was pleased with her work* and _____ .

                                                                    (that)

· ·

E X E R C I S E 16-8

Maintain parallel structure in the following sentences by supplying an *independent clause* parallel with the underlined independent clause.

Example

    Ibrahim enjoyed spending the summer with his relatives in Israel, but *in September he was happy returning to his home in New York.*

1. *Suzanne's head injury seemed slight*; however,

_____ .

2. *In July Randy and Kathy spend two weeks at the ocean*, and

_____ .

3. *Scott was a talented athlete*, for

_____ .

4. Either *you give me an apology*, or

_____ .

5. Mr. Khan was extremely generous; for example,

_____ .

· ·

As you have seen from doing the above exercises, parallel structure tells the reader that ideas are related, that they have similar importance in a sentence. The meaning is made clearer, it is more emphatic, and your ideas flow smoothly into your reader's mind. Consider the power and polish of Lincoln's Gettysburg Address, which was delivered on November 19, 1863 (parallel items here and in the following examples are underlined for easy identification):

    But in a larger sense, *we cannot dedicate—we cannot consecrate—we cannot hallow*—this ground. The brave men, *living* and *dead*, who struggled here, have consecrated it far above our poor power to *add* or *detract*. *The world will little note* nor *long remember what we say here*, but *it can never forget what they did here.*

Although the last sentence is a compound-complex one, its ideas are more easily understood because parallel structure is used:

Subject	Predicate–Modifier–Predicate			Subordinate Clause
The world	will	little	note	
	nor (conjunction)			
	[will]	long	remember	what we say here,
	but (conjunction)			
it	can	never	forget	what they did here.

The same power can be felt in President Kennedy's Inaugural Address (January 20, 1961). Because he expressed equal thoughts in equal grammatical forms, those thoughts were at once brief, strong, and memorable:

Let every nation know, whether it wishes us *well* or *ill*, that we shall *pay any price*, *bear any burden*, *meet any hardship*, *support any friend*, *oppose any foe*, in order to assure *the survival* and *the success* of liberty.

Notice that President Kennedy repeated the article *the* before *survival* and before *success*. In general, to make the parallel statements clear, you should repeat **an article** (*a*, *an*, *the*), **a preposition, a pronoun, a helping verb, a subordinating conjunction,** or **the sign of the infinitive** (*to*, as in *to* fight and *to* win). Repeating words that introduce parallelism adds clarity and emphasis by setting off each parallel element.

For additional practice in achieving parallel structure, do the following exercise.

E X E R C I S E 16-9

In the following sentences, fill in each blank with a word (or words) parallel with the underlined one(s). *Remember to repeat words that introduce (or signal) parallel elements.*

1. Both *my mother* and _____ wanted me to join the

   Peace Corps rather than _____.

2. Because of the fire, *every book*, *every magazine*, and _____ in

   the library *was destroyed* or _____ .

3. Whether Sven was *at home*, *at work*, or _____ , he

   always wore the same *jeans* and _____ .

4. The bullfight was *brief* and _____ .

5. Rick not only *likes cooking* but also _____ .

6. Because of the drought, the *corn* and _____ *withered* and

   _____ .

7. Derek's falcon is trained *to hunt* and _____ small game.

8. My drill sergeant yelled that he was going to make me *physically* and

   _____ tough.

9. Martin was neither *shocked* nor even _____ when he was

   told that he was fired.

10. *Jogging* and _____ are excellent exercises for the

    heart and _____ .

11. They attacked *by land* and _____ .

12. She left for work *after she had bathed* but before _____ .

13. Karim liked *to watch football*, but _____ .

14. All within six months, Clark and Clare *were married*, *were separated*, and

    _____ .

15. *I do not know his arrival time*, nor _____ .

16. I do not know *how to sing* or _____ .

17. Sara had a rash *on her face*, _____ , and _____

    _____ .

18. Alex *ran*, *jumped*, and _____ .

19. The report of the invasion was *on radio*, _____ ,

    and, _____ .

20. *Maxine's husband went to the baseball game*; meanwhile, _____

    _____ .

21. *Since Denise was ill and* _____ , I took her to see a

    doctor.

22. The flag had *blue*, _____ , and _____ stripes.

23. *I have no money, no food, and no home*; in short, _____

    _____ .

24. In one sense, *Melissa won*; in another sense, _____ .

25. I do not care *if you are rich* or _____ .

. . . .

AVOIDING FAULTY PARALLEL STRUCTURE

Faulty parallel structure is of two types.

The first type involves putting unequal (unrelated) ideas in similar grammatical forms. The sentence that is created lacks sound logic.

Example

Princess Diana has captivating eyes, a winning smile, and a stepgrandmother. [Her *captivating eyes* and *winning smile* are facial features; her *stepgrandmother* is not one of those features. Consequently, the three points are not of equal value or of equal significance, and they should not be expressed in parallel structure. The point made about her stepgrandmother should be in a separate sentence.]

The problem that occurs most frequently is one of expressing equal ideas in dissimilar (unequal) grammatical forms.

Examples

The winds came from the south and which grew in strength. [This sentence has a prepositional phrase (*from the south*) parallel with a subordinate clause (*which grew in strength*). The problem could also be seen as that of an independent clause parallel with a subordinate one.]

Possible revisions include the following:

The winds came from the south and grew in strength.

or The winds came from the south, and they grew in strength.

The cat moved slowly, carefully, and with silence. [In this sentence, the single-word adverbs, *slowly* and *carefully*, are parallel with a prepositional phrase, *with silence.*]

The result is faulty parallelism. *With silence* should be changed to *silently.*

The cat moved slowly, carefully, and silently.

To study the problem and solving it are my goals. [*To study the problem* is an infinitive phrase, but *solving it* is a gerund phrase. Once again, faulty parallelism is the result.]

Infinitive phrases should be balanced with infinitive phrases, and gerund phrases should be balanced with gerund phrases:

To study the problem and to solve it are my goals.

or Studying the problem and solving it are my goals.

Having reached the summit of the mountain and since the men were exhausted from the climb, they decided to rest. [In this sentence, *having reached the summit of the mountain* is a participial phrase, but *since the men were exhausted from the climb* is a subordinate clause.]

The faulty parallelism could be corrected by making phrase parallel with phrase or by making subordinate clause parallel with subordinate clause:

Having reached the summit of the mountain and being exhausted from the climb, the men decided to rest.

or Since the men had reached the summit of the mountain and since they were exhausted from the climb, they decided to rest.

E X E R C I S E 16-10

In the blank write *P* if the sentence has effective parallel structure and *X* if the sentence shows faulty parallelism. Rewrite any sentences with faulty parallelism.

_____   1. I knew that he was both unhappy and without friends.

_____

_____

_____   2. Madonna flew to Brazil to find solitude and because she wanted to relax.

_____

_____

_____   3. I plan to swim as well as waterskiing.

_____

_____

_____   4. Sonia had black hair, brown eyes, and tan skin.

_____

_____

_____   5. Kurt liked baseball, football, and he enjoyed tennis.

_____

_____

_____ 6. The police officer ordered the men to turn around, to put their hands on the wall, and then he told them to spread their legs.

_____

_____ 7. Doreen did very well in her studies and which she enjoyed very much too.

_____

_____ 8. I disliked the movie because it contained offensive language, it promoted sexual exploitation of women, and excessive violence.

_____

_____ 9. What Sandra wants most from her car is reliability and getting high gas mileage.

_____

_____ 10. That tiger is quick, powerful, and is beautiful.

_____

_____ 11. If you have worked with Bradley, you know that he is a man of intelligence, tact, and who is totally honest.

_____

_____ 12. Not only the students but also those who taught them enjoyed the summer vacation.

_____

_____ 13. Just as Wes is an excellent dancer, so is Marie.

_____

_____ 14. On Friday Darnell wrote his letter of resignation, and it was submitted.

_____

_____

_____ 15. The soldier not only was brave but also proud.

_____

_____

_____ 16. Suited for raising cattle and sheep and which could grow crops as well, the land seemed an ideal purchase.

_____

_____

_____ 17. The bull's face showed that he was angry and with an intention to charge.

_____

_____

_____ 18. Built of mud and straw, and which had only one opening, the natives' hut housed four families.

_____

_____

_____ 19. We are going to try hard, we are going to win, and being proud of our victory.

_____

_____

_____ 20. If most of the sea turtles are to survive after hatching, the night must be moonless, the tide must be low, and you have got to have few predators.

_____

_____

EXERCISE 16-11

The following paragraphs contain errors in parallel structure. Underline the errors. Then, on separate paper, rewrite the paragraphs so that equal ideas are in equal grammatical structures.

A. My life was always a balanced one. I was born during the first hour of the first day, and it was also the first month of the year 1911. (My mother's pregnancy had lasted exactly nine months, or so she was fond of saying.) At home, at play, as well as when I was at school, I was always a model child. I excelled in reading, writing, and I was also excellent in mathematics. I had exactly three boyfriends and three who were girls. Each day I ate exactly three meals, never more, and I never ate less. Fast on my feet and since I could think quickly, I earned letters in baseball, football, and basketball in high school. My parents, teachers, and friends thought that I was healthy, happy, and behaved normally in every way. Then, just after high school, I enlisted in the United States Army, Navy, and Air Force all in the same day. I knew I had a problem.

B. If you smoke, quitting has many advantages and be tried. For one, not buying cigarettes means to have more spending money. In addition, nicotine stains on your teeth and hands will be eliminated. To quit smoking is eliminating cigarette breath. More importantly, quitting will help you avoid lung cancer, emphysema, and having a heart attack. Your heart will be stronger and at its healthiest. You will be a stronger athlete and, in general, to be healthier. Finally, you will probably please friends and in your family as well as yourself. If you quit smoking, your life will probably be longer and with more enjoyment. Being able to quit will make you proud as well as health.

. . . .

. . . .

Shifts in Person, Number, and Tense

Even as misplaced or dangling modifiers and faulty parallelism prevent a smooth flow of thought in a sentence, needless shifts in person, in number, and in tense also result in incoherence. A sentence—or a paragraph, for that matter—should not have a shift from the third person to the second person, or from the plural to the singular, or from the present to the past tense *unless* there is a logical reason to do so. Unnecessary shifts cause incoherence, irritate your reader, and can seriously alter your intended meaning.

SHIFTS IN PERSON AND NUMBER

You should avoid unnecessary shifts in person and number. When you select a noun or pronoun for use in a sentence (or group of sentences), you create a specific person and number. As a general rule, you should maintain that person and number throughout the writing. In other words, you should not shift abruptly between persons and numbers. Consider the following examples:

1. If a person wants to save money, you need to establish a budget. [The shift here is from the third person (*a person*) to the second person (*you*).]

The problem can be corrected in a number of ways:

If you want to save money, you need to establish a budget.

or If people want to save money, they need to establish budgets.

or If a person wants to save money, he or she needs to establish a budget.

In each of these three revisions, the person is consistent. Shift-in-person problems usually involve a shift from the third to second or from second to third person.

2. If someone wants to enjoy fishing, they need patience. [Although *someone* and *they* are both third person, the former is singular, and the latter is plural in number.]

Possible revisions include the following:

If someone wants to enjoy fishing, he or she needs patience.

or If people want to enjoy fishing, they need patience. [In the first revision, *someone*, *he*, and *she* are all third person singular; in the second sentence, *people* and *they* are both third person plural.]

E X E R C I S E   17-1

Revise the following sentences so that they show consistent person and number.

1. When one considers buying a used car, you should inspect the odometer carefully.

   _____

   _____

2. If a student studies hard, they will usually do well.

   _____

   _____

3. If parents want to inspect the day care center, one should contact Mrs. Harper.

   _____

   _____

4. When drivers fail to obey a traffic signal, you can expect to have an accident.

   _____

   _____

5. If one wants my opinion, they can have it.

   _____

   _____

SHIFTS IN TENSE

In general, you should not shift the verb tense within a sentence (or in a paragraph) unless you have a sound reason for doing so. In the following sentence there is a logical reason for the shift in tense from the present to the past:

> Dr. Johnson is the one scientist who has fully supported this AIDS project since she joined it in 1989.

Again, in the following sentence there is a logical reason for a shift from the past tense to the future tense:

> Pablo told me that he will complete the renovations on my house in June. [The telling took place in the past, but the renovations will take place in the future. Unnecessary shifts in tense, however, result in an incoherent flow of thought.]

The following passage contains an illogical shift from the past tense to the present tense:

> To keep the colonists from starving, Captain Smith realized that he would have to trade with the Indians. For some trifles, such as beads, Smith received a large supply of corn from the Indians. Thus, he saves the Jamestown colony from starvation. [In the last sentence of this passage, *saves* should be *saved*. The historical event should be narrated in the past tense.]

However, when you discuss the plot of a poem, play, novel, film, etc., or the ideas of the author contained in such a work, you should use the present tense. Literary works are, in a sense, open to each generation for new interpretation and thus live in the present. The events surrounding the creation of the work, however, should be narrated in the past tense. Consider these examples:

1. Faulkner's *The Sound and the Fury* and *Go Down, Moses* reveal the sufferings endured by African-Americans in the South and show a profound sympathy for the plight of those people.
2. Faulkner said that he learned honesty, charity, devotion to duty, and a host of other virtues from Caroline Barr, the African-American who raised him. Doubtless, Faulkner's upbringing influenced his depiction of African-Americans in his novels.

In the first example the present tense is used because what the works mean is discussed. The second example is a statement about Faulkner's life and about an influence on his work. Consequently, the past tense is used.

Similar to discussions of the meaning of a literary work, statements of general truth are also in the present tense: Most people realize that smoking causes lung and heart disease.

E X E R C I S E 17-2

Revise the following sentences so that tense is consistent.

1. When Greg lived near Chesapeake Bay, he enjoyed fishing, but he prefers hunting.

   _____

   _____

2. In *Adventures of Huckleberry Finn*, as Huck journeys down the Mississippi River, he had experienced the greed that ruled the lives of many people.

   _____

   _____

3. As a boy, Samuel Clemens (Mark Twain) enjoyed the atmosphere of Hannibal, Missouri; years later, he looks back with nostalgia on his life there.

   _____

   _____

4. Paul yanked on the line, hooked the marlin, battled the giant fish for two hours, and then watches helplessly as the fish finally fights free of the hook.

   _____

   _____

5. In his novel *Main Street*, Lewis presents a portrait of Gopher Prairie, a small midwestern town that was filled with hypocrisy, meanness, and ignorance.

   _____

   _____

· ·

E X E R C I S E 17 - 3

Some of the following sentences are consistent in person, number, and tense usage. Other sentences contain unwarranted shifts in person, number, and tense. Revise any sentences that contain unnecessary shifts.

1. Unless people prepare adequately for retirement years, you may experience financial problems.

   _____

   _____

2. In November each class nominates their officers.

   _____

   _____

3. Each winter I travel to the Cascade Mountains of Washington, climb the snow-capped peaks, and enjoyed the excellent skiing.

   _____

   _____

4. Faulkner asserts in his short story titled "The Bear" that people needed to respect nature.

   _____

   _____

5. When a politician does not listen to voters' concerns, they probably do not stay in office for very long.

   _____

   _____

6. After you have heard the songs on this record, one will experience a mixture of anger and depression.

   _____

   _____

7. During their first meeting, George discussed the Indian ruins of interest in Mexico; his friend Sompong speaks of the ancient temples of Thailand.

   _____

   _____

8. Everyone knows that variety was the spice of life.

   _____

   _____

9. Augustine's *Confessions* and Rousseau's *Confessions* are alike in that both books spoke of the importance of honesty.

   _____

   _____

10. Professor Hunter was excited; he has just been named Teacher of the Year.

    _____

    _____

11. Halley's Comet has continued to arouse interest among stargazers ever since its movements were predicted by Edmond Halley in 1705.

    _____

    _____

12. In writing a paragraph you should always keep one's basic purpose in mind.

    _____

    _____

13. My work for Fibronics Corporation is very exciting, but my supervisor was a fool.

    _____

    _____

14. The Pony Express Company selected young and strong riders, for they had to ride up to seventy-five miles per day.

    _____

    _____

15. I shop at Norm's Department Store because you can get many bargains there.

    _____

    _____

16. When I was a youngster, I enjoyed watching cartoons on television, but now I had no interest in them.

_____

_____

17. Athletes must continually practice if we want to remain competitive.

_____

_____

18. When Hitler announced the German invasion of Russia on June 22, 1941, he says: "The world will hold its breath."

_____

_____

19. Ibsen's *A Doll's House* ended as Nora, the leading character, leaves her snobbish husband and slammed the door behind her.

_____

_____

20. My wife keeps giving me books that dealt with improving your sex life.

_____

_____

· ·

E X E R C I S E 17-4

Rewrite the following paragraph on your own paper so that all unwarranted shifts in person, number, and tense are removed.

(1) I am a baseball player, and we know the meaning of hard work. (2) At the age of eleven, when I started playing the game, I have pitching practice every day after school. (3) I never missed a practice, and you will have to discipline yourself not to miss them. (4) In high school, I pitched more games than any other pitcher on the team. (5) After a game, your sore arms, legs, and back tell us what being on the mound for nine innings means. (6) Now that I was in college, I know that I had to work much harder if pro scouts are going to notice you. (7) He wants to see a pitcher who showed an effort of 110%.

· ·

EXERCISE 17-5

Rewrite the following paragraphs on your own paper so that all unwarranted shifts in person, number, and tense are removed.

(1) During the first few weeks of being a journalist in Saigon (now Ho Chi Minh City), Vietnam, in the early 1970s, I knew that we have an easy life, especially when you compare it with those of the average soldier in the field. (2) Money was never a problem for me because one exchanged my American dollars on the illegal market and get five times the legal rate of exchange. (3) (Walter Jackson, my boss, said that I am sure to get caught, but they were wrong.) (4) I lived in the Continental Palace Hotel, and you always feel that their service was the best in Saigon. (5) I got up around noon, have brunch and a few drinks, and then attend the 4 P.M. military briefing. (6) Around 6 P.M. I wrote my report and send them to my boss. (7) Then I had drinks and a meal at the Continental Palace and go out to enjoy Saigon's nightlife. (8) After a few weeks of observing my routine, my boss says to me that if being a journalist in Vietnam means that they report only on briefings, then one had better look for work elsewhere. (9) The next morning I leave with the troops for the Mekong Delta. (10) After a week with it, I learn the true meaning of the word *journalist*.

. . . .

EXERCISE 17-6

Rewrite the following paragraphs on your own paper so that all unwarranted shifts in person, number, and tense are removed.

(1) There are many actions that was a help in avoiding cancer. (2) You cut the risk of lung cancer 90% if he or she quits smoking. (3) If you drink heavily, the risk of several cancers was greater, especially if one also smokes. (4) If you are pregnant, avoid even dental X-rays unless it is essential. (5) If doctors know that you are pregnant, he can protect the fetus from future leukemia. (6) In general, you should avoid X-rays so that you protected one's own health. (7) If your skin is light or freckles easily, too much sun should have been avoided. (8) Try to avoid air polluted by car smoke, household cleaners, or paint thinner. (9) Be careful with chemicals when you work at farming or were in a factory. (10) Although safety cannot be guaranteed, we can improve our odds.

. . . .

. . . .

End Marks, Dashes, Parentheses, and Quotation Marks

The purpose of punctuation is to make your meaning clear to your readers. For the most part, punctuation marks do nothing more than mirror pauses and stops in your speaking patterns. End marks (periods, question marks, and exclamation points), semicolons, and colons ask you to stop briefly in your reading. Commas ask you to pause briefly and then read on. Dashes and parentheses can be used to set off parenthetical or explanatory information.

Punctuation marks are important because they illustrate dramatically that some ideas are closely related and should be joined. Punctuation marks can also be used to divide ideas into distinct units. Finally, punctuation marks can voice the tone or emotion that you want to get across to your readers.

In this chapter you will learn to use effectively the period (.), the question mark (?), the exclamation point (!), the dash (—), parentheses (), and quotation marks (" ").

THE PERIOD

In general, the period indicates a brief stop in your reading. Study the following rules for the use of the period:

The period is used to end a declarative sentence (one that makes a statement), to end a mild imperative sentence (a mild command), and to end an indirect question.

A **direct question** is one that simply states the question and requires a question mark: *When did Ruth leave?* An **indirect question** merely introduces what has been asked: *I wonder when Ruth left.*

Examples

The English language is used by nearly one billion people each day. [This is a declarative sentence: it makes a statement or an assertion.]

Turn off the light. [This is a mild imperative sentence, a mild command.]

Mrs. Brooks asked whether Tina visited Cape Hatteras. [This sentence is an indirect question. The direct question would be as follows: Mrs. Brooks asked, "Did Tina visit Cape Hatteras?"]

In general, a period is used after abbreviations.

Examples

Mr.	etc.	Inc.	P.M.
Mrs.	lb.	M.D.	J. B. Turner
Ms.	R.N.	Rev.	Ph.D.
Dr.	Dec.	U.S.	Sr.

In your writing in college, such abbreviations as *Mr.*, *Ms.*, and *Dr.* before names, and *Jr.*, *Sr.*, *R.N.*, and *M.D.* after names, are always acceptable. For other titles, usage varies. In informal writing, titles such as *Lt. Col.*, *Fr.* (Father), *Prof.*, *Sen.* or *Gov.* are acceptable before full names, but they should be spelled out before surnames alone.

Examples

Lieutenant Colonel Stevens   Lt. Col. Joel Stevens

Senator Kassebaum   Sen. Nancy L. Kassebaum

You should, however, always spell out the following:

1. People's Names: *George* rather than *Geo.*
2. Geographical Localities: *Maryland* rather than *MD* or *Md.*, *Shaker Heights Park* rather than *Shaker Hts. Pk.*
3. Months and Days: *March* rather than *Mar.*, *Wednesday* rather than *Wed.*
4. Units of Measurement: two *years* rather than two *yrs.*, one *quart* rather than one *qt.*, (**Exception**: An abbreviation for a long phrase such as *miles per hour* is acceptable: 55 *m.p.h.*)
5. Courses of Instruction: *biology* rather than *bio.*, *chemistry* rather than *chem.*

A current trend is to omit the periods in many abbreviations, most frequently in abbreviations for organizations and governmental units. Capitalized initials are used to form these abbreviations.

Examples

FAA   (Federal Aviation Administration)

IRS   (Internal Revenue Service)

| NAACP | (National Association for the Advancement of Colored People) |
| UN | (United Nations) |

When you read a newspaper or monthly news magazine, you will find many other abbreviations without periods:

Examples

CEO	(chief executive officer)
R&D	(research and development)
PC	(personal computer or politically correct)
RVs	(recreational vehicles)

Use a standard (and recently published) college dictionary to make sure whether or not to use a period in an abbreviation. Even then, some dictionaries may offer you a choice: *USA* or *U.S.A.*

Acronyms do not use periods.

An **acronym** is a word coined from the initial letters or syllables of a group of words, and it is pronounced as if it were a word.

Examples

AIDS	(acquired immune-deficiency syndrome)
CORE	(Congress for Racial Equality)
CREEP	(Committee to Re-Elect the President)
NOW	(National Organization for Women)
PACs	(political action committees)
RAM	(random-access memory)

Most acronyms are written in capital letters; however, some acronyms, such as *radar* (radio detecting and ranging), *laser* (light amplification by stimulated emission of radiation), and *yuppie* (young urban professional + ie) have achieved the status of common nouns and should be written in small letters.

Some organizations and governmental units are so well known that their abbreviations or acronyms need not be spelled out in your writing: *NBC*, *CNN*, *CIA*, *IRS*, *NATO*, and *USA* (or *U.S.A.*), for example. **Unless well known, abbreviations and acronyms should be spelled out when first used.** The abbreviation or acronym should be placed in *parentheses* after the term that is spelled out.

Example

When the the Federal Communications Commission (FCC) was created in 1934, its chief concern was regulating interstate communications by radio and wire. In the era of television and satellite communications, however, the role of the FCC has become more complex. [Once the term to be abbreviated has been spelled out, you can use that abbreviation in subsequent sentences and thus achieve brevity and avoid the boredom of excessively repeating a long phrase.]

If a sentence concludes with an abbreviation ending in a period, a second period should not be added.

Example

Paul arrived at 6 A.M.

EXERCISE 18-1

Supply periods as needed in the following sentences.

1. Tom Jacobs, Sr, will receive his MS in computer science from the University of Delaware in June

2. After graduation, Mr Jacobs plans to work for the Environmental Protection Agency (EPA)

3. Rev Dr Martin Luther King, Jr, has inspired millions of people

4. The books arrived COD

5. The accounting world has certainly given us many acronyms: FIFO, GIGO, LIFO, TICTIT, etc

6. Marie left at 6:30 PM

7. My AM/FM radio is not working

8. The US Postal Service asks us to use MA instead of Mass for the abbreviation of Massachusetts

9. I wonder when Willis will return

10. Was Roger named MVP in last night's NFL game?

. . . .

E X E R C I S E 18-2

Some of the following sentences contain errors in the use of the period and abbreviations. Rewrite any sentences that contain errors.

Example

    From: I saw my prof on Fri.

    To: I saw my professor on Friday.

1. My two bros., Robt. and Benj., want to become Drs..

_____

2. Franklin D Roosevelt was born on Jan. 30, 1882, in Hyde Pk., NY

_____

3. I asked for one oz of dye and one qt of water.

_____

4. Before we visited Gettysburg Nat'l Pk, PA, we stopped at the tourist info ctr. on York St.

_____

5. My new Toyota gets 45 m.p.g.

_____

6. Next semester I am taking courses in hist., soc., and psych.

_____

7. I may take a PE course too.

_____

8. Col. Johnson and Gen. Clinton joined us for the Mem. Day observance.

_____

9. Not every physician is a member of the AMA.

_____

10. How many ft. are in a yd.?

_____

. . . .

THE QUESTION MARK

The question mark (?) is used as follows:

The question mark ends a sentence which is a direct question.

> **Example**
>> What does the abbreviation *SSA* mean?

A question mark is not used at the end of an indirect question.

> **Example**
>> I wonder what the abbreviation *SSA* means.

However, a direct question may contain an indirect question in it. In that case, you need a question mark.

> **Example**
>> Did Lynn ask what the abbreviation *SSA* means?

An interrogative clause (direct question) may be found in a declarative sentence.

> **Examples**
>> Lynn asked, "What does the abbreviation *SSA* mean?"
>> *or* "What does the abbreviation *SSA* mean?" Lynn asked.
>> It was on Thursday (or was it Friday?) that we learned about the accident.

A question mark can convert a declarative or an imperative sentence into a question.

> **Examples**
>> Kathy is not going to the Michael Jackson concert?
>> You do not mind flying in a thunder storm?

A question mark may be used to show that the writer is not certain about the accuracy of a number or date.

> **Examples**
>> Aeschylus (525?-456 B.C.) was a famous Greek dramatist.
>> The manager of the bookstore said that he ordered thirty (?) books.

E X E R C I S E   1 8 - 3

Supply question marks (and periods) as needed in the following sentences.

1. I do not know what this message means

2. Have you seen the plans for the new building

3. Ted asked, "When will the trip begin"

4. The students wanted to know if the class was canceled

5. The shipment arrived on Friday (or was it Thursday)

6. I wonder what Roger wants us to do

7. For how many years did Magic Johnson play for the Los Angeles Lakers

8. *Star Trek VI* is an exciting film, isn't it

9. "Who started this rumor" she asked

10. Nearly two hundred thousand people—is it possible—suffer from AIDS in the United States

. . . .

THE EXCLAMATION MARK

In general, the exclamation mark (!) appears at the end of a statement that indicates strong emotion, such as amazement, alarm, shock, fear, etc.

Examples

Yes! He's the killer!

Ouch!

Stop!

Run for your life!

"Hurry!" he screamed.

The exclamation mark should not be used with mild interjections or commands.

Examples

Please follow the instructions with care.

Yes, the new computer network will help us greatly.

E X E R C I S E 1 8 - 4

Supply exclamation marks, as well as any other needed punctuation marks, in the following sentences.

1. Captain Hastings shouted the order, "Take cover"
2. Even so, some soldiers were struck by the exploding shells
3. Cries of "I'm hit" and "Medic" could be heard
4. The explosions ended as suddenly as they had begun
5. Five men had been killed, and eight men had been wounded in just twenty seconds

. . . .

E X E R C I S E 1 8 - 5

Supply periods, question marks, and exclamation marks as needed in the following paragaph.

At about 1:30 PM last Friday, Maj Ruth Miller, MD, Capt Mark Lewis, RN, and I were on our way to work at Franklin VA Hospital when we observed the crash The USMC F-4 jet skidded to a halt between two giant oak trees in a field near the intersections of I-95 and Route 40 Two police officers pulled the pilot and the co-pilot from the jet two minutes before we arrived As we approached the flyers, the pilot, Col G E Slater, yelled, "How's my co-pilot Treat him first" An examination revealed that the co-pilot, Lt Col Rex Williams, was dead Just then, a police officer screamed, "Fire Fire Run" With the pilot yelling "My legs My legs" Dr Miller and I carried him a safe distance from the jet, which thirty seconds later exploded in flames After stabilizing the pilot, we rushed him to the hospital.

. . . .

THE DASH

The dash (or a pair of dashes) is used to signal a sudden shift in thought and to set off appositives and other explanatory material in a sentence.

The dash (or a pair of dashes) may be used to indicate a sharp break in thought.

Examples

She was my—but who cares about it now?

I disliked—no, I hated—the man.

The dash (or a pair of dashes) may be used to dramatically set off appositives or other explanatory material.

Examples

The dash—two unspaced hyphens in typing—gives strong emphasis to the material that is set off.

Four sophomores—Paula Baldwin, Suzanne Murphy, Gary Hernandez, and Alex Kwoh—will be exchange students next year.

The dash is also used to set off an introductory or a concluding list or explanation.
Note: Most writers prefer to use a colon (:) after a statement that introduces a formal list of items.

Examples

"Dreadful, dismal, doleful, dolorous, and dollar-less"—these words were used in the *Pennsylvania Journal* to describe America's condition prior to the Revolutionary War.

As a result of the fire, he lost nearly everything that he owned —clothes, furniture, and artworks.

To our sister republics south of our border, we offer a special pledge—to convert our good words into good deeds, in a new alliance for progress, to assist free men and free governments in casting off the chains of poverty. (From President Kennedy's Inaugural Address, January 20, 1961)

The overuse of the dash can make your writing appear choppy and disorganized. Do not use a dash when a period, a comma, or other mark of punctuation is more appropriate. In addition to altering punctuation marks, you may need to add or subtract words and shift phrases and clauses to correct the overuse of the dash. Study the following example:

From: After I got to my doctor's office—my doctor was not in—I had to wait two hours. During that time, other patients—most of them had the flu—coughed, sneezed, and groaned—but not me—all I needed was a flu shot. When I did see Dr. Savin, I told him that the shot might not help—the germs had gotten a head start.

To: After I got to my doctor's office, I had to wait two hours because my doctor was not in. Showing signs of having the flu, other patients coughed, sneezed, and groaned—but not me. All I needed was a flu shot. When I did see Dr. Savin, I told him that the shot might not help—the germs had gotten a head start.

EXERCISE 18-6

Add a dash (or dashes) as needed in the following sentences.

1. The gibbon, the gorilla, and the orangutan all of these animals are in danger of extinction.

2. The victims of HIV infection number thousands no, they number around a million in the United States.

3. Nearly six million cars are registered in the Los Angeles area a car for every two people living there.

4. Washington possessed qualities that made him an outstanding general courage, resourcefulness, and intelligence.

5. Hawaii's major exports sugar, pineapple, and molasses account for a small part of the state's income when compared to that received from tourism.

PARENTHESES

While the dash emphasizes the material that is set off, parentheses de-emphasize the enclosed material. They are used to enclose examples, explanations, passing remarks, and other information not essential for a clear understanding.

Examples

Many American Presidents (John F. Kennedy and George Bush, for example) were war heroes.

Space probes (space vehicles that neither carry human beings nor orbit the earth) have greatly enhanced our knowledge of the universe.

Cape Fear (it is a remake of the 1962 film starring Robert Mitchum) features outstanding performances by Robert De Niro and Nick Nolte.

Parentheses may also be used to set off dates, to set off numbered points in a list, and to enclose a citation (or reference). Study the following examples:

Dates: In 1945 the United States dropped atomic bombs on Hiroshima (August 6) and Nagasaki (August 9).

Numbered list: Solid wastes are disposed of in three basic ways: (1) in a landfill, (2) through incineration, and (3) by recycling.

Citation: Chapter 12 (pp. 323-42) contains a good introduction to the American political system.

EXERCISE 18-7

Add parentheses in the following sentences.

1. The Republic of Zambia formerly Northern Rhodesia has English as its official language.

2. The War of 1812 actually 1812 to 1814 was ended by the Treaty of Ghent.

3. Sophocles 495?-406? B.C. was a great Greek dramatist.

4. In three cities Los Angeles, Houston, and New York the flu epidemic has caused thousands of deaths.

5. During his long life he was born in 1885, he has seen more changes than he cares to remember.

6. In *Final Exit* p. 110 Derek Humphry writes that his first wife, Jean Humphry, died in less than an hour by taking overdoses of codeine and Seconal.

7. Hepatitis an inflammation of the liver caused by a virus or a toxin is a serious and sometimes fatal disease.

8. An essay has several essential parts: 1 an introduction stating your subject and purpose, 2 a body supporting and expanding your purpose, and 3 a conclusion reinforcing your purpose.

9. According to Henry Lee, President George Washington 1789-1797 was "first in war, first in peace, and first in the hearts of his countrymen."

10. The multi-million dollar Reagan Library $56.8 million, to be exact will house fifty-five million documents.

. . . .

QUOTATION MARKS

The Use of Quotation Marks

Quotation marks are either a pair of punctuation marks ("...") used to enclose a direct quotation, or a pair of single punctuation marks ('...') used to enclose a quotation within a quotation. What is quoted may be taken from someone's oral or written remarks.

Use double quotation marks to enclose direct quotations: the exact spoken or written words of someone.

Examples

On seeing her picture on the new five pound note, sixty-four-year-old Queen Elizabeth II remarked, "It makes me look so old, but I guess I am old."

Note that the quotation starts with a capital letter. If a quotation, such as the above one, is cut in two, the second part of it would not start with a capital. Two sets of quotation marks would be required.

"It makes me look so old," Queen Elizabeth II remarked, "but I guess I am old."

If the above quotation were in fact two sentences and thus two quotations, a capital letter would start the second sentence:

"It makes me look so old," Queen Elizabeth II remarked. "But I guess I am old."

All of the above examples contain direct quotations. Indirect quotations *speak about* what the author has said or written. Since an indirect quotation does not give the author's exact words, no quotation marks are used:

Queen Elizabeth II recently remarked that her picture on the new five pound note shows her sixty-four years.

Single quotations should be used to enclose a quotation within a quotation.

Example

> "In thinking about education," Professor Horner said, "we should start with the words of Confucius: 'To know that we know what we know, and that we do not know what we do not know, that is true knowledge.'"

The punctuation at the end of this sentence looks odd, but it is correct. The single quotation ends the internal quote, and the double quotation ends the total quotation. The period, as well as the comma, is always placed inside the quotation marks.

Double quotation marks enclose the titles of such works as the following: songs, short poems, short stories, articles in magazines, essays, speeches, chapters or sections of books, and episodes of a radio or television series:

"Don't Worry, Be Happy"	(song title)
"We Are the World"	(song title)
"Mending Wall"	(poem)
"The Red Wheelbarrow"	(poem)
"The Jolly Corner"	(short story)
"The Open Boat"	(short story)
"The Right (?) to Bear Arms"	(magazine article)
"Trouble for America's 'Model' Minority"	(magazine article)
"Impressions of Japan"	(essay)
"Hell and Its Outskirts"	(essay)
"Warning: Household Chemicals"	(speech)
"I Have a Dream"	(speech)
"Discover Moses and the Bulrushers"	(Chapter 1 in *Huckleberry Finn*)
"The Nature and Origin of Religion"	(Chapter 1 in *Treatise on the Gods*)
"Simka Returns"	(from the TV series *Taxi*)
"Cooking with Eggs"	(from the TV series *The Frugal Gourmet*)

Note: Quotation marks are not used to enclose a merely descriptive title of a speech, such as Lincoln's Gettysburg Address.

Use double quotation marks to enclose words used in a special sense or to enclose invented words.

Examples

> Not only did the plumber fix my leaking pipes, but he also "plumbed" the depths of my heart.

> When asked what they were doing in the park, the defendants said that they were "wilding."

When you refer to a word as such—i.e., as a word—use underlining (italics). In defining a term, use underlining for the term and use quotations for the actual definition if you have taken the definition from a dictionary.

Examples

From what language do we get the word *ennui*?

From what country does a person come who spells his first name *Georg* instead of *George*?

According to *Webster's New World Dictionary*, a *misogynist* means "one who hates women"; a *misanthrope* means "one who hates all people."

By *eternity*, I mean now. [Notice that in this last example the writer is making up a personal definition; hence, no quotes enclose *now*.]

Placement of Other Marks of Punctuation

The usual practices regarding the placement of other marks of punctuation inside or outside quotation marks are the following:

Place periods and commas inside quotation marks.

Examples

An essay that had a profound effect on Dr. Martin Luther King was Thoreau's "Civil Disobedience."

"The spirits of our fathers rose and told us to avenge our wrongs," Chief Black Hawk said, "or die."

Place colons and semicolons outside quotation marks.

Examples

On Lexington Green on April 19, 1775, some unknown person fired the "shot heard around the world": from Massachusetts to New York, from Pennsylvania to London, from Paris to Vienna and Berlin.

The accomplice in the murder received "life without parole"; the man who pulled the trigger received "death by lethal injection."

When a question mark or an exclamation mark is part of the quotation, place the mark inside the quotation marks.

Examples

Herb's question was a simple one, "When do we begin?"

"Who cares?" Catherine replied.

"Take cover!" the police officer shouted.

When a question mark or an exclamation mark is not part of the quotation, place the mark outside the quotation marks.

Examples

Who said, "Give me liberty, or give me death"?

Were you as inspired as I was when Kate sang "America, the Beautiful"?

Stop calling me "Big Boss"!

EXERCISE 18-8

The following sentences contain errors in the use of quotation marks and other punctuation marks covered in this chapter. Rewrite the sentences so that they follow standard punctuation practices.

1. Frank said that "he had never had a serious illness"

_____

_____

2. Was the most famous of the Civil War songs the Battle Hymn of the Republic.

_____

_____

3. Mike Royko's essay titled Death to the Killers has certainly received much attention recently!

_____

_____

4. Who said To be or not to be—that is the question.

_____

_____

5. "Prior to starting", Francis said "I have one question for you to answer"?

_____

_____

6. In Faulkner's short story titled The Bear, the author often repeats the following words: courage, sacrifice, and truth.

7. In 1982 in *Time* Roger Rosenblatt wrote "Children of War;" in a recent issue of the same magazine the focus shifted in an essay called Child Warriors.

8. According to the dictionary, "infantry" comes from words meaning *very young person, a child, an infant.*

9. Children may not make perfect soldiers, Alessandra Stanley writes, but they make perfectly good ones.

10. Tom remarked It was Will Rogers who said "The income tax has made liars out of more Americans than golf."

11. I believe that President Kennedy in his "Inaugural Address" got Americans to think about space exploration as holding the future of the world?

12. Obscenity is not protected under the "First Amendment" to the "Constitution", the judge replied.

13. The right of the people to keep and bear arms, as stated in the Second Amendment, does not mean that a private citizen has a right to possess a Stinger missile.

_____

_____

14. *The Oz Books* and *Who Makes the Movies* are the essays that I enjoyed most in Gore Vidal's book called "The Second American Revolution".

_____

_____

15. When the men from the "ACE Moving Company" ran over my cat *Fluffy* in the driveway, I had a *moving* experience.

_____

_____

. . . .

E X E R C I S E 1 8 - 9

Finish the following sentences. Include all needed punctuation marks.

1. Dr Hunter said, _____

2. _____Ted asked

3. That information is contained in Chapter 3 titled_____

4. _____is my favorite song

5. The nurse screamed,_____

6. _____was the sign post-ed on the front door of the Arts and Sciences Building.

7. Mrs Potter said that_____

8. _____, Jeffrey said.

9. We students wondered if_____

10. _____, the mob yelled.

. . . .

EXERCISE 18-10

Add needed punctuation to the following sentences.

1. Paul, Tina asked, why don't you call me tonight

2. According to my dictionary, a pretext means an excuse; a reason means a deduction based upon known or presumed facts.

3. Fight Fight Fight the cheerleaders yelled

4. Lt Col Flanders had been a POW for nearly five years

5. With songs like Love Me Tender and Heartbreak Hotel, Elvis Presley broke the silence of what was known as the silent generation

6. Concerning President Nixon's role in the Watergate scandal, Senator Sam Ervin said to witness after witness: What did the President know, and when did he know it

7. What do you hope to learn asked the instructor What do you hope to teach responded the student

8. Rev George A Stallings, Jr, a priest of the Washington, DC, diocese, has broken with the Roman Catholic Church to establish the Imani Temple, a church that will address the needs of African-Americans

9. The term Imani comes from a Swahili word meaning faith

10. Does he spell his last name Bell, Belle, Beal, or Beale John asked And how is it pronounced he added

· · · · · · · · · · · · · · · ·

The Comma

Like end marks and quotation marks, commas help make your meaning clear to the reader. In general, commas signal pauses similar to the pauses in your own speech patterns. Consider how a comma or the lack of a comma can change the meaning of each of the following sentences:

> Attacking the lion frightened Jason and Corey.

> Attacking, the lion frightened Jason and Corey.

Or consider the following sentence:

> When you see a lion get in your car.

Because a comma is omitted, the sentence does not read correctly. In fact, the sentence becomes a subordinate clause fragment. What the writer wanted to say was the following:

> When you see a lion, get in your car.

In written English a few simple rules need to be followed regarding comma usage.

SETTING OFF INDEPENDENT CLAUSES

Use a comma between two independent clauses when they are joined by coordinating conjunctions (and, or, for, so, nor, but, yet) or correlative conjunctions (neither...nor, either...or, etc.).

Examples
> I wanted to fly home, but I had to take the bus.
> Either you pay the rent, or you will be evicted.

Commas may be used alone between independent clauses when those clauses are very short.

Example
> "I came, I saw, I conquered." (Julius Caesar)

Do not use a comma between two predicates joined by a coordinating conjunction or a correlative conjunction.

Examples
> The "Deadhead" fans cheered and applauded when the Grateful Dead came on stage.
> Rosemary neither sought nor got Gregg's help.

You may omit the comma when the main clauses are joined by a coordinating conjunction and when the clauses are very short.

Example
> They stopped and they listened.

E X E R C I S E 19-1

Supply commas as needed in the following sentences.

1. Carol was not early nor was she dressed properly.
2. The warm days of summer finally came and all of us were happy.
3. Chris ran quickly and jumped into the subway car.
4. John was not pleased with his grade but he knew he deserved it.
5. My parents do not want me to enlist in the Navy yet I am determined to join.
6. The basic laws of physics appear complex but are simple.
7. Marie studied and she passed.
8. Either you pay your bills or you can have no more credit.
9. I lived I loved I learned.
10. I was pleased to accept the job offer for the work conditions and the salary were attractive.

SEPARATING ITEMS IN A SERIES

In general, use commas to separate three or more coordinate (parallel) words, phrases or clauses. You may omit the final comma as long as no ambiguity results.

Examples

1. Among female novelists, Toni Morrison, Joyce Carol Oates, and Alice Walker are my favorites. [In this sentence commas separate the three parallel proper nouns used as subjects.]

2. The cave was cold, damp, and dark. [Commas are used to separate three adjective complements in a series.]

3. The Trump story was featured on radio, on television, and in newspapers. [Commas are used to separate a series of three prepositional phrases used as adverbs.]

4. During the 1990 version of the rock opera *Tommy*, Phil Collins sang superbly, Billy Idol pranced brilliantly, and The Who played exceptionally well. [Commas are used to separate a series of independent clauses.]

In a series of two or more coordinate adjectives modifying a noun or pronoun, use commas to separate the adjectives. However, if the adjectives are joined by a conjunction, no comma is used.

Examples

1. A large, menacing dog greeted me with a growl. [*Large* and *menacing* are two coordinate adjectives modifying the noun *dog*. A comma is needed to separate the two adjectives. No comma comes between the final adjective and the word(s) modified.]

2. A large and menacing dog greeted me with a growl. [In this instance, since the adjectives are joined by a coordinating conjunction, no comma is needed.]

3. Sheila was a truthful, dependable, devoted friend. [Commas are needed after the coordinate adjectives *truthful* and *dependable*. A comma is not needed after *devoted* since it comes immediately before the noun it modifies.]

Some adjectives seem so closely connected that they need no commas between them: ten little old ladies *and* three rare American coins. *If you are unsure of whether to use a comma in such cases, change the order of the adjectives:* old little ten ladies *and* rare American three coins. *If the sound is strange, you may omit the commas in the original phrase.*

EXERCISE 19-2

Supply commas as needed in the following sentences.

1. It is a bright sunny October day.

2. Hawaii Kauai Maui Molokai and Oahu are the five major islands that comprise the state of Hawaii.

3. She enjoyed good health had plenty of money and possessed much wisdom.

4. This semester I am studying English astronomy history and art.

5. My agent told me that I must get additional car insurance.

6. The flags flew the guns roared and the troops moved forward.

7. The land we walk on the water we drink and the air we breathe are all endangered by pollution.

8. The company was blessed with intelligent energetic loyal employees.

9. Where he came from what he wanted and where he went remained a mystery.

10. George Clinton Levi Morton Hannibal Hamlin and Elbridge Gerry were four men with one thing in common: they were all vice presidents of the United States.

. . . .

SETTING OFF INTRODUCTORY WORDS, PHRASES, AND CLAUSES

Use a comma after the following introductory words: conjunctive adverbs, transitional expressions, yes or no and other mild interjections.

Study the following examples:

    1. **Conjunctive Adverbs**

        However, I will be able to attend the afternoon meeting.

        Additionally, Ms. Johnson will be attending the meeting.

        Note: The comma should be omitted after an adverb that closely modifies the predicate or the sentence as such: Maybe she will win.

2. **Transitional Expressions**

For instance, well over 400 new films were released in the United States in each of the last three years.

In summary, the film industry is not suffering an economic decline.

3. *Yes* or *No* **and Other Mild Interjections (***indeed, oh, well, why***)**

Yes, I know that I am late.

Well, why didn't you leave on time?

E X E R C I S E 19-3

Supply commas as needed in the following sentences.

1. For example I like to read such magazines as *Captain America Spider-Man* and *Silver Surfer.*

2. Oh I thought you knew that China has the largest population in the world.

3. In conclusion acid rain continues to be a major threat to the forests of America.

4. No I do not know what caused the accident.

5. Indeed I will complete the project on time.

6. Perhaps we can help you.

7. Unfortunately the shooting victim did not recover from his wounds.

8. In addition twenty-seven million people in the United States are unable to read well enough to adequately function in society.

9. In short the nation needs to do more to help people who have reading problems.

10. In brief we can do better.

. . . .

Usually, introductory participial, infinitive, and prepositional phrases require a comma after them.

Study the following examples:

1. **Introductory Participial Phrase**

Knowing that the battle was lost, the Iraqi general ordered his troops to surrender.

2. **Introductory Infinitive Phrase**

   To succeed in the stock market, you would do well to have a good financial advisor.

3. **Introductory Prepositional Phrases**

   Beyond the Appalachian Mountains in the early 1800s, the West was a virgin land.

Commas do not follow phrases that function as subjects of sentences. Study the following examples:

1. To get a college education is my goal. [The infinitive phrase functions as subject.]

2. Getting a college education is my goal. [The gerund phrase functions as subject.]

3. In the woods is fine. [The prepositional phrase functions as subject.]

In general, a comma is not needed after a very short introductory phrase: In September Jabar will visit us. However, a comma may be needed for clarity: At twenty-one, people can legally drink alcohol in Maryland.

EXERCISE 19-4

Supply commas as needed in the following sentences.

1. To win the marathon you will need to endure much pain.

2. Having returned from a four-week vacation Paula was refreshed.

3. Convinced that his cause was just Ted decided to pursue the matter in the courts.

4. Watching an exciting football game causes my blood pressure to rise.

5. At the start of the festivities in Dallas President Kennedy appeared relaxed.

6. Pleased by the results of the poll Mary Landis felt that she could win the race for governor.

7. After studying all night for the history test Tom was too tired to concentrate.

8. Becoming one of the nation's best professional photographers is my ambition in life.

9. Built over two centuries ago the mill was still in excellent condition.

10. To be an honor student and a fine athlete required all of Barbara's talents.

· ·

In general, an introductory adverb clause is followed by a comma. However, a brief introductory adverb clause does not need to be followed by a comma as long as no confusion results from the omission.

Examples

1. When Andrew Carnegie came to the United States from Scotland, he arrived without a penny in his pocket.

2. While working in the steel industry, Carnegie became a multimillionaire. [This introductory clause is an elliptical adverb clause, one whose subject is implied rather than expressed.]

3. Before Carnegie died he had given much of his money to fund public libraries and colleges. [The comma is not required after a short introductory adverb clause.]

EXERCISE 19-5

Supply commas as needed in the following sentences.

1. When William Faulkner was awarded the Nobel Prize for Literature many critics were surprised.

2. Because Hawaii has an inviting climate and beautiful beaches the state attracts millions of tourists each year.

3. While exploring the steamy jungles of Malaysia Mr. Thompson contracted malaria.

4. When Tim left he forgot his car keys.

5. Though aspirin has had many medical uses a new use was recently discovered: stroke prevention.

· ·

SETTING OFF NONESSENTIAL WORDS, PHRASES, OR CLAUSES

Nonessential words, phrases, and clauses are those that may be omitted from a sentence without changing its essential meaning. Though every part of a sentence should have meaning, nonessential elements are *not basic* to the intended message. They give helpful but not necessary information. Nonessential elements are also called *nonrestrictive*.

Essential or restrictive elements must be in the sentence; if they are not there, the meaning of the sentence is seriously altered.

Examples

Physicians who receive their medical degrees from foreign universities must be certified to practice medicine in the United States. [Since the subordinate adjectival clause (*who receive their medical degrees from foreign universities*) is essential to the meaning of the sentence, no commas are placed around it.]

March 26, 1979, which was the highpoint of Jimmy Carter's presidency, witnessed the signing of the Egyptian-Israeli peace treaty by President Sadat and Prime Minister Begin. [The subordinate clause (*which was the highpoint of Jimmy Carter's presidency*) is not essential to the message of the sentence, for it does not narrow the focus of that message. As a result, commas must be placed around the clause.]

Remember: Ask youself if the sentence element is absolutely necessary to the meaning of the sentence. If it is necessary, place no commas around it; if it is not necessary, place commas around it.

Place commas around nonessential phrases and clauses.

Examples

Imelda Marcos, dressed entirely in black, smiled as she entered the Manhattan courtroom. [The modifying participial phrase (*dressed entirely in black*) is not essential to the meaning of the sentence.]

The bald eagle, with its majestic appearance, is but one of many animals facing extinction in the United States. [The prepositional phrase (*with its majestic appearance*) is not essential, for it can be omitted without any damage to the basic meaning of the sentence.]

Mr. Baker, who has been teaching for twenty years, was named Teacher of the Year for the sixth time. [The modifying adjectival clause (*who has been teaching for twenty years*) is not essential to the meaning of the sentence.]

In this photo the girl dressed in red is my sister. [Since the participial phrase (*dressed in red*) is essential to the selection of the girl, no commas are used around it.]

The physician whom you are looking for is in the emergency room. [The subordinate clause (*whom you are looking for*) is essential in order to indicate which physician is intended. No commas are needed around the clause.]

In general, place commas around transitional and parenthetical expressions.

Transitional expressions include such words or phrases as *finally, however, moreover, therefore, after all, in fact, for example, in summary*, and *on the other hand*. Transitional expressions help to make clear the relationships that exist between ideas, and parenthetical expressions give supplemental or additional information, but neither is essential to the meaning of the sentence.

Examples

1. **Transitional Expressions**

   Blues guitarist B. B. King has recorded 300 singles since 1949; his albums, moreover, number seventy. He has won five Grammy awards; he has, in addition, received a medal from President Bush for outstanding contributions to American music. B. B. King is, in short, an exceptionally popular and talented musician.

2. **Parenthetical Expressions**

   The Bank of Credit & Commerce International was, according to the CIA's Robert Gates, "the bank of crooks and criminals." A full investigation of the bank's illegal operations, the U.S. Justice Department thinks, may take years.

Notes: If a transitional or parenthetical expression comes at the end of a sentence, place a comma before that expression:

> The Persian Gulf may need decades to recover from the pollution it suffered during the recent war, experts say.

In general, a parenthetical expression that shows contrast requires a comma or commas:

> India's Taj Mahal, not Donald Trump's, is a tomb.
>
> Proceed with caution, never with haste.

Reminder: In general, when a transitional or parenthetical expression is used to join independent clauses in a compound sentence, that expression is preceded by a semicolon and followed by a comma: Alex was the stronger athlete; nevertheless, his opponent won the race.

Other Nonessential Words and Phrases

Other nonessential words and phrases that require commas are the following:

1. **Direct Address: Names**

   You, Captain Davis, will lead Alpha Company.

   What's the answer, Paula?

   My colleagues and distinguished guests, I am honored to introduce to you the man who saved us all from polio.

   Mr. Pavlov, when did you leave Russia?

2. **Attached Statements Forming Questions**

   He can assume command, can't he?

   It is true, is it not, that sulfuric acid is the key element in acid rain?

   The report suggests, does it not, that our forests are in danger?

3. **Nonessential Appositives**

   An appositive is a noun or a noun phrase that follows another noun or noun phrase and expands its meaning. A nonessential appositive contains additional but not essential information about the noun or noun phrase modified and hence requires commas:

   Curtis Strange, a golfer envied by professionals and amateurs alike, won the U.S. Open in 1988 and 1989. [The appositive, *a golfer envied by professionals and amateurs alike*, is interesting information, but it is not essential to the meaning of the sentence. Commas must precede and follow the phrase.]

   H. L. Mencken, Baltimore's most famous writer, is best known for his series of books titled *The American Language*. [The appositive, *Baltimore's most famous writer*, gives descriptive but not essential information. Commas are thus required.]

   The British scientist Charles Darwin is best known for his book *Origin of Species*. [In this sentence both *Charles Darwin* and *Origin of Species* are appositives, but they are essential to the meaning of the sentence. In this case, then, no commas are used. Consider how the sentence reads if the appositives are removed:

   The British scientist is best known for his book.

   Clearly, the removal of the appositives seriously alters the meaning of the sentence.]

4. **Absolute Phrases**

An absolute phrase is one that is not grammatically connected to a specific part of a sentence; in effect, an absolute phrase modifies the whole sentence. In general, an absolute phrase is composed of a noun or pronoun plus a participle (and any words associated with the participle). A comma follows the absolute phrase if the phrase comes at the start of the sentence; a comma precedes the absolute phrase if the phrase comes at the end of the sentence.

Their mission being hopeless, the men abandoned the attempted rescue of the hostages.

Weather permitting, graduation exercises will be held in Wilson Stadium.

The pilot made an emergency landing, the fuel having been exhausted.

EXERCISE 19-6

Supply commas as needed in the following sentences.

1. What is your opinion Mr. Owens?

2. Theodore Dreiser's novel *The Financier* according to one critic is filled with "irrelevant facts."

3. Thomas Huxley not Charles Darwin popularized the theory of evolution.

4. His confession made the defendant asked for mercy.

5. The Cuban missile crisis which was the most serious of all Cold War crises paved the way to the first arms limitation treaty between the United States and the Soviet Union.

6. Of Boris Yeltsin the leader of the Russian Republic Britain's Margaret Thatcher has said that "He is like an Irishman."

7. The Russian Republic along with other members of the old Soviet Union has become part of a new federation of independent nations.

8. Katherine Bates an English professor at Wellesley College wrote "America, the Beautiful" in 1893 her words inspired by the view from Pike's Peak.

9. Arnold Schwarzenegger a thin and weak child decided early that his future rested with bodybuilding.

10. A reporter for the *Baltimore Sun* Alice Steinbach won a Pulitzer Prize for her feature writing in 1985.

11. Las Vegas Atlantic City notwithstanding is still a favorite of gamblers.

12. Much more than American pressure however will be needed for peace to break out in the Middle East.

13. In 1990 the Greyhound Company which went greatly in debt during a strike filed for bankruptcy.

14. The fire victims clad only in their underwear rushed from the burning home.

15. John F. Kennedy was the youngest man ever elected president of the United States; on the other hand Ronald Reagan was the oldest man ever elected to that office.

. . . .

OTHER STANDARD USES OF THE COMMA

In addition to the uses noted thus far, there are several other conventional practices regarding comma usage:

1. **In Dates**

   September 17, 1974, was the date of his birth. [Notice that commas are needed after *17* and after *1974*. However, no commas are needed in the following constructions: He was born on 17 September 1974. He was born in September 1974.]

2. **Between Names and Degrees or Titles**

   Charles Hyland, R.N., was on duty.

   Marie Willis, Ph.D., earned her degree at Harvard University.

   Jozef Cardinal Glemp, Archbishop of Warsaw, was the speaker.

   David Dinkins, Mayor of New York, attended the meeting.

   [No comma is used between a name and II, III, etc.: Queen Elizabeth II.]

3. **In Addresses**

   Her address is 1212 Old Niles Lane, Baltimore, MD 21228.

4. **In Salutations and Closings in Letters**

   In informal correspondence, use a comma after the salutation:

   Dear Tony,

   Dear Uncle Jim,

In formal correspondence, use a colon (:) after the salutation:

Dear Senator Sarbanes:

Dear Mr. Richmond:

Use a comma after the complimentary close in all correspondence: Sincerely yours, Faithfully,

5. **In Numbers of More Than Four Digits**

In numbers of more than four digits, use commas to separate the numbers by inserting a comma every three digits, starting from the right:

1,500 (The comma is optional with four digits.)

15,000

150,000

1,500,000

Long numbers in addresses (12389 Frederick Road), telephone numbers (1-301-000-9854), zip codes (21390-7865), or years (1500) do not require commas.

6. **For Direct Quotations**

When expressions such as *she remarked*, *he said*, and *they yelled* are used in conjunction with a direct quotation, commas set off the quotation:

"I hope to see you in March," Isak remarked.

Roger said, "Isn't the meeting in May?"

"In fact," Beryl added, "the meeting is scheduled for the afternoon of June 15."

Langston yelled, "Get your dates straight!"

TO ASSIST CLARITY IN OTHER WAYS

Commas are helpful in making meaning clear in other ways:

Examples

Johnson took the train to New York; Paulson, the bus to Atlanta. (Here a comma points to the omission of a word.)

All who failed, failed miserably. (In this instance, a comma assists a smooth reading of a sentence that has adjoining, repeated words in it.)

EXERCISE 19-7

Insert commas as needed in the following sentences.

1. Andrey Sakharov who was born on May 21 1921 and died on December 14 1989 received the Nobel Prize for Peace in 1975.

2. Someone once remarked "Those who can do; those who can't teach."

3. Laurence Olivier the Baron of Brighton was the fifth actor in British history to be buried in Westminster Abbey.

4. The Federal Home Loan Bank Board is located at 1700 G St. N. W. Washington D.C.

5. Created on June 24 1948 the Selective Service System has its national headquarters in Washington D.C. and can be reached at 1-202-724-0820.

6. Hirohito Emperor of Japan reigned from December 25 1926 to January 7 1989.

7. The official motto of Maryland is "Manly deeds womanly words."

8. Maryland has a total area of 10460 square miles and a population of approximately 4700000.

9. Maryland's official bird is the Baltimore oriole; official dog the Chesapeake Bay retriever; official fish the Rockfish; official flower the Black-eyed Susan; official fossil the *Ecphora Quadricostata* an extinct snail.

10. One Marylander once remarked "Having an official fossil is one thing but why don't we have a giant dinosaur rather than a lowly snail?"

. . . .

EXERCISE 19-8

The following exercise covers all uses of the comma. Insert commas as needed.

1. If the earth's average temperature were to rise even by a few degrees the implications for sea-level dwellers would be enormous.

2. In the 1990s AIDS continues to be a serious threat to many developing nations especially African nations none of which has been able to fully deal with the crisis.

3. The *Exxon Valdez* ran aground on March 24 1989 in Prince William Sound Alaska; however the effects of the oil spill that followed the grounding have yet to be fully realized.

4. When Ferdinand Marcos died on 28 September 1989 in Honolulu Hawaii after having ruled the Philippines for twenty years he stood accused of having stolen at least $100000000 from the people of the Philippines.

5. Just before dying Marcos said "My yearly salary was only $5000 and I presently have no funds at all."

6. Corazon Aquino the former president of the Philippines noted that the actual theft may have been billions of dollars.

7. According to some scientists an aspirin-size piece of a white dwarf a star whose atoms have been greatly compacted weighs about one ton.

8. Hydrogen is the most abundant element in the universe; the next most abundant helium; the least abundant perhaps technetium promethium astatine or francium.

9. Thomas Alva Edison an American inventor who lived from 1847 to 1931 held the patent for the electric light the phonograph the mimeograph and various motion picture cameras and projectors.

10. John Kennedy's Inaugural Address given on January 20 1961 included these moving words: "In your hands my fellow citizens more than in mine will rest the final success or failure of our course. Since this country was founded each generation of Americans has been summoned to give testimony to its national loyalty."

11. According to statistics released by the United Nations there are 1914789000 radios and 749424000 televisions in use in the world today.

12. Moreover most of the radios and televisions are in the United States.

13. The total population in the United States increased by about 9 percent from 1980 to 1990, but the number of Hispanics increased by about 33 percent the largest increase by any segment of the American population.

14. Approximately two million Hispanics in the United States according to the National Academy of Sciences are illegal immigrants.

15. To solve the illegal immigration problem the United States will need the full cooperation of Central and South American nations especially Mexico.

EXERCISE 19-9

In the following paragraph, cross out any incorrectly used commas, and add commas as needed.

On October 4 1957 the U.S.S.R. launched *Sputnik 1* into orbit around the earth and the U.S. launched *Explorer 1* its first satellite on January 31 1958. Since those launches other nations such as France Japan and China have sent satellites into orbit. In fact hundreds of artificial satellites, now orbit the earth. Communications satellites in particular, have changed the way we live. Orbiting the earth every 24 hours these satellites are used by many businesses industries and governments not to mention by ordinary people in their homes. For example when anchorman, Bernard Shaw, correspondent Peter Arnett, and reporter John Holliman, broadcast from Baghdad to the world the start of the Gulf War communications satellites made the live transmissions possible. "This feels like we're in the center of hell!," said CNN's Bernard Shaw his tone reflecting the tension-filled atmosphere. As a result, of communications satellites 22300 miles high countless viewers shared that tension. J. C. Penney's satellite network which cost the company $8 million allows viewers around the country to view product displays, and fashion shows broadcast from the company's headquarters in Manhattan. According to Paul Rush a vice president of the company "It's been an astounding success." Communications satellites make it possible for the eighteen nationwide printing plants of *The Wall Street Journal*, to receive the total contents of the paper for processing. When a wife in Alaska telephones her soldier-husband stationed in Korea, and says "Paul you have a son" communications satellites made the call possible.

. . . .

· · · · · · · · · · · · · · · ·

The Semicolon and Colon

Now that you have learned to use end marks, quotation marks, and commas effectively, you have only two punctuation marks left to learn: the semicolon (;) and the colon (:). Effective use of the semicolon and the colon will help you to write unified and coherent sentences.

THE SEMICOLON

The semicolon is more than a comma and less than a period. Put another way, the semicolon signals a pause greater than a comma but less than a period. The semicolon is especially useful in pointing out a contrast between two independent clauses or the equality between two independent clauses. The contrast or equality (balance) signaled by the semicolon is the mark of parallel structure. The rules for the use of the semicolon are as follows:

Use a semicolon between independent clauses not connected by a comma and a coordinating conjunction (and, or, for, but, nor, so, yet).

Examples

During the 1980s college campuses experienced few demonstrations; most students were more interested in studying a cause than in promoting one.

Huck Finn liked his life on the Mississippi River; his two guardians preferred life in a small town.

Note: If the independent clauses are very short, you may use commas to join them. Example: Cats hissed, dogs barked, Christina ran.

EXERCISE 20-1

Each of the following sentences is compound; each contains two independent clauses. Use a semicolon to separate the main clauses.

1. I must forgive you you must forgive me.

2. Mr. Franklin's history course is hard Mr. Whitney's is easy.

3. Mr. Slater took the train to Newark Mrs. Slater took the bus.

4. What we know of Shakespeare's life can be stated in a few pages what we know of the life of Queen Elizabeth I requires books to document.

5. George Washington enjoyed many pleasures at Mount Vernon he endured a great deal of hard work as well.

. . . .

EXERCISE 20-2

Make compound sentences of your own by adding a semicolon and another independent clause to the independent clause provided in the following items.

1. My sister is planning to become a banker _____

   _____

2. I know what being poor means _____

   _____

3. Watch out for cracks in the ice_____

   _____

4. Gloria usually gets what she wants_____

   _____

5. Mr. Nelson's front yard was a sea of flowers and shrubs _____

   _____

. . . .

Use a semicolon to connect two independent clauses joined by a conjunctive adverb.

In general, a comma follows the conjunctive adverb. **Note:** A comma does not follow every conjunctive adverb that joins two main clauses. Let your ear be your guide to the pauses you want.

Among the conjunctive adverbs are the following: thus, also, however, therefore, then, nevertheless, in fact, for example, in fine, in sum, moreover, as a result, still, in conclusion, meanwhile, likewise, futhermore, otherwise, consequently, besides, accordingly, further, finally.

Remember that a transitional phrase, such as *in conclusion*, can function as a conjunctive adverb.

Examples

Adventures of Huckleberry Finn was published in England in 1884; however, the American edition did not appear until 1885.

You should study very hard; otherwise you may not pass the test.

E X E R C I S E 20-3

Each of the following sentences contains two independent clauses joined by a conjunctive adverb. Punctuate the sentences correctly.

1. Frank was my friend nevertheless he did not help me.

2. The captain wanted to reach port before dark accordingly he called for more speed.

3. The Dutch traders wanted their new home to be like the one they had known in Holland consequently they called their settlement New Amsterdam.

4. In several books Mark Twain attacked people who lusted after money still he struggled all his life to become wealthy.

5. I do not think that the construction work will be finished this month further I suspect that we will need three more months to finish the job.

E X E R C I S E 20-4

Add an appropriate conjunctive adverb and independent clause to each of the following independent clauses. Be sure to place the semicolon and comma (if needed) correctly. You may want to refer to the list of conjunctive adverbs.

1. My brother Bob had a severe headache _____
   _____

2. The chick pecked and pecked from inside its shell _____

    _____

3. This drug has some short-term and very positive results _____

    _____

4. I have an excellent exercise program _____

    _____

5. Jerry walked slowly and silently into the haunted house _____

    _____

. . . .

When two main clauses are joined by a coordinating conjunction (and, or, for, nor, so, but, yet) *and when these clauses are long and have other punctuation within them, use a semicolon to separate the main clauses. In such cases, the semicolon helps you to achieve maximum clarity.*

Example

> Citizens of the United States can travel freely from city to city, from state to state, and from America to other countries; but in some other countries, such travel cannot be taken for granted.

Use a semicolon to separate items in a series if there are commas within them.

Ordinarily, commas are used to separate items in a series.

Example

> On our cruise we visited St. Maarten, Martinique, and St. Thomas.

In some sentences that have items in a series semicolons are needed to make relationships clear.

Examples

> At the conference I met Kelly Clark, president of Davis and Jones, Inc.; Mr. Gerald Martin, general manager, Hancock Industries, Ltd.; Ben Cheever and Debbie Levine, two former associates of mine; and Mary Whitfield, head of Barker Productions, Inc.
>
> Australia has the oldest known rocks, 4.4 billion years old; the oldest known fossils, 3.5 billion years old; and the oldest known petroleum, 1.4 billion years old.

EXERCISE 20-5

Apply the four semicolon rules to the sentences below.

1. The suspect gave the officer three addresses: 9898 Tate Lane, Los Angeles, California, 2223 Main Street, Mayview, Delaware, and 712 Freemont Drive, Elkton, New York.

2. Laura expects to vacation in France however she does not know her departure date.

3. At the ceremony were Fred Telltale, winner of the Free Speech Award, Carol Writewell, recipient of the Short Story Gold Medal, and Marcus Uno, a former student of mine, winner of the Silver Trophy for Poetry.

4. We visited Disney World in Florida my brother Lex and his family travelled to Pennsylvania to ski.

5. You have only one week to read this long novel consequently you had better start reading it right away.

6. In the prison camp he saw hours become days, days become weeks, weeks become months, and months become years nevertheless he retained the hope of being rescued.

7. Daniel failed his final examination in astronomy as a result he plans to repeat the course in the summer.

8. The Catholic church in Brickville was built in 1815 it was dedicated on Christmas day in that year.

9. After years of internal fighting, Cambodia has become one of the poorest nations in Asia meanwhile, comparatively speaking, Thailand has become one of the richest.

10. Bette Davis was certainly an acclaimed actress for example she received ten Academy Award nominations and won twice.

THE COLON

The colon (:) calls attention to something to follow, or it may call attention to or introduce the strong connection that exists between two statements. Put another way, the colon looks ahead to the completion of a thought. The rules governing the use of the colon are the following:

Use a colon to introduce a list after such words as the following *or as follows or after a noun that identifies the list.*

Examples

During the summer I read the following: *Megatrends 2000*, *The New Russians*, and *The Trials of Life*.

In my English class there are only three students: Dominick Robbins, Dallas Tucker, and Tim Selman.

Do not use a colon between a predicate and its objects or between a preposition and its objects.

Examples

Change: Howard enjoyed: fishing, hunting, and hiking.

To: Howard enjoyed fishing, hunting, and hiking.

Change: Janet's breakfast consisted of: ham, eggs, milk, and toast.

To: Janet's breakfast consisted of ham, eggs, milk, and toast.

A colon may be used to separate two main clauses, the second of which clarifies or makes more concrete the first one.

Examples

Philip Slater's conclusion in *The Pursuit of Loneliness* is an unhappy one: American culture is suffering from serious social ills at every level.

The jury's decision was unmistakably clear: the defendant was guilty as charged.

Use a colon to introduce a formal question or quotation.

Examples

The question is: how much money will the trip cost?

President Kennedy declared: "If a free society cannot help the many who are poor, it cannot save the few who are rich."

Colons are also used to separate parts of a title and numerals referring to the time.

Examples

The Pursuit of Loneliness: American Culture at the Breaking Point has caused many Americans to question the health of their society.

I expect to see you at 11:15 A.M.

E X E R C I S E 2 0 - 6

In the blank write *C* if the colon is correctly used; write *X* if the colon is incorrectly used. Rewrite all incorrectly punctuated sentences.

_____ 1. On the game show I won: a washing machine, a television set, and a new car.

_____

_____

_____ 2. I have three favorite writers: Isaac Asimov, Lewis Thomas, and Stephen Jay Gould.

_____

_____

_____ 3. I was concerned with: the new home's total cost and monthly payments.

_____

_____

_____ 4. Marco plans to visit four countries: Burma, Thailand, Japan, and South Korea.

_____

_____

_____ 5. Thomas read: *Freedom to Learn, On Becoming a Person,* and *Human Destiny.*

_____

_____

E X E R C I S E 20-7

Write five sentences using the colon. In your sentences use the phrases as indicated below.

(the following:)

1. _____

_____

(favorite sports:)

2. _____

_____

(promised three things:)

3. _____

_____

(these gifts:)

4. _____

_____

(three wishes:)

5. _____

_____

. . . .

E X E R C I S E 20-8

The following sentences contain errors in the use (or non-use) of the comma, the semicolon, and the colon. Make corrections above the errors.

1. Last week I saw three movies, *The Rocketeer; Terminator 2: Judgment Day;* and *Robin Hood; Prince of Thieves.*

2. Concerning the nature of government, New Jersey's James Florio has stated his position clearly, "The issue isn't more or less government. It's dumb versus smart government."

3. Moreover; astrology may be the study of the stars and the planets and their influence on human behavior, however; astronomy is the *scientific* study of the heavenly bodies.

4. Iran was previously known as Persia, on the other hand, Iraq was formerly known as Mesopotamia.

5. Weather includes the following, rain, snow, wind, and temperature.

6. President James K. Polk in his Inaugural Address delivered on March 4, 1845, made these curious remarks; "All distinctions of birth or of rank have been abolished. All are entitled to equal rights and equal protection."

7. On March 4, 1861, President Lincoln stated in his Inaugural Address, "I have no purpose directly or indirectly to interfere with the institution of slavery in the states where it exists. I believe I have no lawful right to do so and I have no inclination to do so."

8. At 8;45 P.M. Dr. Diori returned to his patient to see if the medication was working, unfortunately; his patient had died.

9. At the farmers' market I bought: tomatoes; corn; radishes; and lettuce.

10. In recent years a number of women have sought and won the highest elected office in their nations; Margaret Thatcher, former prime minister of Great Britain, Gro Brundtland, former Norwegian prime minister, Corazon Aquino, former president of the Philippines, and Violeta Chamorro, president of Nicaragua.

· ·

E X E R C I S E 20-9

The following paragraph contains errors in the use of commas, semicolons, and colons. Make corrections above the errors.

When Americans think of the Gulf War, they can take comfort in knowing that their troops were led by two great generals, Colin Powell, Chairman of the Joint Chiefs of Staff, "Stormin' Norman" Schwarzkopf, Commanding General, Allied Forces. From the very birth of the United States, moreover; the nation has been blessed with some outstanding generals. In 1775 George Washington took command of: the ill-equipped and ill-trained Continental Army, by 1781 he had transformed it into a fighting force superior to that of Great Britain. In the War of 1812, Andrew Jackson found his army outnumbered two to one, however, he led his troops to a decisive victory over the British at the Battle of New Orleans. During the Mexican War, Zachary Taylor defeated the huge army of General Santa Ana; and captured Monterrey in 1847. Called "Unconditional Surrender" Grant by his troops; Ulysses S. Grant defeated the Confederate troops at Vicksburg and Chattanooga in 1863, as a result; President Lincoln named him supreme commander a year later. By 1865 Grant had followed victory with victory, Lee was left with no choice except to surrender. During World War II Dwight D. Eisenhower became: Supreme Allied Commander and the first United States five-star general, he led his troops to victory over Germany in May 1945. Washington, Jackson, Taylor, Grant, Eisenhower—all of them went on to become presidents of the United States, perhaps Colin Powell or Norman Schwarzkopf will do the same.

. . . .

. . . .

Capital Letters, Apostrophes, and Underlining

In this chapter you will learn how and why writers use capital letters, apostrophes, and underlining (or *italics*). You will learn certain mechanical conventions (or rules) that writers have adopted over the years. These rules help to make the writing clearer and the reading easier.

CAPITAL LETTERS

The rules for the use of capital letters are not really rules at all, but the practices used by writers to make readers take careful notice of certain words. For example, the first letter of the first word of a sentence is capitalized to alert the reader to the start of a sentence. Proper nouns, such as Jamaica, Maria Lukoski, and Operation Desert Storm, are capitalized to show their importance. Capitals can also show what a word means. There is a key difference between jack and Jack, between being an odd fellow and belonging to the Odd Fellows (a fraternal group), and between china and China. What practices should you follow?

First Words

Capitalize the first letter of the first word of each sentence that you write.

Example

An up-to-date dictionary will indicate whether a word is a proper noun by capitalizing its first letter.

If a colon is followed by more than one sentence, a capital letter begins each sentence.

Example

The committee had three main questions: What was known? Who knew it? When was it known?

However, consider the following sentences:

> I enjoy three sports: swimming, jogging, and wrestling.
>
> He knew that he would lose the race: he had sprained his ankle.

The noun phrase, *swimming, jogging,* and *wrestling,* is a mere list. In the second sentence, the colon is followed by a single independent clause, one which simply fulfills the meaning contained in the first one.

Capitalize the first letter of the first word of a quoted sentence.

Example

> After the fifty-six men had signed the Declaration of Independence, Benjamin Franklin said: "If we do not hang together, we shall all hang separately!"

Capitalize the first letter of the first word, the last word, and any other significant words in a title. Do not, however, capitalize articles (a, an, the), short conjunctions (and, or, if, etc.), and short prepositions (at, in, of, etc.) unless the title starts with one of them.

Example

> *Of Mice and Men* (book)
>
> *Tender Is the Night* (book)
>
> *The Sea Around Us* (book)
>
> "Alternate Sources of Fuel" (chapter title)
>
> "The Road Not Taken" (poem)
>
> *Star Trek VI* (film)

Be sure to capitalize the first letter of a subtitle:

Examples

> *Unreliable Sources: A Guide to Detecting Bias in the News Media* (book)
>
> *Poison Pen: The Unauthorized Biography of Kitty Kelley* (book)

A and *The* are capitalized because they begin a subtitle following the colon.

E X E R C I S E 2 1 - 1

Put a line through all words that need capitals in the following sentences. Above each crossed-out word write the capitalized form of the word.

1. I very much enjoyed reading the following books: *men who hate women & the women who love them, half of man is woman,* and *fire in the belly.*

2. i have two key concerns: does she love me? and if so, why does she love me?

3. every man and woman who has served in the military can recall these famous sentences: "if it moves, salute it. if it doesn't move, pick it up. if you can't pick it up, paint it."

4. kennedy's time in office, as he said in 1961, was one of challenge: "we face a challenge in our own hemisphere, and indeed wherever else the freedom of human beings is at stake."

5. writers can come up with some fascinating titles: *from front porch to back seat: courtship in twentieth century america, love and other infectious diseases,* and *some people, places and things that will not appear in my next novel.*

. . . .

PROPER NOUNS

Capitalize the first letter of a proper noun. A proper noun is the name of a *specific* person, place, or thing. Adjectives formed from proper nouns must also be capitalized. Words that refer to *general classes* of people, places, or things are common nouns and are not capitalized.

Example

Proper Nouns	Common Nouns
Nelson Mandela	man
Empire State Building	building
Silver Star	medal
the Renaissance	rebirth
Marxism	socialism

Remember that adjectives made from proper nouns must be capitalized. For example, from the proper noun *Freud* comes the proper adjective *Freudian* (as in *Freudian* theories), and from the proper noun *Shakespeare* comes the proper adjective *Shakespearean* (as in *Shakespearean* plays). Below is a style sheet for capitalization. Use it as a guide.

Style Sheet for Capitalization

Capitals	No Capitals
President George Washington	a president
Chief Justice Rehnquist	a judge
Queen Elizabeth II	a queen
Charles F. White, M.D.	a physician
Senator Tom Cook, Sr.	a senator
Houston, Texas	a city, a state
Sun Belt; Lake District; the South	geographical name or location
South China Sea, Indian Ocean	a sea, an ocean
Panama Canal	a canal
Brooklyn Bridge	a bridge
Statue of Liberty	a monument
New Jersey	a battleship
Los Angeles Times	a newspaper
Mars	a planet, a deity
Christ, Allah, Jehovah, Pan, Shiva	names of deities
Sunday	a day
July	a month
Martin Luther King, Jr., Day	a holiday
Rosh Hashanah, Christmas, Ramadan	religious holidays
World War II, Vietnam War	wars
the Talmud, the Gospels, the Koran	sacred writings
a Christian, a Jew, a Moslem	a follower of a religion
Democratic Party, Republican Party	political parties
National Association for the Advancement of Colored People (NAACP)	an organization promoting equal rights
Internal Revenue Service (IRS)	a government agency
University of Georgia	a university

Capitals	No Capitals
History 101	a history course
English, French, Spanish	a language or people
Madison Avenue, U.S. Route 40	an avenue, a highway
United States Constitution	a constitution
Slick hair cream, Pepsi, Coca-Cola	a brand name, a trademark
Baltimore Orioles	a baseball team
"America, the Beautiful"	a patriotic song
Nuclear Test-Ban Treaty	a treaty
Cat's Cradle	a novel, a book
United Nations	a multi-national organization
Old Man Winter, Mother Nature	winter, nature
DDT	an insecticide
Roe vs. Wade	a court trial (or decision)

Notes:

1. Capitalize words showing family relationship when those words are used in a title before a name (*Aunt Joan, Uncle Fred*) or by themselves as names (*Mother and Father, I love you.*). Do not capitalize words showing family relationship when those words follow a possessive pronoun or noun (*my brother, Tony's aunt*).

2. Do not capitalize seasons, but do capitalize months, days, and holidays.

3. Do capitalize geographical regions such as the *East* or the *Midwest*, but do not capitalize directions: Should I go *south* or *north* on Route 332?

E X E R C I S E 21-2

Put a line through all words that need capitals in the following sentences. Below each sentence, write the capitalized forms of the words. The spaces match the number of capitalizations you will need to make.

1. James baldwin's go tell it on the mountain is a novel with many autobiographical elements.

_____ _____ _____ _____

_____

2. The british museum has the largest collection of books in london, england.

_____ _____ _____ _____

3. The american red cross has an excellent reputation.

_____   _____   _____

4. Father, did my grandfather fight in the battle of the bulge in world war II.

_____   _____   _____   _____

5. God is known by many names: heavenly father, adonai, and yahweh, among many others.

_____   _____   _____   _____

6. Have you ever met an eskimo?

_____

7. I will be in new york on the first friday in august.

_____   _____   _____   _____

8. My favorite magazines are _time_ and _changing times._

_____   _____   _____

9. Although uncle frank was a member of the green bay packers, my uncle also enjoyed playing baseball and basketball.

_____   _____   _____   _____

_____

10. The most interesting chapter in joseph campbell's _the hero with a thousand faces_ is "the meeting with the goddess."

_____   _____   _____   _____

_____   _____   _____   _____

_____

11. Please, mom, let's leave now.

_____

12. Kuwait is a country located at the head of the persian gulf on the arabian peninsula.

_____   _____   _____   _____

13. The baltimore museum of art has an excellent collection of art from asia and the middle east.

_____   _____   _____   _____

_____   _____

14. One of the most important court decisions in american history came out of *miranda vs. arizona.*

———————   ———————   ———————

15. My favorite opera is *don giovanni.*

———————   ———————

. . . .

E X E R C I S E 21-3

For additional practice, capitalize as needed in the following sentences. First, put a line through all words that need capitals. Then, below each sentence, write the capitalized forms of the words. The spaces match the number of capitalizations you will need to make.

1. Did you give your mother a gift on mother's day?

———————   ———————

2. Not too many people can sing "the star spangled banner" well.

———————   ———————   ———————   ———————

3. Approximately 1000 years ago leif ericson founded a colony named vinland on the north american coast.

———————   ———————   ———————   ———————

———————

4. The spanish-american war started in 1898 after the battleship *maine* blew up in the port in havana, cuba.

———————   ———————   ———————   ———————   ———————

———————   ———————

5. The young women's christian association was founded in 1866 in boston, massachusetts.

———————   ———————   ———————   ———————

———————   ———————

6. Based on the teachings of mohammed, the moslem religion is called islam.

———————   ———————   ———————

7. Did the war of 1812 last longer than one year?

_____

8. Benjamin franklin once said: "in this world, nothing can be said to be certain, except death and taxes."

_____   _____

9. In egyptian mythology the queen of the underworld is isis.

_____   _____

10. When I asked mr. minh if he had seen *born on the fourth of july*, he replied: "no, i lived it. I lost my right leg in 1971 during a battle in quang tri province."

_____   _____   _____   _____

_____   _____   _____   _____

_____

. . . .

E X E R C I S E 21-4

Use each of the following words in a sentence. You may have to add a word (or words) to the capitalized one in order to write your sentence. For example, you could change *Bell* to *Liberty Bell*.

Example

uncle   My uncle owns three antique automobiles.

Uncle   I will visit Uncle Jonas next week.

1. china _____

2. China _____

3. war _____

4. War_____

5. mother _____

6. Mother _____

7. college _____

8. College_____

9. day _____

10. Day _____

. . . .

E X E R C I S E 21-5

In the following sentences, put a line through the words that are incorrectly capitalized. Write the correct forms in the spaces below the sentences. The spaces match the number of corrections you will have to make.

1. When I was in High School, I did not enjoy courses in History and Art, but now that I am in College, I like them.

   _____ _____ _____ _____

   _____

2. My favorite season is Summer because I enjoy Water Skiing on the Chesapeake bay.

   _____ _____ _____ _____

3. My Grandparents like to read such Magazines as the *Saturday Evening Post* and the *Reader's Digest*.

   _____ _____

4. The Trophy that Ross received for being on the winning Baseball team was made of Silver.

   _____ _____ _____

5. During the Holidays this coming Winter we are going to visit our Nieces and Nephews in California.

   _____ _____ _____ _____

. . . .

APOSTROPHES

The apostrophe (') has three important uses: (1) to show possession, (2) to show the omission of letters or numbers, and (3) to form some plurals. The apostrophe helps you to write (and speak) with succinctness and speed. In informal English you say *I'm* rather than *I am*, *they shouldn't* rather than *they should not*, and *Roxanne's friends* rather than *the friends of Roxanne*.

To Show Possession

When you show possession (ownership), you are using the possessive case.
The possessive case of nouns not already ending in *s* is shown by using a phrase starting with the preposition *of* (*the power of God*) or using an apostrophe and an *s* (*God's power*). Indefinite pronouns such as *anybody*, *anyone*,

everybody, everyone, nobody, one, no one, somebody, and *someone* show possession with the addition of an apostrophe and an *s* (for example: *somebody's book*). To determine ownership, just ask this question: "Who or what owns or possesses the person(s) or thing(s)?" Consider this phrase: *the dogs of Ben Fowler. Who owns the dogs? Ben Fowler.* To show possession you add an apostrophe and *s* to *Fowler: Ben Fowler's dogs.*

E X E R C I S E 21-6

Change the following phrases into possessives with an apostrophe and an *s.*

Example

    Change: the speeches of the men

    To: the men's speeches

1. **Change:** the weather of Vermont   **To:** _____

2. **Change:** the laws of America   **To:** _____

3. **Change:** the money of someone   **To:** _____

4. **Change:** the manners of Andy   **To:** _____

5. **Change:** the decision of no one   **To:** _____

E X E R C I S E 21-7

In the following phrases add an apostrophe and *s* to show possession. Write your new phrase in the blank.

1. George clothes   _____

2. boy bicycle   _____

3. nation people   _____

4. baby cry   _____

5. everybody opinion   _____

6. apple taste   _____

7. clergymen prayers   _____

8. Donna smile   _____

9. Rickie lyrics   _____

10. judge authority   _____

In general, to form the possessive case of nouns ending in s, add the apostrophe only.

Examples

two boys' gloves, Jesus' miracles, Los Angeles' smog, several birds' nests, Euripides' plays, Mr. Lessings' book, the Smiths' children.

Exception: If the noun is singular and ends in an *s* sound, add an apostrophe and *s* *if a new syllable that is easily pronounceable is formed.*

Example

Mr. Harris's job, the goddess's power, Russ's girlfriend, Mr. Gomez's plan, the actress's debut

E X E R C I S E 21-8

Change the following phrases into possessives with an apostrophe. Write your new phrase in the blank.

Example

Change: the plight of the victims
To: the victims' plight

1. **Change:** the cries of the infants   **To:** _____

2. **Change:** the help of my brothers   **To:** _____

3. **Change:** the victory of the troops   **To:** _____

4. **Change:** the shows of the networks   **To:** _____

5. **Change:** the pride of the winners   **To:** _____

· ·

E X E R C I S E 21-9

In the following phrases add *'s or '* to form the possessive case. Write your answer in the space provided.

1. the library rare books   _____

2. George Burns jokes   _____

3. Tim shirts _____

4. cigarettes stale odor _____

5. the bells music _____

6. someone else baby _____

7. Minnesota Vikings victories _____

8. doctors medicine _____

9. the president office _____

10. your sister graduation _____

11. the enemies feelings _____

12. the busybodies gossip _____

13. our Irish setter broken leg _____

14. the politician speeches _____

15. the boss memo _____

. . . .

E X E R C I S E 21-10

Combine each of the following pairs of sentences into *one* sentence by using the possessive case.

Example

From: William owns a classic car. It is a 1966 Ford Mustang.

To: William's classic car is a 1966 Ford Mustang.

1. **From:** Hawaii has natural resources. They include sand, surf, and sun.

   To: _____

2. **From:** *The Rocketeer* has a long history. It starts with a 1930s comic book hero.

   To: _____

3. **From:** Rubin had virtues. They were patience, tolerance, and humility.

   To: _____

4. **From:** Europe has only one species of wild monkey. That monkey is the Barbary ape.

   To: _____

   _____

5. **From:** Count Basie had a key influence on his jazz career. The influence was his mother.

   To: _____

   _____

6. **From:** This bookstore has twenty thousand volumes. They are, in the main, histories.

   To: _____

   _____

7. **From:** Margaret has one goal. It is to become a chemist.

   To: _____

   _____

8. **From:** The truck had faulty brakes. They caused the accident.

   To: _____

   _____

9. **From:** Our zoo has four elephants. They are from India.

   To: _____

   _____

10. **From:** The mink has beautiful fur. It is highly valued by fur dealers.

    To: _____

    _____

. . . .

An apostrophe is **not** *used with the following possessive pronouns:* **his, hers, its, ours, yours, theirs, whose.**

Example

The car was *hers*. **Not:** The car was her's.

Its cover is missing. **Not:** Its' cover is missing.

Whose horse won? **Not:** Who'se horse won?

To Show the Omission of Letters or Numbers

Apostrophes are also used to show the omission of letters or numbers. Words or numerals formed in this way are termed **contractions.** For example: *it's* for *it is, didn't* for *did not,* and *'92* for *1992.* You use contractions in relaxed conversations with your friends and in informal writings, such as personal letters and notes. On formal occasions, however, contractions are generally avoided. Such occasions might include engaging in a formal debate, writing a college research paper, or composing a job application letter. Following is a partial list of commonly used contractions:

I'm (I am)	I'd (I would)
you're (you are)	he'd (he would)
he's (he is, has)	she'd (she would)
she's (she is, has)	you'd (you would)
it's (it is)	aren't (are not)
we're (we are)	can't (cannot)
they're (they are)	doesn't (does not)
I've (I have)	hasn't (has not)
you've (you have)	haven't (have not)
we've (we have)	couldn't (could not)
they've (they have)	wouldn't (would not)
I'll (I will, shall)	shouldn't (should not)
you'll (you will, shall)	where's (where is)
who's (who is)	I'd (I had)
won't (will not)	he'd (he had)
let's (let us)	you'd (you had)
o'clock (of the clock)	

Note that the contraction *won't* (*will not*) is not formed in the regular way. Take care to observe the following differences in usage:

1. *its* — Example: The dog has *its* bone.
   it's — Example: *It's* Monday.
2. *your* — Example: *Your* gift is appreciated.
   you're — Example: *You're* my true friend.
3. *their* — Example: I have *their* books.
   there — Examples: I was *there* in December.
   There are two families living in that house.
   they're — Example: *They're* back.
4. *whose* — Example: *Whose* party did you attend?
   who's — Example: *Who's* going to the party?

Words such as *it's* and *its* may sound the same and have a similar appearance, but they have different uses in a sentence. Be sure to use them correctly.

E X E R C I S E 21-11

In the following sentences insert apostrophes in the contractions.

1. Im the winner.
2. Hed never smile.
3. Its five oclock.
4. I cant leave.
5. Wheres Karen?

6. She doesnt care.
7. Lets go now.
8. Youll be sorry.
9. Shes happy.
10. Theyve the tickets.

11. He couldnt come.
12. Youre correct.
13. She hasnt arrived.
14. Were pleased.
15. Ted wont be back.

. . . .

E X E R C I S E 21-12

In the following sentences cross out the incorrect word.

1. (Whose, Who's) the owner of the Panama Canal?
2. I think that (its, it's) time to see Kevin.
3. Did you bring (your, you're) lunch with you?
4. (Whose, Who's) personality do you like best?
5. She (lets, let's) them take (their, there, they're) time.
6. *The Wizard of Oz* has never lost (its, it's) ability to enchant people young and old.
7. I hope that (its, it's) not going to rain today.
8. (Their, There, They're) flight departs at 6:15 A.M.
9. (Your, You're) going to enjoy hearing my news.
10. (Whose, Who's) the woman appointed by President Reagan to the Supreme Court?
11. (Their, There, They're) are three possible answers to this question.
12. I hope that (their, there, they're) ready to play today.
13. (Its, It's) no surprise to me.
14. Will (your, you're) brother agree to the plan?
15. I know (whose, who's) team lost.

. . . .

EXERCISE 21-13

Using the apostrophe in a contraction, write five sentences.

1. _____

   _____

2. _____

   _____

3. _____

   _____

4. _____

   _____

5. _____

   _____

. . . .

By using contractions in the five sentences above, you have written what is termed informal speech. Though you should be able to use contractions correctly in your informal writing, you should avoid using them in formal college papers unless you are quoting a passage that contains contractions.

To Form Some Plurals

Lastly, the apostrophe and an *s* is used to form the plurals of letters, numerals, signs and symbols, abbreviations, and of words referred to as words. You must underline (*italicize*) letters, numerals, and words when you are specifically referring to them as such. However, the apostrophe and the *s* are not underlined. *Caution:* Many writers omit the apostrophe to form the plural of numerals, capitalized abbreviations without periods, and capital letters. What is important is consistency and the avoidance of confusion. For example, you would not want to write *As* when you mean *A*'s.

1. **Letters:** The word *Honolulu* contains two *o*'s, two *l*'s, and two *u*'s. Sister Miriam taught me my ABC's [or ABCs] in first grade.
2. **Numbers:** The 1960's [or 1960s] saw America undergo many social changes.
3. **Signs and Symbols:** Do not use *&*'s in place of *and*'s.
4. **Abbreviations:** How many YMCA's [or YMCAs] have you stayed at?
5. **Words Referred to as Words:** You have used thirty *and*'s in this brief paragraph!

E X E R C I S E 21-14

Using the following words, letters, and numbers in parentheses, write appropriate plurals in the blank spaces. Underline (*italicize*) as needed.

1. Her (5) _____ and (3) _____ look too much alike.

2. I count six (+) _____ among the answers.

3. Teresa used so many (however) _____ in her argument that I was unable to find a clear answer to the question.

4. You have too many (of) _____ , (by) _____ , and (and) _____ in this essay.

5. Throughout his essay he spelled the word *separate* with three (e) _____.

6. The (1980) _____ and the (1990) _____ appear similar politically.

7. How many (M.D.) _____ does this hospital employ?

8. The word *Massachusetts* has two (a) _____ , four (s) _____ , and two (t) _____ .

. . . .

UNDERLINING

Italic type (or *italics*) is that typeface that is slightly slanted to the right and somewhat thinner than that type used, for example, in most of this book. You indicate italics in your written or typed prose by underlining (though, of course, your word processing software and printer may have italic print capability). As with capital letters and apostrophes, the use of underlining (italicizing) follows certain established guidelines:

Underline Certain Publications, Titles, and Names

Books, Plays, and Long Poems (published separately):

Books: *Soul on Ice, The Great Gatsby, Vietnam Diary*

Plays: *Hamlet, Goin' a Buffalo, Death of a Salesman*

Long Poems: *Iliad, The Divine Comedy, The Song of Hiawatha*

Newspapers, Magazines, and Pamphlets

Newspapers: *USA Today, Wall Street Journal, New York Times*

Magazines: *TV Guide, Sports Illustrated, New Republic*
Pamphlets: *Understanding AIDS, Growing Roses*

Films, Television/Radio Series, Long Musical Works, and Recordings

Films: *The Babe, Dances with Wolves, Terminator 2*
Television Series: [CBS] *Evening News, 20/20, L.A. Law*
Long Musical Works: *Tommy, Messiah, Carmen*
Recordings: *Born in the USA, Thriller, House of Hope*

Paintings and Sculptures

Paintings: Pollack's *Number 1*, de Kooning's *Excavation*
Sculptures: Rodin's *The Age of Bronze*, Giacometti's *Man Pointing*

Ships, Trains, Aircraft, and Spacecraft

Ships: *Queen Elizabeth II (QE 2), Titanic, Saratoga*
Trains: *The Jeffersonian, The Yankee Clipper*
Aircraft: *Spirit of St. Louis, Air Force One, Hindenburg*
Spacecraft: *Mercury 3, Apollo 11*, [space shuttle] *Discovery*

Remember that quotation marks enclose the titles of songs, short poems, short stories, magazine essays, speeches, sections of books, and episodes of a radio or television series.

Lastly, by tradition certain works do not require quotation marks or italics. Such works include the Bible (and its books), other sacred writings, and various national documents. Examples: Old Testament, Mark, Exodus, Koran, Bill of Rights, United States Constitution, and Emancipation Proclamation.

E X E R C I S E 21-15

For the following items, use quotation marks or underlining as needed. **Note:** Some of the items require neither quotation marks nor underlining.

1. Record Album: Dangerous

2. Newspaper: Minneapolis Star

3. Book of the Bible: Genesis

4. Ship: Lusitania

5. Short Poem: A Supermarket in California

6. Book: I Know Why the Caged Bird Sings

7. Essay: Pee-wee's Misadventure

8. Part of the Bible: the New Testament

9. Film: Memoirs of an Invisible Man

10. Television Series: 60 Minutes

11. Play: A Raisin in the Sun

12. Short Story: A Rose for Emily

13. National Document: the Gettysburg Address

14. Name on a Boeing 747:   Spirit of America

15. Spacecraft: Vostok 1

16. Sculpture: Bust of Diego

17. Pamphlet: Cruise the Chesapeake Bay

18. Song: Don't Worry, Be Happy

19. Painting: Musical Instruments

20. Magazine: National Geographic

. . . .

E X E R C I S E 21-16

Underline as needed in the following sentences. **Note:** Some words may need to be enclosed in quotation marks.

1. The Queen Mary, which was once the most luxurious passenger ship afloat, is now a hotel and museum.

2. Amtrak's service on The Potomac and The Colonial was excellent.

3. Among Bob Dylan's great albums are Oh Mercy, Blood on the Tracks, and Blonde on Blonde.

4. Of all the books in the Bible, Psalms interests me the most.

5. Great Expectations is a novel with one of the most captivating openings in all of Dickens.

6. Among the British ships that engaged the enemy in famous battles in World War II were the Ark Royal and the King George V.

7. A Chorus Line was the longest-running Broadway musical production in theater history.

8. In *Time* magazine for June 18, 1990, the essay When Allah Beckons points out that boys are honored to be God's soldiers.

9. Baraka's play titled *Dutchman* is as current today as it was when it was presented in New York City in 1964.

10. During the 1950s Alistair Cooke hosted the award-winning television series called *Omnibus*; today he hosts a series called *Masterpiece Theater*, which is on National Educational Television.

11. Among the museum's paintings depicting Christ are Titian's *Entombment* and El Greco's *Lamentation*.

12. The author of such books as *The Hero with a Thousand Faces* and *Myths to Live By*, Joseph Campbell found similarities among the following: the film *Star Wars*, Native American beliefs, and the Gospels of Matthew, Mark, Luke, and John.

13. Owen's favorite magazines are *People Weekly*, *Field & Stream*, and *Popular Science*.

14. Without doubt, my favorite opera is *The Marriage of Figaro*.

15. Few of us will forget the short flight of the space shuttle *Challenger* on January 28, 1986.

. . . .

Other Uses of Underlining

Underline Certain Foreign Terms and Expressions

Foreign words and phrases that are not yet considered as part of the English language are underlined (italicized).

Example

Marie was graduated *summa cum laude*.

The Spaniards' route through the Los Alamos desert was called the *jornada del muerto*, the "journey of death."

English has a great capacity for taking foreign words and making them part of everyday American speech; such words are not underlined. Examples: papoose (Native American), mesquite (Mexican Spanish), pretzel (German), Santa Claus (Dutch), and Kris Kringle (German).

Underline Letters, Words, Numbers, and Symbols Treated as Such

Letters, words, numbers, and symbols that are referred to as such should be underlined (italicized).

Examples

Among the Dutch contributions to American English are *boss*, *cole slaw*, *sleigh*, and *waffle*.

In the word *Tennessee* there are four *e*'s, two *n*'s, and two *s*'s.

Quotations marks may also be used to point out that you are treating a word as a word; however, underlining may be preferred over the distracting use of too many quotation marks.

Underline to Emphasize a Word or Words

Underlining may be used to give emphasis to a word or phrase in a quotation; however, you should note that the underlining is your own by adding in parentheses the words *italics mine* or *emphasis mine*.

Example

According to Justice Holmes, "A Constitution is made for people of *fundamentally differing views*" (emphasis mine).

You may also give emphasis to a word or words of your own by using underlining.

Example

I have heard of brotherly love, sisterly love, motherly love, fatherly love, erotic love, self-love, and love of God. *But what, exactly, is love?*

Caution: Excessive use of underlining results in a loss of emphasis. Underlining to achieve emphasis should be used *sparingly*.

E X E R C I S E   21-17

In the following sentences, use underlining as needed. Cross out any underlining (italicizing) that is not needed.

1. When my sister started to choke on some food, I was glad I had read the pamphlet titled First Aid for Foreign Body Obstruction of the Airway.

2. On May 7, 1915, an unterseeboot (U boat) torpedoed the Lusitania, a British liner.

3. One hundred and fifty-nine people were killed when the Scandinavian Star, a *Danish ferry*, caught fire on April 7, 1990.

4. A 1776 copy of the *Declaration of Independence* sold for $1,595,000 at a 1990 auction.

5. At the same auction, a first edition of Cervantes' novel Don Quixote sold for $1,650,000.

6. The *word* dog has no known origin.

7. The *name* is spelled with an i—Francis, not with an e—Frances.

8. The scientific term for the *common wolf* is Canis lupus, and America's *timber wolf* belongs to the subspecies Canis lupus occidentalis.

9. My instructor had an essay published in a *journal* called Feminist Studies.

10. One of the nation's most celebrated *newspapers*, the Los Angeles Herald Examiner, ceased publication in 1990.

11. Citizens of the Commonwealth of Independent States (formerly the Soviet Union) are free to buy most *American magazines*, from the New Yorker to the New England Journal of Medicine.

12. I suspect that M*A*S*H will be rerun on television for many years to come.

13. Why has such a book as Final Exit become a best-seller?

14. He writes his 9's as if they were 7's.

15. An epic is a poem that begins in medias res, a *Latin* term meaning "in the midst of things."

. . . .

E X E R C I S E 21-18

In the following paragraph, supply capital letters, apostrophes, and underlining as needed.

Perhaps no other united states writer had a more varied career than h. l. mencken, popularly known as baltimores bad boy. Born on september 12, 1880, he was a journalist for the baltimore sunpapers for over forty years. In addition, he edited two magazines: smart set and american mercury. He published the american language, a series of books that pointed out the differences between the english language and the american one. A play titled heliogabalus, a book of poetry titled ventures into verse, and many short stories were among his works. Among menckens literary criticism was an essay titled "the sahara of the bozart," an attack on the souths culture after the civil war. (The term bozart was used to show how far the south had wandered from the beaux arts, a french phrase meaning "beautiful letters.") He wrote a series of books titled prejudices, a book on religion called treatise on the gods, and a book on morality titled treatise on right and wrong. His autobiography, happy days, was a best-seller in 1940. When he died on january 29, 1956, he was not finished publishing, for he left books to be published after his death. Mencken did not want these works published so long as those people written about in them were still alive. One of the books, the diary of h. l. mencken, was published by alfred a. knopf in 1989. On january 29, 1991, seven other volumes of menckens works were unsealed—exactly thirty-five years after his death—as his will had indicated. These books about authors and journalism will be published in the 1990s.

. . . .

. . . .

Strategies for Improving Spelling

If you have trouble spelling words correctly, you are not alone. However, you can improve your spelling skills by taking a few simple steps. Taking those steps is important, for you want to avoid the confusion that results from misspellings. In short, you want to present yourself as a writer interested in communicating with clarity and precision.

STEP 1: RECORD AND LEARN THE CORRECT SPELLINGS OF YOUR MISSPELLED WORDS

Keep a record of the correct spellings of your own misspelled words. Among others, your instructors will point out your misspellings. By studying, pronouncing, writing, and repeating the correct spellings, you should avoid making the same spelling errors in the future. At the same time, you should try to figure out the source(s) of your misspellings.

Misspelling is often the result of mispronunciation.

Have you added an unneeded syllable to a word?

Athlete, for example, is composed of two spoken units (or syllables). However, if you mispronounce the word by adding a third syllable, the written result may be *athalete* or *athelete*.

Have you omitted a needed letter?

For example, if you omit the first *t* in your pronunciation of *quantity*, you are likely to misspell the word as *quanity*.

A college-level dictionary can help you to pronounce a word correctly. Although English is noted for its irregular spellings, most words are, in fact, spelled by the way they are pronounced.

E X E R C I S E 22 - 1

Using the dictionary as necessary, circle the correct spelling in each of the following pairs of words.

1. canidate, candidate
2. mischievous, mischevious
3. miscellaneous, misslaneous
4. minature, miniature
5. grievous, grevious
6. cantlope, cantaloupe
7. labratory, laboratory
8. environment, envirnment
9. disasterous, disastrous
10. Bangkok, Bankok

. . . .

For many other words, correct pronunciation does not guarantee correct spelling. For example, the following words (**homonyms**) have sound-alike syllables but are spelled differently: *to, too, two*; *hear, here*; *peace, piece*. For such words, follow Step 2.

STEP 2: MATCH SPELLING AND MEANING WHEN YOU USE WORDS HAVING SIMILAR SOUNDS

As you learned in previous chapters, *it's* is the contraction for *it is*; *its* is the possessive case of the pronoun *it*. *They're* is the contraction for *they are*; *their* is the possessive case of the pronoun *they*; *there* is most often used as an adverb of place. As these examples show, you need to match the spelling of a word with its meaning and function in a sentence.

The following list contains some frequently misused sound-alikes. Pay particular attention to those words that have caused you problems in the past.

Troublesome Words	Selected Definitions
1. *accept*: (verb)	to receive or to take an offering of some kind
except: (preposition)	excluding, but
2. *advice*: (noun)	a recommendation or opinion for a course of action
advise: (verb)	to suggest or to recommend
3. *affect*: (verb)	to influence or to cause a change in; to stir the emotions of
effect: (verb)	to produce a result; (noun) a result
4. *all ready*: (adverb-adjective combination) totally prepared	
already: (adverb)	by this time; before; previously
5. *all together*: (adverb-adverb combination) as a group	
altogether: (adverb)	entirely, completely

Troublesome Words	**Selected Definitions**
6. *altar*: (noun)	a structure on or before which religious rites are conducted
alter: (verb)	to change
7. *angel*: (noun)	an immortal, spiritual being that serves God
angle: (noun)	a point of view; the figure formed by two lines diverging from a common point
8. *break*: (verb)	to crack with (or without) separating into pieces; to destroy; (noun) a crack; a beginning
brake: (noun)	a device for slowing or stopping movement; (verb) to slow or stop the motion of
9. *breath*: (noun)	air inhaled and exhaled in respiration
breathe: (verb)	to inhale and to exhale air
10. *capital*: (noun)	wealth; major or governing city; (adjective) principal, chief
capitol:(noun)	a building in which a state or national legislature meets
11. *coarse*: (adjective)	rough, of inferior quality
course: (noun)	a program of studies (or one unit of such studies); onward movement in a specific direction; duration
12. *complement*: (noun)	something that completes or makes whole;
(verb)	to complete, to supply what is needed or lacking
compliment: (noun)	expression of praise; (verb) to praise or commend
13. *corps*: (noun)	a branch or unit of the armed forces
corpse: (noun)	a dead body
14. *council*: (noun)	a body of people acting as advisors or lawmakers
counsel: (noun)	advice given to someone, one who gives advice; (verb) to advise
15. *desert*: (noun)	a dry, barren region which can support little or no vegetation; (verb) to abandon, to leave
dessert: (noun)	usually a sweet food that is the final course of a meal
16. *diner*: (noun)	one who eats; a restaurant fashioned like a railroad car
dining: (verb)	eating, taking dinner
dinning: (verb)	making loud noises lacking harmony

Troublesome Words	Selected Definitions
17. *dyeing*: (verb)	coloring a material (with a dye)
dying: (adjective)	nearing death, done prior to death; (verb) ceasing to live
18. *formally*: (adverb)	in accord with accepted customs or conventions
formerly: (adverb)	taking place earlier in time; previously
19. *hear*: (verb)	to learn (by the ear), to be told of
here: (adverb)	in this place (as opposed to *there*: at that place)
20. *later*: (adjective/adverb)	comparative degree of *late*
latter: (adjective)	the second of two mentioned items; nearer to the end
21. *loose*: (adjective)	not firmly secured, not packaged together
lose: (verb)	to be defeated, to be unable to locate
22. *passed*: (verb)	moved beyond, ran past
past: (noun)	the time before now; (adjective) having taken place in an earlier time, over
23. *peace*: (noun)	not at war, a time of calm
piece: (noun)	a part of a larger quantity; an artistic work; (verb) to connect the pieces of
24. *personal*: (adjective)	of a particular person or individual; done in person
personnel: (noun)	group of persons employed in the same business or organization
25. *principal*: (adjective)	chief or primary in importance; (noun) chief or primary person
principle: (noun)	a basic rule, truth, law, or code
26. *stationary*: (noun)	not moving, not changing position
stationery: (noun)	writing paper or materials (pencils, paper, envelopes, etc.)
27. *than*: (conjunction)	used to introduce the second item of a comparison
then: (adverb)	at a particular time in the past; soon or immediately following
28. *to*: (preposition)	in the direction of or toward
too: (adverb)	also; very, extremely
two: (noun/adjective)	1 + 1, a cardinal number

Troublesome Words	Selected Definitions
29. *weather*: (noun)	the condition of the atmosphere regarding wind, humidity, etc.; (verb) to experience or stand up against and pass safely through (a storm, a tragedy, etc.)
whether: (conjunction)	either—introduces the first of two (or more) alternatives, the second of which may be stated or implied
30. *were*: (verb)	past tense of the verb *to be*
where: (conjunction/adverb)	indicates at or in a particular place

E X E R C I S E 22-2

Cross out the wrong word in each of the following sentences. Refer to the list above as needed.

1. In December 1991, Gorbachev finally (accepted, excepted) the fact that the U.S.S.R. had become a country of the (passed, past).

2. In fact, the Soviet Union had been (dyeing, dying) for several years.

3. By late 1991, Gorbachev was (all ready, already) a president without a nation.

4. (Formally, Formerly), the people of the U.S.S.R. had not known freedom.

5. Gorbachev, however, allowed his people to (breath, breathe) the fresh air of freedom and democracy.

6. (Complements, Compliments) for his largely (personal, personnel) efforts came from all over the world.

7. For his work to (altar, alter) the (coarse, course) of the Soviet Union, he was awarded the Nobel (Peace, Piece) Prize.

8. The (affects, effects) of freedom on the Soviet people (were, where) not long in coming, however.

9. The Soviet Union began to (break, brake) apart and eventually was left a (corps, corpse) among nations.

10. Despite Gorbachev's (advice, advise), not even a (loose, lose) Soviet "Union" could be maintained.

11. In the end, the (principal, principle) leader of democracy in the U.S.S.R. became the victim of the (principals, principles) he himself had supported.

12. Boris Yeltsin became the key leader of the new Commonwealth of Independent States (formerly the Soviet Union), and the (capital, capitol) was moved from Moscow to Minsk.

13. The (later, latter) city is not even located in what historically has been called Russia!

14. (Weather, Whether) this new association of nations will survive or (weather, whether) it, (to, too, two), will die is an open question.

15. Clearly, though, the people have (deserted, desserted) the (passed, past) in favor of an uncertain future.

16. Can that future be worse (than, then) what they have known?

· ·

E X E R C I S E 22-3

From the list of sound-alike words, select ten that give you the most difficulty. Use each of those words in a sentence.

1. _____

2. _____

3. _____

4. _____

5. _____

6. _____

7. _____

8. _____

9. _____

10. _____

· ·

Memory devices (**mnemonics**) can assist you in spelling words correctly, as well as in remembering their meanings. For example, for *stationery*, you might think of *letters*; for *stationary*, you might think of *standing* still.

E X E R C I S E 22-4

Create your own memory devices for the following words:

1. angel_____

2. angle_____

3. capital _____

4. capitol _____

5. complement _____

6. compliment _____

7. council_____

8. counsel _____

9. personal_____

10. personnel _____

11. principal _____

12. principle _____

13. than _____

14. then _____

. . . .

STEP 3: LEARN THE BASIC SPELLING RULES

Another step that you can take is to learn several simple spelling rules that apply to most of the words you use frequently. To apply the rules, you need to know that the **vowels** of the alphabet are *a, e, i, o,* and *u.* The **consonants** are the remaining letters.

IE AND EI WORDS

Although the following rhyme has exceptions, it is useful:

> (1) Write *i* before *e,*
>
> (2) Except after *c,*
>
> (3) Or when sounded like *a*
>   As in n*ei*ghbor and w*ei*gh.

Examples

    (1) Write *i* before *e*

achieve	field	priest
siege	belief	grief
relief	yield	brief
mischief	retrieve	

E X E R C I S E 22 - 5

Using this rule and the words above as guides, complete the following:

1. bel_____ve

2. fr_____nd

3. p_____ce

4. th_____f

5. v_____w

· ·

Examples

    (2) Except after *c*

      ceiling   deceive   receipt

E X E R C I S E 22 - 6

Using the above rule and words as guides, complete the following:

1. conc_____ve

2. perc_____ve

3. rec_____ve

· ·

Examples

    (3) Or when sounded like *a*/As in n*ei*ghbor and w*ei*gh

beige	feign	heir	reign
eight	freight	neighbor	their

EXERCISE 22-7

Using the above rule and words as guides, complete the following:

1. h_____nous

2. r_____n

3. r_____ndeer

4. sl_____gh

5. w_____ght

. . . .

There are exceptions to the *ie* and *ei* rule, and these words must be learned by memorization or with the aid of a mnemonic device.

Exceptions: caffeine, foreigner, leisure, seize, counterfeit, forfeit, neither, sheik, either, height, protein, sleight, weird.

EXERCISE 22-8

Without looking at the lists of *ie* and *ei* words, apply the rules that you have learned to the following words. If the word is spelled correctly, write *C* in the blank. Correct all misspellings. (Exceptions are not included among the words.)

1. acheive_____

2. deceive_____

3. nieghbor_____

4. percieve _____

5. heir _____

6. thief _____

7. cieling _____

8. retreive_____

9. reciept _____

10. receive _____

11. thier _____

12. seige_____

13. breif _____

14. mischeif _____

15. beleive_____

16. fiegn _____

17. seige _____

18. beige_____

19. concieve _____

20. frieght _____

. . . .

Words Ending in <u>E</u>

In general, with a word ending in e, you drop the final e when the added ending (**suffix**) begins with a vowel such as *able*, *al*, *ance*, or *ing*.

Examples

conceive + able = *conceivable*

arrive + al = *arrival*

insure + ance = *insurance*

love + ing = *loving*

In general, keep the final e when the added ending begins with a consonant such as *ful*, *less*, *ment*, or *ty*.

Examples

hope + ful = *hopeful*

leisure + less = *leisureless*

announce + ment = *announcement*

safe + ty = *safety*

There are some exceptions, and nine of the most common ones are listed below. They need to be memorized.

acknowledge becomes *acknowledgment*

acre becomes *acreage*

argue becomes *argument*

dye becomes *dyeing*

judge becomes *judgment*

nine becomes *ninth*

mile becomes *mileage*

true becomes *truly*

whole becomes *wholly*

When a word ends in ce or ge with a c or g softly pronounced, keep the final e before *able* (but not *ible*) and *ous*.

Examples

notice becomes *noticeable*

peace becomes *peaceable*

enlarge becomes *enlargeable*

disadvantage becomes *disadvantageous*

courage becomes *courageous*

E X E R C I S E 22-9

As necessary, retain or drop the final *e*'s to form words spelled correctly. When in doubt, use your dictionary.

1. replace + able = _____

2. entitle + ment = _____

3. love + able = _____

4. sincere + ly = _____

5. use + age = _____

6. force + ible = _____

7. blame + less = _____

8. entire + ty = _____

9. assure + ance = _____

10. definite + ly = _____

11. isolate + ing = _____

12. price + less = _____

13. produce + ible = _____

14. procure + able = _____

15. refine + ment = _____

16. suspense + ion = _____

17. refuse + able = _____

18. advise + ment = _____

19. use + ful = _____

20. refine + ing = _____

. . . .

Words Ending in Y

Usually, a word ending in a *y* which is preceded by a consonant changes the *y* to *i* before all added endings. When adding the ending *s*, change the *y* to *ie*.

Examples

bully + s = *bullies*

marry + s = *marries*

thirty + eth = *thirtieth*

study + ous = *studious*

fussy + ness = *fussiness*

spy + ed = *spied*

rely + ance = *reliance*

If the *y* is preceded by a vowel or when the ending is *ing*, keep the *y*.

Examples

deny + ing = *denying*

study + ing = *studying*

employ + ment = *employment*

alley + s = *alleys*

slay + er = *slayer*

Exceptions to this rule are the following: lay + ed = *laid*, pay + ed = *paid*, say + ed = *said*.

E X E R C I S E 22 - 10

As necessary, retain or drop the final *y*'s to form words correctly spelled. If in doubt, use your dictionary.

1. deploy + ment = _____

2. harmony + s = _____

3. luxury + ous = _____

4. comply + ed = _____

5. delay + ing = _____

6. twenty + eth = _____

7. marry + age = _____

8. comply + ance = _____

9. beauty + ful = _____

10. enjoy + able = _____

. . . .

Doubling a Final Consonant

Occasionally, a word ending in a consonant doubles the consonant when a suffix is added.

When a single vowel precedes the final consonant in a one-syllable word, double the final consonant when adding a suffix beginning with a vowel.

Examples

span + ed = *spanned*

let + ing = *letting*

ton + age = *tonnage*

If a word has more than one syllable, the final consonant is doubled when (1) a single vowel precedes the final consonant, (2) the stress falls on the last syllable of the word and stays on that syllable after the ending is added, and (3) the ending starts with a vowel.

Examples

commit + ed = *committed*

commit + ing = *committing*

commit + ment = *commitment* (ending does not start with a vowel)

refer + ed = *referred*

refer + ence = *reference* (the stress does not stay on the final syllable after the ending is added)

occur + ence = *occurrence*

EXERCISE 22-11

As needed, double the final consonants in the following words to form correctly spelled words. If in doubt, check your dictionary.

1. submit + ed = _____

2. zip + ing =_____

3. repair + ing = _____

4. hop + ed =_____

5. stoop + ing =_____

6. hook + ed =_____

7. remit + al = _____

8. begin + er = _____

9. sleep + ing = _____

10. leap + ing = _____

11. log + er = _____

12. infer + ence = _____

13. patrol + ed = _____

14. wrap + ing = _____

15. allot + ed = _____

. . . .

A Final Note on Prefixes and Suffixes

As you have learned, a **suffix** is a word element added to the end of a word. A **prefix** is a word element added to the start of a word. In general, if the prefix ends with the same letter that starts the word, retain both letters: dis + similar = *dissimilar*, mis + spell = *misspell*. Retain both letters if the suffix of a word starts with the same letter that ends the main word: final + ly = *finally*, lean + ness = *leanness*.

E X E R C I S E   22-12

Form correctly spelled words by adding prefixes or suffixes as indicated. If in doubt, use your dictionary.

1. ir + redeemable = _____

2. un + needed = _____

3. im + measurable = _____

4. cool + ly = _____

5. il + legible = _____

6. mean + ness = _____

7. coincidental + ly = _____

8. dis + service = _____

9. over + rate = _____

10. drunken + ness = _____

. . . .

Use a hyphen (–) between prefix and main word and between suffix and main word to avoid (1) a lack of clarity, or (2) difficulty in reading. For example, there is a large difference between *to resign a job* and *to re-sign* a contract; *hell-like* is much easier to read than *helllike*. The hyphen is also used after the prefixes *all*, *self*, and *ex* ("former") and with the suffix *elect*. Examples: *all-important, self-denial, ex-senator, governor-elect*. Finally, hyphens are used when compound numbers from twenty-one to ninety-nine are spelled out. Examples: forty-seven, sixty-three.

E X E R C I S E 22-13

If the following words are correctly spelled, write *C.* If they are not correctly spelled, add or remove hyphens as needed.

1. thirty two   _____

2. expresident   _____

3. president elect   _____

4. mis-step   _____

5. unnecessary   _____

6. selfemployed   _____

7. shelllike   _____

8. re-cover   _____

9. un-nerve   _____

10. alltime   _____

. . . .

To become an effective speller requires patience and work on your part. However, you can become the speller you want to be by following the steps outlined in this chapter. In addition to the "Troublesome Words" listed earlier, you can study and learn the following list of frequently misspelled words on the next page.

Words Often Mispelled

1. absence	51. friend	101. sacrifice
2. accept	52. government	102. salary
3. across	53. grammar	103. sandwich
4. actually	54. guarantee	104. scene
5. address	55. guidance	105. schedule
6. adolescent	56. heroes	106. secretary
7. aggressive	57. immediately	107. seize
8. alcohol	58. independent	108. separate
9. a lot of	59. intelligence	109. sergeant
10. always	60. interest	110. similar
11. among	61. interfere	111. sincerely
12. annual	62. interpret	112. sophomore
13. answer	63. jewelry	113. stomach
14. apology	64. judgment	114. studying
15. arguing	65. knowledge	115. subtle
16. argument	66. laboratory	116. succeed
17. article	67. length	117. success
18. aspirin	68. license	118. surprise
19. athlete	69. loneliness	119. syllable
20. basically	70. maintenance	120. technical
21. beginning	71. marriage	121. technique
22. believe	72. mathematics	122. temperature
23. business	73. meant	123. therefore
24. calendar	74. missile	124. till
25. cemetery	75. necessary	125. tobacco
26. challenge	76. niece	126. together
27. chief	77. ninety	127. tomorrow
28. coming	78. ninth	128. tragedy
29. committee	79. nuclear	129. truly
30. commitment	80. obstacle	130. until
31. completely	81. occasionally	131. usage
32. criticize	82. occurrence	132. useful
33. definitely	83. opportunity	133. using
34. definition	84. parallel	134. usually
35. describe	85. pastime	135. vacuum
36. description	86. permanent	136. valuable
37. develop	87. possess	137. vegetable
38. difference	88. possible	138. view
39. disease	89. practically	139. vitamins
40. easily	90. privilege	140. Wednesday
41. eighth	91. professor	141. weird
42. embarrassed	92. psychology	142. wintry
43. equipped	93. quizzes	143. woman
44. etc.	94. really	144. women
45. excellence	95. religious	145. worshiped
46. existence	96. repetition	146. writing
47. familiar	97. receive	147. written
48. February	98. restaurant	148. yacht
49. foreign	99. rhythm	149. yield
50. forty	100. ridiculous	150. zealous

INDEX

A

A/an/and, 67-68, 84
A/an/the
  to identify nouns, 10-11
  repeated for parallel statements,
    227
Abbreviations, period usage in, 243
Absolute phrases, comma usage
  with, 270
Accept/except, 310
Acronyms 244-245
  defining/using, 244-245
  period omission in, 244
Active voice, 32-33
Adjective(s), 3, 64-73, 76-79
  bad, worse, worst, 77
  clauses acting as, 131-135
    nonrestrictive, 131-135
    restrictive, 131
  comparison of, 76-79
  complement, 62-63, 111, 114, 118
  defined, 3, 64
  definitive, 67-68
  demonstrative, 68-69
  descriptive, 65-66
  good, better, best, 77
  indefinite, 69
  infinitives acting as, 117-118,
    120-121
  interrogative, 69
  little, less, least, 77
  numerical, 68
  participles acting as, 111-117
  possessive, 69-72, 294-298
  prepositional phrases acting as,
    99-100
  proper, capitalization of, 288-289
  many (much), more, most, 77
Address, commas used in direct, 269
Adverbs, 3, 73-76, 79, 81
  badly, worse, worst, 79
  clauses acting as, 134-137
    comma usage with, 134-135
  defined, 3, 73
  infinitives and infinitive phrases
    acting as, 117-123
  little, less, least, 79
  much, more, most, 79
  of time, manner, place, degree,
    73-74
  prepositional phrases acting as,
    99-101
  well, better, best, 79
Advice/advise, 310
Affect/effect, 310
Agreement of pronoun and
  antecedent, 196-203
  defined, 196
  with antecedents joined by *and*,
    197-198
  with antecedents joined by *or*,
    either...or, etc., 198
  with antecedents plural in form
    but singular in meaning, 200
  with collective nouns, 199-200
  with singular indefinite pronouns,
    198-199
Agreement of subject and predicate,
  44-46, 56-57, 170-184
  when a subject complement is
    present, 178
  when phrases come between sub-
    ject and predicate, 171-172
  with a subject joined by a correla-
    tive conjunction, 172-173
  with a subject that is the name of
    a book, play, etc., 180
  with collective nouns, 176-177
  with indefinite pronouns, 174-175
  with nouns plural in form but
    singular in meaning, 180-181
  with relative pronouns, 182
  with subjects joined by *and*, 172
  with *The number* and *A number*,
    181
All ready/already, 310
All together, altogether, 310
Altar/alter, 311
Among/between, 102

Angel/angle, 311
Antecedent, defined, 13, 196
Apostrophes, 69-71, 294-302
    and possessive pronouns, 71-72,
        294-295, 298
    to form some plurals, 301-302
    to show possession, 69-71,
        294-298
    with contractions, 299-301
Appositives, defined, 24, 106, 144
    commas to set off, 106, 108, 269
    emphatic pronouns used as, 24
    using correct case in, 187-188
Articles, 67-68
    definite, 67
    indefinite, 67
As/like, 103
Auxiliary (helping) verbs, 55-56

B
Bad[ly], *worse*, *worst*, 77, 79
Be (*to be*), 32, 46, 56, 57-58, 62-63
    as linking verb, 62-63
    in passive voice, 32-35
    in progressive tenses, 48-55
    in subjunctive mood, 57-58
    conjugation of, 46
    subjective case after, 186-187
Beside/besides, 102
Between/among, 102
Both...and, 88-89
Brake/break, 311
Breath/breathe, 311
But/yet, 84-85

C
Capital/capitol, 311
Capitalization, 12, 286-294
    of first word of a quoted sentence,
        287
    of main words in a title, 287
    of proper adjectives, 288-289
    of proper nouns, 12, 288-290
    starting sentences with, 286

Case
    one of four properties of nouns
        and pronouns, 13-14
    objective, (direct/indirect objects)
        60-61, (object of preposition)
        95-96,
        (personal pronouns) 18-20,
        185-188,
        (for subject of infinitive)
        120-121, (*who/whom*) 21-22,
        192-194
    possessive, (adjectives) 69-71,
        294-298, (before gerunds) 106,
        (pronouns) 71-72, 185-186,
        188-189, 193, 298
    subjective case, (personal pro-
        nouns) 18-20, 185-187,
        (*who/whom*)
        21-22, 192-194
Clause (defined), 142-143
Clauses, 124-143
    adjective, 126, 131-134
    adverbial, 127, 134-137
    dangling subordinate, 216
    dependent (*See* Clauses, subordi-
        nate)
    independent, 124-126, 142-150
    nonrestrictive, 131-135
    noun, 137-140
    restrictive, 131-133
    subordinate, 126-150
Coarse/course, 311
Collective nouns (defined), 14-15,
        176
    subject-predicate agreement with,
        176-177
    pronoun-antecedent agreement
        with, 199-200
Colon, 281-283
    defined, 281
    introducing a formal question or
        quote, 281
    introducing a list, 281
    separating parts of a title, 282
    separating two independent
        clauses, 281

Commas (260-275) with
  absolute phrases, 270
  addresses (location), 271
  adjectival clauses, 132
  adjectives, 111, 262
  adverbial clauses, 134-135
  appositives, 106, 269
  compound sentence, 84, 88, 90-
    91, 260-261
  compound subject, 88
  coordinate clauses, phrases,
    words, 262
  coordinating conjunctions, 84,
    260-262
  dates, 271
  degrees and titles, 271
  direct address, 269
  infinitives, 118
  interjections, 263
  introductory clauses, phrases,
    words, 263-266
  nonrestrictive words, phrases,
    clauses, 267-270
    (See also 131-135)
  numbers, 272
  parenthetical expressions, 268
  quotation marks, 255, 272
  salutations and closings in letters,
    271-272
  series, 262
  transitional words, 90, 263, 268
  verbals and verbal phrases, 106,
    111, 267
Comma splices, 160-165
Common nouns, 12
Common tenses, 48
Comparative degree, 76-81
  avoiding double, 79
  adjectives and adverbs having no,
    79
Comparison, using correct case in,
  187
Complements
  adjective, 62-64, 111, 114, 118
  subject, 62-64, 178
Complement/compliment, 311

Complete subject and predicate, 4-8,
  30
Complex sentences, 126-141
Compound-complex sentences, 145
Compound sentences, 83-94, 125,
  144
Compound subjects and predicates,
  7, 83
Conjunctions (defined), 3, 82
  coordinating, 83-87
  correlative, 88-89
  subordinate, 126-127
Conjunctive adverbs, 89-91
  list of, 90, 278
  punctuation with, 90-91
Consistency in
  person, 234-235
  number, 234-235
  tense, 236-237
Consonant(s)
  difference between vowels and,
    315
  doubling final, 321
  keeping final *e* when suffix begins
    with, 318
  word ending in *y* preceded by a,
    319-320
Contractions, 299-301
  list of commonly used, 299
  of look- and sound-alike words,
    299
Coordinating conjunctions, 83-87
  defined, 83
  list of, 83
  using commas with, 84, 260-261,
    262
  for correcting comma splices,
    160-162
Coordination, 82-93, 221-233, 276-
  280
  with conjunctive adverbs, 89-91,
    277-278
  with coordinating conjunctions,
    83-87, 221-222
  with correlative conjunctions,
    88-89, 221-222
  with semicolons, 276-280

Corps/corpse, 311
Council/counsel, 311

D
Dangling modifiers, 214-220
Dash(es)
  overuse of, 250-251
  to indicate a sharp break in
    thought, 250
  to set off an introductory or a con-
    cluding list, 250
  to set off appositives, 250
Dates, commas used in, 271
Declarative sentences, 150
Definite article, 67-68
Definitive adjectives, 67-73
Demonstrative adjectives, 68-69
Demonstrative pronouns, 20-21
Descriptive adjectives, 65-66
Desert/dessert, 311
Diner/dining/dinning, 311
Direct address, commas used in, 269
Direct object, 60-61
Direct question, 242-243, 247
Direct quotations, punctuation of,
    253-254, 255-256
Dyeing/dying, 312

E
-e, dropping or keeping final,
    318-319
Effect/affect, 310
ei/ie spelling rule, 315-317
  exceptions to, 317
Either...or, 88-89, 172-173, 198
Elliptical clauses, dangling, 216
Emphatic pronouns, 23-25
Emphatic tense, 48, 55
Except/accept, 310
Exclamation marks, 4, 248-249
  avoiding overuse of, 151
  with quotation marks, 255-256
Exclamatory sentences, 151

avoiding overuse of, 151
Explctive(s) (*there, it*),
    defined, 178
  subject-predicate agreement with,
    178
  noun clause after, 138

F
Finite verbs, 105-106
Formally/formerly, 312
For/so, 85
Fragments (*See* Sentence fragments)
Fused sentences, 165-169
  defined, 165
  ways to correct, 166
Future perfect progressive tense, 48,
    51-55
Future perfect tense, 38, 44-46
Future progressive tense, 48-49
Future tense, 36, 44-46

G
Gender, 15-18
Gender bias, avoiding, 199
Gerunds, 106-107
Gerund phrases, 108-111
Good, better, best, 77
Grammatical functions of words, 1-4

H
Hear/here, 312
Helping (auxiliary) verbs, 55-56
Hyphenated words, 323

I
ie/ei spelling rule, 315-317
  exceptions to, 317
Imperative mood, 57
Imperative sentences, 151
Indefinite adjectives, 69
Indefinite articles, 67-68
Indefinite pronouns, 22-23, 25

subject-predicate agreement with, 174-176

pronoun-antecedent agreement with, 198-200

Independent clauses (*See* Clauses)

Indicative mood, 57

Indirect objects, 60-61

Indirect question, 242-243

Infinitives, 40, 117-120

Infinitive phrases, 120-123

dangling, 215

In/into, 102

Interjections, 4, 248, 264

Interrogative adjectives, 69

Interrogative adverbs, 74

Interrogative pronouns, 21-22, 25

Interrogative sentences, 150, 247-248

Intransitive verbs, 62

Irregular verbs

conjugation of, 45-46

defined, 40

list of, 40-42

Italics (underlining), 302-306

defined, 302

rules for use of, 302-306

Its/it's, 299

J

Joining words, 3-4 (*See also* conjunctions, conjunctive adverbs, preposition)

Just as...so, 88-89

L

Later/latter, 312

Like/as, 103

Linking verbs, 62-63

participle after, 111-112

possessive personal pronouns after, 72

subjective case after linking verb *be*, 186-187

subject-predicate agreement with, 178

Little, less, least, 77, 79

Look- and sound-alike words, 67-68, 83-84, 299, 310-313

a/an, 67-68, *and*, 83-84

accept/except, 310

advice/advise, 310

affect/effect, 310

all ready/already, 310

all together/altogether, 310

altar/alter, 311

angel/angle, 311

break/brake, 311

breath/breathe, 311

capital/capitol, 311

coarse/course, 311

council/counsel, 311

desert/dessert, 311

diner/dining/dinning, 311

dyeing/dying, 312

formally/formerly, 312

hear/here, 312

its/it's, 299

later/latter, 312

loose/lose, 312

passed/past, 312

peace/piece, 312

personal/personnel, 312

principal/principle, 312

stationary/stationery, 312

than/then, 312

their/there/they're, 299

to/too/two, 312

weather/whether, 313

were/where, 313

whose/who's, 299

your/you're, 299

Loose/lose, 312

M

Many (much), more, most, 77, 79

Misspelled words, list of often, 323-324

Mnemonics (for correct spelling), 315

Modifiers (*See* Adjectives, Adverbs)
    Dangling, 214-220
    Misplaced, 210-214
Mood
    indicative, 57
    imperative, 57
    subjunctive, 57-59

N

Neither...nor, 88-89, 172-173, 198
Nonfinite verbs, 105-106
Non restrictive clauses, 131-135
Non restrictive verbal phrases, 111
Nor/or, 84, 172-174, 198
Not only...but [*also*], 88-89, 172-173
Noun(s), 2, 10-13
    capitalization of, 12-13, 288-294
    clauses, 127, 137-140
    collective (*See* Collective nouns)
    common, 12-13, 288-290
    plural, 13-18
    possessive adjectives formed
        from,   69-72, 294-298
    prepositional phrases acting as,
        100
    proper, 12-13, 288-294
    singular, 13-18
    test to identify, 10-11
    third person, 14
    verbal, (gerunds) 106-111, (infini-
        tives) 117-118, 120-121
Number, singular and plural, 13-18,
        56-57, 170-171, 196
    of indefinite pronouns, 22-23,
        174-176, 198-199
    shifts in, 234-235
Numerical adjectives, 68

O

Objective case (*See* Case)
    in comparisons, 187
Objects (*See* Case)
On/onto, 103
Or/nor, 84, 172-173, 198

P

Parallelism, 221-233 (*See also* 82-94,
        144-145)
Parentheses, 251-253
Participles (*See* Verbals)
    past (*See* Past participles)
    present (*See* Present participles)
Parts of speech (listed/defined), 1-4
Passed/past, 312
Passive voice, 32-35, 112
Past emphatic tense, 55
Past participles, 40
    in future perfect tense, 38, 44-46
    in passive voice, 32-35
    in past perfect tense, 38, 44-46
    in present perfect tense, 37, 44-46
    in subjunctive mood, 58
    in verbals, 111, 118
    of irregular verbs, 40-43
    of regular verbs, 40, 44-45
Past perfect progressive tense, 48,
        51-55
Past perfect tense, 38, 44-46
Past progressive tense, 48-50
Past tense, 35-37
    of irregular verbs, 40-44
    of regular verbs, 40, 44-45
Peace/piece, 312
Perfect tenses
    present, past, future, 37-39, 44-46
    present, past, future progressive,
        48-49, 51-55
Periods, 242-246
    with quotation marks, 255
Person, 13-18
    shifts in, 234-235
Personal/personnel, 312
Phrase(s)
    absolute, comma usage with, 270
    defined, (prepositional) 96,
        (verbal) 105
    introductory, comma usage with,
        263-266
    non restrictive, comma usage
        with, 267-271
    prepositional, 95-104
    verbal, 105-123

Positive degree
    defined, 76
    of adjectives, 76-78
    of adverbs, 79-80
Possessive case (See *Case*)
Predicates
    complete, 6-7, 30
    simple, 6-9, 30-32
Prefixes, spelling rules for, 322-323
Prepositional phrase(s)
    comma after introductory, 263-
        266
    defined, 95-96
    functions of, 98-102
    infinitives mistaken for, 117-119
    nonrestrictive, comma usage with,
        267-268
    subject-predicate agreement and,
        171
Preposition(s),
    defined, 3-4, 95-96
    list of common, 95-96
    object of, 3-4, 95-96
    special usage problems with,
        102-104
        among/between, 102
        beside/besides, 102
        in/into, 102
        as/like, 103
        on/onto, 103
Present emphatic tense, 55
Present participles, 40
    in progressive tense, 48-55
Present perfect progressive tense, 48,
    51-52
Present perfect tense, 35-37
Present progressive tense, 48-50
Present tense, 35-36, 44-46
    of *to be*, 46, 56
    of *to do*, 56
    of *to have*, 56
Principal/principle, 312
Progressive tenses, 48-55
Pronoun(s)
    and antecedent agreement,
        196-203

antecedent of, defined, 13, 196
    correct case usage with (See Case)
    defined, 2, 13
    demonstrative, 20-21
    emphatic, 23-24
    indefinite, 22-23, 194
    interrogative, 21-22
    list of, 24-25
    personal, 18-19, 186
    properties of, 14-18
        gender, 15
        number, 14
        person, 14
    reciprocal, 24, 194
    reflexive, 23-24
    relative, 126-127, 131, 137-138,
        182, 192-194
    shifts in person and number of,
        234-235, 238-241
    vague, general, and unclear refer-
        ence of, 204-209
Punctuation
    Colon (See Colon)
    Commas (See Commas)
    Dashes (See Dashes)
    Exclamation marks (See
        Exclamation marks)
    Parentheses (See Parentheses)
    Periods (See Periods)
    Question marks (See Question
        marks)
    Quotation marks (See Quotation
        marks)
    Semicolon (See Semicolon)
    (See also Apostrophes,
        Capitalization, and Italics)

Q
Question marks, 4, 150, 247-248
    with quotation marks, 255-256
Questions
    indirect, 242-243, 247-248
    direct, 242-243, 247-248
    quoting and, 247, 255-256
Quotation marks, 253-259

Quotations, 253-259
 direct and indirect, defined, 253
  punctuating direct, 253
 for certain titles, 254
 for special-sense words, 254
 quotations within, 254
 other marks of punctuation with,
  255-259

R

Reciprocal pronouns, 24-25
Reflexive pronouns, 23-25
Regular verbs
 conjugation of, 44-45, 48, 55
 defined, 40
Relative pronouns
 agreement with antecedents of,
  182-183
 case of, 192-194
 introducing adjectival clauses,
  126, 131-132,
 introducing noun clauses, 127,
  137
Repetition of article, preposition,
  etc.,
 in parallelism, 227
Restrictive clauses, 131-133
Run-on sentences, 160-169

S

-*self* and -*selves*, 23-25
Semicolon, 276-280
 with conjunctive adverbs, 89-91,
  162, 166, 277-279
Sentence fragments, 155-160
Sentence(s)
 classes of, 150-151
 comma splice, 160-165
 consistent person, number, tense
  in, 234-241
 defined, 4-7
 fragments, 155-160
 misplaced/dangling modifiers in,
  210-220

parallelism in (*See* Parallelism)
pronoun-antecedent agreement in
  (*See* Agreement of pronoun
  and antecedent)
pronoun case usage in (*See* Case)
punctuating (*See* Punctuation)
run-on, 160-169
subject-predicate agreement in
  (*See* Agreement of subject
  and predicate)
types (patterns) of, 64, 82-83, 124-
  126, 142-150
vague, general, and unclear pronoun reference in, 204-209
Shifts in
 person, 234-235
 number, 234-235
 tense, 236-237
Sign of the infinitive (*to*), 117
Simple predicates, 6-7, 8-9, 30-32
Simple sentence, 64, 82-83, 124,
  143-144
Simple subjects, 4-5, 30-32
So/for, 85
Sound-alike words (*See* Look- and
  sound-alike words)
Spelling
 rules, 315-323
 apostrophes and, 69-71, 294-302
 mnemonics for correct, 315
 word list, 323-324
 See also Look- and sound-alike
  words
Subject-predicate agreement (*See*
  Agreement of subject and
  predicate)
Subjects (*See* Simple subjects,
  Complete subject...)
Subjunctive mood, 57-60
Subordinate clauses, 126-150 (*See
  also* Clauses)
Subordinate conjunctions, 126-127
Subordination, effective, 151-154
Suffixes
 and hyphens, 323

and words ending in a consonant,
321-322
and words ending in *e*, 318-319
and words ending in same letter
as, 322
and words ending in *y*, 319-320
Superlative degree
of adjectives, 76-79
of adverbs, 79-81
See also good, bad[ly], *little, many
(much), well*

T
Tense(s)
common
simple present, simple past,
simple future, 35-37
present perfect, past perfect,
future perfect, 35-38
consistent, 236-237
defined, 35
emphatic, 55
progressive
present, past, future, 48-51
present perfect, past perfect,
future perfect, 48, 51-55
Than/then, 312
The, 10-11, 67-68
Their/there/they're, 299
There is/are, was/were, 178-179
These/those, 20-21, 68-69
This/that, 20-21, 68-69
Titles, capitalization of, 287-288
To
as preposition, 95, 312
as sign of the infinitive, 40,
117-119
To be (See *Be*)
To do
as helping verb, 55
present tense of, 56
To have
present tense of, 56
in perfect tenses, 37-38, 44-46,
51-55

To/too/two, 312
Transitional expressions (*See*
Conjunctive adverbs)
Transitive verbs, 60-61
Troublesome words, list of, 310-313
(*See also* 299)

U
Underlining (*See* Italics)

V
Verbals
gerunds, 106-111
participles, 111-117
infinitives, 117-123
Verb(s) (*See also* Participles, Tense)
active voice form of, 32, 44-46
agreement of subject and (*See*
Agreement of subject and
predicate)
common tense formation of, 44-46
defined, 2, 30-31
emphatic tense formation of, 55
helping (auxiliary), 55-56
infinitive (*to* form), 40-42, 117-118
intransitive, 62
irregular, 40-44, 45-46
linking, 62-63
objects of, 60-61, 187
passive voice form of, 32-35
phrases (*See* Verbals)
predicate, 6-9, 30-63
principal parts of a, 40-42
progressive tense formation of, 48
regular, 40, 45
tense consistency and, 236-237
transitive, 60-61
Voice, active and passive, 32-35
Vowels, 315
suffixes starting with, 318-321

W
Weather/whether, 313
Were/where, 313

Which/what/whose (interrogative
  adjectives), 69
Who/whom/what/which
  using interrogative pronouns,
    21-22, 25, 192-194
  using relative pronouns, 126-127,
    192-194
Whose/who's, 299

Words often misspelled (list),
  323-324

Y
-*y*, dropping or keeping final,
  319-320
Yet/but, 84-85
Your/you're, 299